# Research and the Teacher

78

# Research and the Teacher

**Graham Hitchcock**

*and*

**David Hughes**

London & New York

First published in 1989 by Routledge
11 New Fetter Lane, London EC4P 4EE

Published in the USA by Routledge
29 West 35th Street, New York NY 10001

Reprinted 1991, 1992 and 1993

Printed and bound in Great Britain by Mackays of Chatham PLC, Kent

*British Library Cataloguing in Publication Data*

Hitchcock, Graham, 1952–
    Research and the Teacher: A
    Qualitative Introduction to
    School-based Research
    1. Education. Research. Qualitative Methods
    I. Title II. Hughes, David

370'.7'8
ISBN 0–415–02432–3
ISBN 0–415–02433–1 (Pbk)

*Library of Congress Cataloging-in-Publication Data*

Hitchcock, Graham, 1952–
    Research and the Teacher: A Qualitative Introduction to School-based
    Research/Graham Hitchcock and David Hughes
    p. cm.
    Bibliography: p.
    Includes indexes.
    ISBN 0–415–02432–3
    ISBN 0–415–02433–1 (pbk.)
    1. Education-Research. 2. Interaction analysis in education.
I. Hughes David, 1938–  II. Title.
LB1028.H535 1989
370'.7'8–dc19

# Contents

Contents

# Figures

# Acknowledgements

No book is written in isolation and the authors have benefited from contact and discussions with a number of colleagues and friends over recent years. We would especially like to thank Jim Crump, Kate Herrick, and Malcolm Lee who have discussed a number of ideas contained in this book with us and provided valuable feedback. Special thanks go to Robin Talbot, who provided much support and encouragement during the book's early stages. We have also received much critical evaluation of our ideas by being involved in a variety of curriculum development exercises over recent years. We would like to acknowledge the keen eye and dry wit of the anonymous reviewer of our first draft who helped us towards a clearer appreciation of what we were about and how to go about it.

We would like to thank the teachers on in-service courses both past and present for their complaints, criticisms, and praise alike. We are also grateful to those teachers with whom we tried out some of the materials contained in this book. They have constantly faced us with the realities of their teaching worlds to which we have always tried to respond.

During a time of constraints and cut-backs we have received considerable support from the staff of High Melton Library. Particular thanks go to the inter-library loans staff, who have dealt with our unending requests over the years so quickly and with a smile. We also gratefully acknowledge financial assistance and support from the DMIHE Institute Research and Staff Development Committee and its current chairperson, Dr Trevor Kerry. The whole of this enterprise would have been made more difficult were it not for the considerable typing skills of Beverly Nesbitt, Lynn Eaton, Joan Smith, and the staff of the secretarial units at High Melton and Waterdale, who all struggled to make sense of our scripts. In particular special thanks go to Kathie Jowitt who typed the final version of the book in an expert fashion.

Our greatest debt, however, is to our immediate families, especially our wives, June and Helen, who have borne with the inevitable sacrifices writing such a book entails, as well as acting as professionals and critics. All we can say is 'thank you' in more ways than one. However, at the end of the day we share both individually and jointly any shortcomings and omissions that remain.

Graham Hitchcock, David Hughes                                    June 1988

**Publisher's Acknowledgements**

The authors and publishers would like to thank the following for permission to reproduce copyright materials.

Routledge & Kegan Paul for the observation categories of the teacher record, p. 17, from M. Galton and B. Simon (eds) (1980) *Progress and Performance in the Primary School.*
Falmer Press, the Taylor and Francis Group, for floorplan of Harmony Preschool, p. 84, and for flow chart for 'Sue', Harmony Preschool, p. 47, from S. Lubeck (1985) *Sandbox Society: Early Education in Black and White America – A Comparative Ethnography.*

# Part I

# The Context and Practice of Research

# Chapter one

# Introduction

There has perhaps never been a less propitious moment to present an introductory textbook on teacher research than the present time. Rapid and far-reaching changes are affecting the teaching profession and the everyday world of classroom learning. Increasingly education is seeing the intrusion of a market philosophy. Education is encouraged to forge closer links with industry and the world of work. Meanwhile many groups of children are still massively underachieving in our educational system. The Core Curriculum and GCSE will involve schools and individual teachers in rethinking the very shape of the curriculum. Catch phrases like anti-racist teaching, non-sexist teaching, multicultural education, or girl-friendly schooling are increasingly being heard in places where one would never have expected to hear them. Despite, and in part because of, these momentous changes and the increasing pressures which they inevitably place upon teachers we are asking teachers to do something else: to engage in research. Research, as we will go on to define it here, is seen as an essential and important aspect of the teacher's professional responsibilities. The aim of this book is therefore to equip training teachers and serving teachers in a wide variety of contexts from both the reception class to the further education lecture, with a knowledge of just how they might go about researching their own and immediate situations. In doing this we will stress the need for acquiring a working knowledge of the social science frameworks from which social and educational research develops. We will explore both the context and practice of school-based teacher research as well as the most appropriate methodological tools and techniques for achieving this. The book is written from a firm conviction that research is of immense value in improving practice. But what do we mean by research?

We use the term research here to describe what we might call 'systematic inquiry': inquiry that is characterized by a certain amount of rigour and governed by sets of principles and guidelines for procedures. Social research therefore refers to both the collection and analysis of information on the social world, in order thereby to understand and explain it better. Educational research is informed by social research more generally and refers to both the collection and analysis of information on the world of education. Teacher research refers to the research that the practising teacher is able to conduct in the context of immediate professional practice. This utilizes and modifies the insights and procedures of social and educational research in applying them to school circumstances. In this sense research does have a number of benefits. Doing research will encourage a systematic approach to the collection of information and furthermore will help to develop a respect for evidence which in turn will lead to more critically informed opinions. Those involved in doing research will have the opportunity to rethink taken-for-granted assumptions. A distinction may instantly be drawn between professional researchers and teacher researchers.

Despite the fact that the number of teachers with research experience has grown over recent years, teachers are not professional academic researchers, they are teachers. For many terms *teacher* and *research* are mutually exclusive. Doubts are raised about the knowledge base from which teachers might carry out research. Their jobs are so demanding, it is argued, that they simply have no time in which to do any research. Furthermore, they have not received any training in the skills required and lack the appropriate objectivity or distance from the subject of their research. While many argue quite rightly that teachers should be made more familiar with the assumptions and methods of educational research so that they might better evaluate its products, the process of doing research itself is best left to professional researchers.

In contrast we have taken a rather different view of the relationship between teaching and research. While not underestimating the difficulties involved in teachers undertaking research we emphasize the importance, positive value, and excitement of teacher school-based research. There is also an important sense in which teacher research viewed as a critical, reflexive, and professionally oriented activity might be regarded as a crucial ingredient in the teacher's professional role. This ought to have the effect not only of enhancing the teacher's professional status but also of generating self-knowledge and personal development in such a way that practice can be improved.

Another view which is often expressed is that teachers themselves have little regard for the findings of conventional educational research, seeing it as having limited, if any, practical value. They are especially critical, it is contended, of the divorce (as they perceive it) between theory and practice, and to the abstract and alien language of the social sciences of which conventional educational research is part. The obscurity of the language and the high level of generality implied in much research has often resulted in teachers perceiving this work as being remote and divorced from their needs and situations. This has led some to argue that while teachers should engage in systematic inquiry into their practice, such research should have a strictly pedagogic intent, and teachers need not become over-involved in the methodological issues of social science.

Here again we will argue a different viewpoint. While research into education, especially that undertaken by teachers, has its own individual focus, schools inhabit the same social world that is explored by all social scientists. That being the case, educational research cannot divorce itself completely from the methodological issues that social science research raises, nor from understanding the language in which such research is conducted. As such it is important for teachers considering undertaking research into their own practice at whatever level to acquire an appreciation of the frameworks within which research has been discussed and practised in the social sciences. Any piece of social or educational research is informed by some basic underlying assumption and employs certain procedures. It is vital therefore to know what these are in order both to carry out research and to assess in any meaningful way the products of such research. Our ideas are reinforced by the increasing amount of research which is now being conducted by teachers, some of it coming out in print, and by the enthusiastic way in which some of the teachers we have worked with have tackled the methodological and substantive issues raised by investigations of such topics as gender and schooling, multicultural issues, parental involvement, and mainstreaming children with special educational needs. An understanding of models of research design in education and the human sciences is important since both conventional educational research and that which is applied to the solution of particular problems undertaken by professional academics and others has always been closely linked to educational policy and training. The modern teacher needs, in our view, to be equipped to understand the methodologies and language that underpin research in order not only to make sense of both current policy and initial and in-service training approaches, but also to be able to apply a selective and critical attitude towards its relevance and application in practice. A common response by teachers who have undertaken a course with a methodological or research component is that it has improved their ability to contribute to discussions on school policy in a more critical and effective manner.

The impetus for such a book as this now becomes clear. Over the years there has been a growing recognition of the importance of providing training and practising teachers with a knowledge of research orientations in order to enable them to become involved in conducting small-scale school-based research. The idea for this book derives from our own experience with teachers in a variety of contexts conducting small-scale research as part of initial teaching training, INSET work, or work towards a professional qualification. There was a clear need to provide teachers with a background to social research which recognized both the specific context of the teacher researcher and the purpose of school-based research and that offered guidance, advice, and instruction on the most appropriate tools and techniques. While there are many textbooks available they all seemed to sacrifice one or other of these needs. Our solution was to think in terms of three areas: research and the notion of the teacher researcher, the methodologies and techniques available, and the context and practice of school-based teacher research. These areas correspond to Parts I, II, and III of the book respectively.

Throughout the educational world the teacher researcher movement has been developing rapidly. For example the *Classroom Action Research Network* (CARN) founded in 1977 by John Elliott at the Cambridge Institute of Education together with a group of teachers and educationalists was established as a support group for teacher research and indeed now has worldwide links. Furthermore, teachers are becoming involved in larger collaborative projects either with outside academic researchers or as part of a school- or authority-based staff development programme. A body such as the *Primary Schools Research and Development Group,* founded in the mid-1960s to bring together all those with a professional interest in primary education, including teachers, college and university lecturers, advisers, and specialists in particular areas such as remedial education, special needs, or child psychology, demonstrates the growth of interest in the involvement of all parties in the educational equation. This interest manifests itself in holding conferences, publishing articles and journals, and undertaking collaborative research between teachers and such bodies as the now defunct Schools Council. Its recent survey on morale in the primary school sector, *The Primary Teacher: A Profession in Distress,* is a good example of its work, and shows the value of research sponsored by sources other than the government, the LEA, or other traditional sources, in which practising teachers are actively involved in framing the issues to be researched.

We intend therefore that this book be both read and used. The readers and users will come to it from a variety of backgrounds, and with different professional needs. Some readers will already have views on the contributions that systematic inquiry or research can make to their own circumstances. Some may be involved in obtaining further qualifications and find that one of the course components is methods of educational research. Others still may be involved in school-based 'action research' or 'evaluation' and need to use some of the approaches described in this book to aid their work. Yet others may simply wish to develop their own skills as teachers and their ability to become more reflective about their practice. Finally other readers will also come to the book with varying degrees of familiarity with the contribution that the social sciences in general, and educational research in particular, have made to the study of education. At the end of the book we aim to have built upon these initial foundations and provided a sound basis from which teachers can legitimately and realistically conduct small-scale school-based research.

## What counts as research? Some definitions

'Research' is often prefixed by words like 'pure', 'basic', 'applied', or 'action'. What do each of these terms mean, and what are the connections, if any, between them? A distinction is often drawn between 'pure' and 'applied' research. Pure research is not primarily concerned to develop understanding of practical problems but rather to advance knowledge within a particular area of human life or one academic discipline.

Applied research, though in no way less rigorous in its approach, focuses its attention on certain issues from the beginning. An example is modern research into learning theory, which, while extending general knowledge has, as one of its objectives, the application of its findings to a number of areas. The point is that applied research seeks generalizations from a large number of cases and that the link between the research findings and their application need not be immediate. Another feature of applied research is that the link between those who do the research and those who apply it need not normally be a close one. The dissemination of information is often second-hand via books, articles, and teaching.

Action research, on the other hand, might be described as inquiry conducted into a particular issue of current concern, usually undertaken by those directly involved, with the aim of implementing a change in a specific situation. Cohen and Manion have drawn out the distinctions between action research and applied research by suggesting that the conditions which usually govern applied research are somewhat more relaxed in action research since the latter focuses upon a specific situation or problem in a specific setting (Cohen and Manion 1986: 209).

In contrast, by 'evaluation' we mean the systematic study of a particular programme or set of events over a period of time in order to assess effectiveness. This research can be a case of simple appraisal carried out by an individual teacher into an aspect of curriculum, or a nationally conducted survey such as that currently being undertaken by the National Foundation for Education Research into the Technical and Vocational Education Initiative (TVEI). The emphasis in evaluation is with the assessment of the effectiveness of a particular programme or how well it has worked in terms of its aims.

Underlying these various definitions of research are debates about the relationship between research and practice. Nowhere is this more crucial than in the teacher researcher movement. Is the role of educational or teacher research to provide tips for teachers? Is the goal of research the development of more effective teaching strategies? Alternatively ought research to throw light on the social and cultural processes which affect a student's learning or help teachers and policy-makers obtain a better understanding of the context in which teaching and learning takes place? It is clear that teacher research can embrace any of these aims. Teachers may find themselves engaged at different times in a variety of types of research each having rather different aims. For example, they may become involved in applied or pure research if undertaking a research degree or they may find themselves involved in some form of collaborative action research or evaluation as part of a staff development programme within a single school. Common to all these types of research is a commitment to reflection upon what goes on in schools and classrooms. Our concern in this book is with providing teachers with the means by which this can be achieved. Despite the increase in teachers' involvement in research into educational practice over recent years the question of how this is to be done and the methodology which should be adopted is still unclear. Furthermore, teachers hardly ever possess the technical skills of professional social science researchers. The situation is further confused since no one methodology now dominates educational research. This means that there is now a greater range of research techniques that the teacher may legitimately draw upon. The overriding question, however, is which one to use?

Teachers will need to become familiar with the advantages and limitations of particular techniques in order to consider their applicability to certain situations. There are a number of practical constraints which stem from the nature of the teacher's role that will also affect both the choice of any particular technique and the way in which it can be used. We place each of the techniques we discuss in the context of school and classroom life and provide guidelines on the choice of technique. Perhaps the most often heard reservation about teacher research is that teachers invariably possess neither the skills nor the resources to carry out satisfactory and acceptable research. While this book cannot do anything to change the resources available to teachers it can help to provide knowledge of the contemporary situation and the ways in which these resources may be made use of. It is to be hoped that having worked through the sections on techniques teachers will develop an appreciation of the skills involved in doing research. Our experience of working with teachers who have conducted small-scale school-based research, and the products of teacher research now emerging, Hustler *et al.* (1986) suggest that teacher research can generate rich, illuminating, and important insights into the way in which we teach and learn in our society. These insights ought to have a crucial place in the formulation of policy and practice.

This book is written from the viewpoint of those who regard qualitative techniques as of unique value to teachers in achieving a better understanding of what happens in their classrooms and schools. By qualitative methodology we mean approaches that enable researchers to learn, first hand, about the social world they are investigating by means of involvement and participation in that world through a focus upon what individual actors say and do. This approach offers a new and considerable potential for teachers yet also brings with it fresh problems. Qualitative as opposed to quantitative research is more amenable and accessible to teachers and has the considerable advantage of drawing both researcher and subject closer into the activity itself. This research orientation focuses upon investigating social behaviour in natural settings and in terms of school-based research requires that close attention be paid to what ordinarily and routinely happens in schools and classrooms. Over the years considerable work has been done on developing and refining the qualitative research techniques on which this approach is based and there is now a growing body of studies which demonstrate the applicability and value of these approaches to the study of education. One of the aims of the book is therefore to provide teachers with an introduction to the use of these techniques in school-based research.

## How to use this book

From what we have said so far it is clear to see that teachers will bring different experiences to this book. They will have different kinds of knowledge and know more or less about social and educational research. The book is, however, meant to be both read and used. It can be read straight through in a chronological fashion, or, depending upon the knowledge, experience, and circumstances of the teacher, sections or chapters can be read in isolation. It may be that those teachers having a firm social science background and knowledge of, for example, sociology or psychology will already have an understanding of the issues raised in Chapter 2. However, since these questions are so complex further discussion of them would not go amiss. While the book can be used as a research manual, the 'menu' of techniques and approaches discussed must be seen in the specific context of the rationale and purpose of the book.

The book is divided into three parts which relate to specific aspects of social and educational research and to the context and practice of teacher school-based research. Part I deals with the notion of research and research design and examines the implications of this discussion for teacher research. Part II unravels a range of issues associated with qualitative methodology focusing upon a number of key techniques and how these might be used in educational settings. Since the context of research the teacher engages in is very different from that of conventional, academic researchers, Part III explores the relationship between teacher research and practice. These three parts are divided into ten chapters.

Chapter 2, as we have indicated, deals with the major assumptions underlying the two main approaches to social research, namely the positivistic scientific model and the interpretative ethnographic model. The chapter unravels what research design means for the teacher researcher approaching this in terms of research design and preparation, data collection, and data analysis. Our reasons for focusing upon interpretative, ethnographic approaches are outlined in preparation for a discussion of a range of qualitative techniques in Part II. Chapter 3 sets the scene by presenting the main principles and procedures of ethnography and fieldwork as these apply to school-based research and provides the framework for the subsequent discussion of interviewing in Chapter 4, collecting and using documentary sources in Chapter 5, studying classroom interaction in Chapter 6, and looking at the spatial arrangements of schools and classrooms in Chapter 7. Once the teacher is familiar with questions of research design and the nuts and bolts aspects of the application and use of a number of techniques in school-based research, it is important to move back to a consideration of the context and practice of teachers doing research. Part III therefore deals with research and practice bearing in mind the contemporary circumstances of teachers. Chapter 8 begins by raising the important questions of access to research situations and the ethical conduct of the teacher researcher given the peculiar nature of teacher school-based research. Since a number of teachers may be unfamiliar with the writing of research reports and the presentation of research findings, Chapter 9 focuses upon finding out and writing up together with the important question of what teachers do with their research, that is the dissemination of research findings. Finally Chapter 10 concludes by taking a look at the contemporary situation of schools by drawing attention to the possible relationships between school-based research, policy and management issues, and considering the future.

### Suggested further reading

Background reading is an essential aspect of any form of study. Clearly the amount of further reading the teacher will be able or need to do depends upon the research being conducted. If the teacher is conducting research as part of a degree or professional qualification evidence of further reading, the location of themes in current work, and a literature review will all usually be required. On the other hand the teacher may need to read up only on the use or application of a particular technique. At the end of each subsequent chapter we have tried to bear the various needs of readers in mind by providing suggestions for further reading. The teacher can follow up any of the references in the text by looking them up in the Reference section at the end of the book. The suggestions for further reading are intended as guides to the main texts and articles available on a particular topic or area. We have concentrated on citing those works which are fairly readily available and have included works by American as well as British researchers. These works will in turn have suggestions for further reading and by following up some of these the teacher will be able to build up a reasonable amount of reading on a particular topic.

This book will undoubtedly please some people but no doubt anger others. It will not convince those who believe that teachers cannot satisfactorily do research. Neither will it persuade those who believe that they have all the answers to teaching that there are far more questions to ask and that teachers themselves can ask these via research. It would be foolish, however, to deny the fact that teaching and research *are* very different enterprises. It would be equally foolish to argue that nothing fruitful could be derived from teachers engaging in the kinds of activities that researchers engage in. At the end of the day teacher research stands or falls on its ability to increase professional awareness of the complex factors which influence learning so as to improve the delivery of our educational practice. With this in mind we will begin our journey by considering the nature and organization of social research and subsequently school-based research. While this journey is certainly not easy we hope it will be rewarding.

# Chapter two

# Models of social research

## Introduction

In this chapter we will unravel the key ideas, background assumptions, and controversies in social research. Social research depends upon some basic principles and foundations and there are a number of different models of social research that have been used in social and educational research. These principles and foundations have been developed over many years across the disciplines of the social sciences. These models of research design act as plans or blueprints for the researcher to follow and it is important that the teacher researcher has a working knowledge of these models because they provide the basis of any research activity. Furthermore there is considerable controversy as to the most appropriate models for researching the social world and subsequently the best techniques to employ. This chapter explores the main approaches to social and educational research that have emerged over the years and the controversies with which they have been associated. The implications of this discussion for school-based research are considered in terms of the ways in which the three stages of research design, data collection, and data analysis apply to school-based research.

Research as we described it in Chapter 1 is concerned with systematic inquiry. Some people have argued that this systematic inquiry must also be scientific in the way in which we see physics or mathematics as scientific. These researchers, described as 'positivists', argue that social research must use the methods and procedures of the natural or physical sciences. Others have argued that the nature of the social world is such that investigation of it must be in principle different from investigation of the physical world. These researchers argued for the importance of discovering the meanings and interpretations of events actors themselves have. They are described as adopting an 'interpretative' approach. We will outline the main features of the contrasting sets of assumptions which underpin each of these approaches to the investigation of the social world. The two models may be described as the positivistic, scientific model and the interpretative, ethnographic model. This book focuses upon describing a range of interpretative and ethnographic research techniques as they may be used by the teacher in school-based research. We will outline our reasons for suggesting that the interpretative tradition in the social sciences overcomes many of the diffficulties of positivistic research and provides a firm base from which the prospective teacher researcher may begin some school-based research. As such we challenge the prevailing viewpoint that the positivistic or scientific model of social research is the only valid mode of research in education and the social sciences.

Research in education has of course had strong links with the research traditions of the social sciences. Indeed psychologists, sociologists, and anthropologists have all contributed to research into educational processes and practices. In many important respects educational research is not distinct from social research more generally. Educational research and education as a discipline both rely upon the tools, techniques, and insights of the social sciences. In turn prospective teacher researchers need to be aware of the complex and complicated themes of social research as well as being responsive to the teaching situation. Ultimately the object of inquiry, the social world, is the same for both professional social science researchers and teachers. The major difference, of course, lies in *why* one wants to do the research in the first place. However, to begin with, the background to any school-based research must be a social scientific one and a realization of the practical and professional context of teaching and learning. As such teacher researchers will inevitably have to achieve an understanding of the elements and principles of social research in order to carry out research into their own professional practice. This research and its products should facilitate reflection, criticism, and a more informed view of the educational process which will in turn help to improve professional practice.

Unfortunately social research is neither simple nor uncontroversial. Social research, individual tools and techniques, and particular models of research have been the subject of many heated debates. These debates are not new and go back to the writings of the great philosophers. The problems surround the ways in which we can produce knowledge of the social world, and the appropriate methods and procedures for the delivery of this knowledge. We will describe these issues in this chapter so that teacher researchers may then consider the particular aspects of individual research techniques, which are the subject of Part II, and the practice of doing school-based research, the subject of Part III.

*Making sense of social reality: two opposing traditions*

Social scientists have looked at the social world in many different ways. They have conducted different styles of research and collected different sorts of data and information by means of a quite staggering array of techniques. The reasons for this diversity go back to the questions raised by the great philosophers. During the Enlightenment two predominant questions arose: what is the character of our knowledge of the world and how might we therefore develop knowledge of the world, that is investigate the world? The Enlightenment philosophers struggled with these questions. Does the social world exist independently of our knowledge of it? Is our knowledge of the world constructed from a particular point of view? How far can we be certain about our knowledge of the world? All these questions will shape and influence social research. For example, if knowledge of the world is to be gained through some kind of observation does this mean that we talk meaningfully only about that which we observe and that we must rely on our senses for accurate information? In terms of social research these philosophical themes may be translated into a series of questions.

1 How do different propositions about social reality influence the investigation of the world?
2 How might researchers establish the truth of their claims?
3 How do different propositions about the social world and views about truth influence methods of data collection?

The answers to these questions have resulted in social researchers employing different logics, models, and techniques to investigate the world. Ultimately these differences are based upon different background assumptions.

There may be said to be two opposing ways of making sense of social reality. One of the best ways of discovering these differences is to examine the ways in which key fundamental assumptions are handled by these two opposing traditions before elaborating the positivistic and interpretative models of social research in more detail. These assumptions are ontological, espistemological, methodological, and technical, and we will examine each in turn.

When the word 'ontology' is used it refers to issues concerned with being. While this may sound somewhat esoteric it basically concerns what people believe and understand to be the case. As far as social research is concerned ontological assumptions are those surrounding the nature of the subject matter of the research, namely the social world. 'Epistemology' refers to the question of knowing and the nature of knowledge. Epistemological assumptions therefore surround such issues as the basis of knowledge, the form which it takes, and the way in which knowledge may be communicated to others. In this sense one can ask questions about the spiritual or religious basis of knowledge and about whether or not knowledge can be obtained only directly from personal experience or indirectly in other ways. 'Methodology' refers to the frames of reference, models, concepts, and ideas which shape the selection of a particular set of data-gathering techniques. Methodological assumptions will therefore surround questions about the appropriate overall framework of any particular piece of social research and whether or not to collect quantitative data through surveys and questionnaires, or qualitative data by means of participation and involvement in the setting being explored itself. Tools and techniques are the means through which researchers carry out their research. A number of 'technical' assumptions are made by researchers about the practicality and appropriateness of certain techniques and instruments for any piece of social research.

It is fair to say that the basic ontological and epistemological assumptions held by any researcher will shape the kind of methodology which those researchers will adopt. The relationship between these sets of assumptions can be expressed diagrammatically.

ONTOLOGICAL ASSUMPTIONS will give rise to
↓
EPISTEMOLOGICAL ASSUMPTIONS which have
↓
METHODOLOGICAL IMPLICATIONS for the choice
of particular
↓
TECHNIQUES OF DATA COLLECTION

These background assumptions are so important yet so complex that responses to questions of an ontological, epistemological, and methodological nature have resulted in two quite distinct perspectives or traditions in social research. This distinction has important implications for educational research because it has meant that not only have schools and classrooms been investigated in different ways but also what are seen to count as valid and appropriate data on schools and classrooms have varied also. In the following sections we will explain the major elements of these two contrasting ways of making sense of social reality in the shape of two traditions which are readily seen in most of the social sciences. It will become clear that understanding the differences between the two traditions is neither simple nor straightforward. To begin with let us proceed by analogy and consider the analogy offered by one American anthropologist.

*Petroleum engineers and explorers*

James Spradley (1980) accepts the existence of the two predominant models of social research which we earlier described as positivistic and interpretative. He likens the differences between positivists and interpretative researchers to those between petroleum engineers and explorers. Spradley argues that most social scientists operate in a fashion that is not unlike the way in which petroleum engineers work. These people are already in possession of some detailed knowledge of a geographical location in which they expect to find oil. In this analogy the social scientist is like the petroleum engineer who knows what he is looking for, how to look for it, and what to expect. Like the petroleum engineer the social scientist works in a linear, sequential, or step-by-step fashion. In contrast to the petroleum engineers, Spradley describes the explorer who is trying to map an uncharted wilderness. However, unlike the petroleum engineer the explorer has little or no prior knowledge of the area. While the main aim of the petroleum engineer's work is the discovery of oil, the explorer's main task is the description of what is found. Spradley likens the positivistic researcher to petroleum engineers and the ethnographer to explorers.

> The ethnographer has much in common with the explorer trying to map a wilderness area. The explorer begins with a general problem, to identify the major features of the terrain; the ethnographer wants to describe the cultural terrain. Then the explorer begins gathering information, going first in one direction, then perhaps retracing that route, then starting out in a new direction. On discovering a lake in the middle of a large wooded area, the explorer would take frequent compass readings, check the angle of the sun, take notes about prominent landmarks, and use feedback from each observation to modify earlier information. After weeks of investigation, the explorer would probably find it difficult to answer the question, 'What did you find?' Like an ethnographer, the explorer is seeking to describe a wilderness area rather than trying to 'find' something.
>
> Most social science research has more in common with the petroleum engineer who already has some detailed maps of the same wilderness area. The engineer has a specific goal in mind; to find oil or gas buried far below the surface. Before the engineer even begins an investigation, a careful study will be made of the maps which show geological features of the area. Then, knowing ahead of the time the kinds of features that suggest oil or gas beneath the surface, the engineer will go out to 'find' something quite specific. A great deal of social science research begins with a similar clear idea of something to find; investigators usually know what they are looking for.
>
> (Spradley 1980: 26)

The debates between 'petroleum engineers' and 'explorers' or positivist and interpretative researchers are far too important to be ignored by the prospective teacher researcher. These debates and controversies while clearly philosophical in nature, and hence for many people suitably obscure and often irrelevant, do have important consequences for educational research. So much so that we have had to state which side of the divide we are on in writing this book. At a time when the functions and organization of schooling are changing at a pace that has rarely been seen before and when dissent is rife, the teacher researcher must be sure about the philosophical basis of her school-based research. We will now unravel these traditions in more detail.

## The positivistic scientific model of social research

From about the late nineteenth century onwards the scientific model employed by the natural and physical sciences like biology, physics, and chemistry quickly became defined as the most appropriate model for investigating the social world. The principal thinkers associated with the development of the application of this view to the social sciences, in this case sociology, are the French philosopher Auguste Comte and the French sociologist Emile Durkheim. For Comte the only way of developing true knowledge of the world was through our sense experiences. This may be described as an empiricist position. 'Empiricism' suggests that the only reliable source of knowledge is through experience, by literally seeing and hearing, which usually took the form of some kind of observation or controlled experimental situation where the researcher could effectively exercise some authority over what was being experienced. One of the implications of this stance was that forms of knowledge based upon religion or superstition were highly speculative and certainly inferior to the knowledge gained from empirical enquiry. Indeed Comte was to describe sociology as 'social physics', a term which betrays much.

Comte's ideas were taken up by the French sociologist Emile Durkheim. Both Comte and Durkheim were concerned to develop an autonomous social science by adopting the philosophy and methodology of the then newly emerging natural sciences. Durkheim put forward a set of 'rules' for sociological methodology, rules which he argues all sociological research must follow. These 'rules' centred around following, as far as possible, the procedure of the natural sciences. This also involves the principle of objectivity. The researcher could and should remain objective. By ensuring a measure of distance from the subjects of the research personal bias could be avoided. For Durkheim the world was external to individuals, existing independently of actors' construction of it. Society was therefore *sui generis,* apart from and over and above the individuals who make it up. In attempting to establish an independent science of society which did not reduce explanation to the level of the individual psychological aspects, Durkheim proposed what might be described as a 'sociological determinism'. 'Society' was all and could force individuals into doing things; it was external to them, and exercised a considerable constraint over its members' activities. Durkheim developed what has been described as the functionalist perspective in sociology. This perspective viewed society as being not unlike a biological organism. Thus society, like a plant, was made up of a series of parts each of which performed an important function. The 'needs' of society were therefore met by the functions carried out by these various parts, or institutions like the family, education, or the economy. For Durkheim the proper investigation of society was to be achieved by adopting this functionalist framework and developing objective procedures for the collection and interpretation of data.

The approach of Comte, Durkheim, and others developed into what most social scientists would describe as positivism and which finds its fullest expression in the empiricist scientific method. While there are many fine-grained philosophical issues which may be discussed about positivism, any definition of positivism will contain two elements. Most people would accept that positivism is based upon the view that the natural sciences provide the only foundation for true knowledge and that the methods, techniques, and modes of operation of the natural sciences offer the best framework for investigation of the social world. Thus a definition of positivism would be that position in the social sciences which aims at objectivity in social inquiry by means of adopting the methods and procedures of the natural or physical sciences. Clearly for this view to be tenable certain propositions and assumptions would have to be made.

Key assumptions are made by positivists about human behaviour. First and most important from this viewpoint human behaviour is predictable, caused, and subject to both internal pressures (for behaviourist psychologists) and external forces (for positivistic sociologists). Second, these aspects can be observed and measured. The notion of causality in human affairs suggests that in fact human actions can, once correctly observed and identified, be predicted. Ultimately positivism therefore assumes that there is no qualitative difference between the natural and social world. As positivism developed in the social sciences two central principles of social research began to emerge and it is worth defining and describing these briefly here. The principles of 'deductive reasoning' and 'falsifiability' became the hallmarks of what is described as the scientific method.

Deductive reasoning suggests it is possible to move, following the scientific method, through from general kinds of statements to particular statements, which can in fact be objective and independent of experience. One of the key figures in the philosophy of science is Karl Popper; his book *The Logic of Scientific Discovery* has been immensely influential. He has argued that theories and subsequently explanations cannot be regarded as being scientific in the true sense, unless they are falsifiable; hence it can be argued that the main criteria of whether or not a statement has any scientific status resides in its testability. This means that scientists must do two things: (1) they must frame their theories in a way that leaves them open to falsification, and (2) they must be prepared to disregard such theories if either they are not open to falsification *per se*, or they prove wrong in the light of falsifying evidence. Popper's ideas have been highly influential and the testing and falsification procedures he describes have been widely accepted as the basis of good scientific practice.

Those social scientists who hold to this positivistic tradition are for many reasons likely to concentrate upon the collection of large amounts of data since the concern is with establishing patterns and regularities in that data and testing theories about that data by means of falsification procedures. As a result this approach to social research will be quantitative in orientation. Again to draw on Durkheim's work as an example, his study of suicide relies upon the suicide statistics and the suicide rates of various countries in Europe from which Durkheim is able to discover patterns and regularities which back up his hypothesis about the relationship between suicide and the degree of integration of the individual in society. From his observation that more single people committed suicide than married people, more people belonging to the Protestant faith committed suicide than Catholics, and that the suicide rate went up at times of social and economic crises like wars and depressions, he was able to generate a theory of suicide. Durkheim's book stood for a long time as the classic model of scientific sociological research.

A further term has recently come into use to describe the positivistic, scientific model of social research: a 'nomothetic' approach tends to be a major feature of positivistic, objective social research. Simply put, a nomothetic approach argues that the generalizations or theories emerging from a piece of research must be applicable to a large number of cases or situations. This is often expressed in a desire to search for universal general laws. But conversely, introspective, biographical, individual or small-group studies are seen to be suspect.

From what we have said so far it is now possible to identify the major assumptions of science and how the scientific method provides the most widely used model for social research. It is fair to say that a large proportion of research in both education and the social sciences has adopted to a greater or lesser extent this scientific method as the model for its research design. It is also fair to say that the driving force of much of this research was the desire to emulate in social research the precision and level of understanding characterized by the physical sciences. The general principles underlying positivism then come together in the scientific method. The concern to measure and quantify social behaviour in order to explain the regularities of such phenomena and the relationships that may be observed between them by matching the sophistication and rigour of the physical sciences in order to develop general, universal law-like statements is what the scientific method is all about. This is where we find Spradley's petroleum engineers. Figure 2.1 summarizes the basis of the scientific method.

| Positivism |
| :---: |
| Natural science base |
| Objectivity |
| Causality |
| Quantification |
| Falsification |
| Nomothetic |

**Figure 2.1**  The basis of the scientific model of social research

We can now approach the operation of this scientific model of social research in a bit more detail. Figure 2.2 outlines the kinds of stages which a typical piece of social research based upon this scientific model would take. What stands out most clearly here is the linear or sequential pattern of this research and the reliance upon hypotheses. Before we move on to discuss some of the problems with this model, the kinds of criticisms which have been made of it, and the development of an alternative tradition, we will pause to consider this framework.

The assumptions of science and the background ideas which direct scientific inquiry have resulted in a model of research for the investigation of the social world. However, while these general assumptions are accepted by natural scientists and social scientists working within the positivistic tradition, the subject matter of the natural sciences and that of the social sciences obviously varies fundamentally. This observation has formed the basis for the main criticisms of positivism in social science. However, the scientific method might be said to involve a set of widely accepted procedures which if followed, it is claimed, will produce knowledge of certain phenomena and theories which can explain such phenomena. If we take a closer look at Figure 2.2 we will see how these procedures take the form of a series of fairly well-defined stages which follow a sequential and ordered pattern. All of the features and assumptions we have discussed so far come together within the framework of this scientific model.

Sometimes this model is described as employing the 'hypothetico-deductive' technique, HD for short. What this complex-sounding idea means in practice

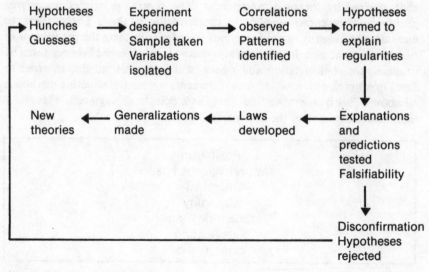

**Figure 2.2**  The scientific model

turns out to be quite simple. Often the researcher will have an idea, a hunch, or a vague notion about a possible connection or relationship between a set of events. The researcher will then put forward a hypothesis about this, that is a more formalized set of ideas about the situation in question. The scientific method then involves subjecting this hypothesis to a series of tests in order to prove or disprove the original hypothesis. Figure 2.2 shows the ways in which this process works out in practice. However, it is important to remember that this model is only an idealized view of what the scientific method consists of. In reality doing science and producing results is often a much more haphazard and problematic affair than this model would seem to suggest. Neither does the model capture all of the ways in which all social scientists making use of the scientific method have ever worked. This then is only an approximation but an approximation which bears a good resemblance to practice.

Once the researcher has established a hypothesis a test of some description is designed in order to reveal the main variables or factors which appear to be influencing the event under investigation. The classic kind of test here is the experiment. An experiment is used in the natural sciences in order to identify, control, and quantify the factors which affect a situation. By doing this the researcher can establish causality, the cause and effect of the factors and thereby isolate the variables or key factors which seem to be exercising the most influence. The researcher can look at the results of the experiment and identify any patterns or regularities. Once this has been done the researcher can look at the hypotheses which have been formed in order to explain these regularities in the light of the early hunches and less well-developed hypotheses. The next process is described as falsifiability which involves the falsification or corroboration of the hypotheses by placing it alongside the facts produced by the experiment or other method. If the hypothesis is proved then the researcher can go on to develop more formalized laws and generalizations about the actions which might eventually result in new theories. Alternatively if the hypothesis is not corroborated and is in effect falsified, the original hypothesis must be rejected and the whole process begun again. In this sense 'scientists' are not unlike the petroleum engineers described by Spradley.

## Evaluation of positivism and the scientific method

As a result of the importance and widespread acceptance of the scientific method and the positivistic assumptions which underpin it we have spent some time unravelling this tradition. This is only one, albeit the most influential, model of social research and has played a crucial role in providing a basis for much educational research. One of the features of the social sciences over the last few years has been an ongoing and often acrimonious debate between those who argue that positivism and the scientific method provide the only acceptable route to knowledge of the social world and those who reject all or part of this claim.

Some important question marks hang over the scientific method as we have described it. These criticisms have developed from within other perspectives or traditions in the social sciences, educational research, and the teacher researcher movement. Some of these criticisms appear so far reaching that the term 'anti-positivists' is applied to some of these researchers. It is useful to consider the kinds of criticisms which have been made under three broad headings. The nature of the social scientists' subject matter, forms of explanation, and the value of positivistic, quantitative methodology.

### The nature of the social scientists' subject matter

Perhaps no other aspect of the debate over positivism has received more attention that the distinction which is drawn between the subject matter of the natural sciences and that of the social sciences. Positivism within the social sciences seems to be based upon an implicit assumption that there is no qualitative difference between the natural and the social worlds such that the methods and procedures of the natural scientist can unproblematically be applied to the investigation of the social world. The essential qualitative difference between the natural and social worlds is the central platform of the anti-positivistic stance and the interpretative tradition. These researchers argue that the hard, often mechanistic, and calculating view of research cannot be squared with the fact that human beings may be said to exercise choice and express their own individuality in many different ways. Anti-positivists and interpretative social scientists, some of whom we will discuss shortly, take issue with the tendency of positivism and the implicit assumptions of the scientific method with its emphasis on correlation, laws, and objectivity, to make human beings out to be 'things' whose actions are unproblematic, clearly self-evident, quantifiable, and able to be objectively investigated.

The social world, it is argued, is a meaningful world where actors constantly construct and reconstruct the realities of their own lives. Any order found there is created by actors themselves who make use of concepts, rules, and interpretations. This is why many researchers have criticized the scientific method on the grounds that it makes use of preconceived ideas and hypotheses against which to test the data thereby imposing categories upon the observations of an event prior to discovering the meaning of those events to the actors involved themselves.

The problems involved in failing to distinguish between the natural and the social worlds for purposes of research spill over into other areas, notably forms of explanation and the value of quantitative methodology. The criticisms that we have just been discussing have implications for the forms of explanation social scientists may legitimately adopt and the techniques of data collection they employ in order to be able to make those explanations. Since these two sets of criticisms are linked we will consider them together.

## Forms of explanation and the appropriateness of positivistic methodology

The scientific method involves a rather specific approach to the collection and testing of data. The scientist using this method and adopting the key assumptions which we have outlined searches for relationships between events which can be observed. The data are examined in terms of some preformulated hypothesis and the data subjected to verification procedures so that the original hypothesis is either confirmed or rejected. Clearly the use of quantifiable data such as the results of social surveys, responses to questionnaires or official statistics will prove to be more amenable to these sorts of procedures. The typical forms of explanation which have been used by these researchers and the sorts of data and data collection techniques employed has generated considerable discussion. Three concerns emerge at this point: (1) the difference between causes and meanings, (2) the differences between quantitative and qualitative data, and (3) the question of generalization.

## Causes and meanings

It is frequently argued that the search for objective causal links between sets of events leads to a deterministic position where certain factors are viewed as causing events. For example, differences in performance in IQ tests could be said to be the cause of differential educational achievement of different groups of children. Indeed educational researchers have used IQ and other test performance scores as indications of differences in innate ability which are said to bear directly upon school achievement. While most people would now agree that 'school failure' is certainly a multifaceted phenomenon, only recently have researchers begun to challenge much of the positivistic research which suggested that it was not. The problem lies in the distinction between causes and meanings.

The cause-and-effect relationship is one that clearly operates in the natural world. Heat causes water to boil which has the effect of giving off steam leading to evaporation. In contrast the social world is composed of meanings and interpretations which result in the meaningful relationships we describe as action. A meaningful relationship exists when a relationship can be demonstrated between an actor's subjective state, for example in terms of a particular motive on the one hand and an overt, observable piece of behaviour on the other. What is missing from positivistic explanations, the critics have argued, is a demonstration of how the action in question is accounted for and explained by the person or persons involved. This would require an explication of the rules, shared meanings, and interpretations human beings routinely work with in conducting their everyday lives. The social world therefore needs to be investigated in terms of meanings and actions rather than causes and effects.

### Quantitative and qualitative data

An acceptance of the assumptions underlying the scientific method has meant that quantitative-oriented research tended to be the norm. Thus social surveys, structured interviews and questionnaires, and the use of official and unofficial statistics are the sources of data and methods which have been predominant. Quantitative data can be measured more easily, patterns can be established more clearly, and therefore any patterns which are discovered and generalizations made will be accurate since they are located within a large body of materials. The use of mathematical models and the notion of 'correlation', that is establishing the degree of fit, agreement, or association between various factors or variables in a piece of research, works much better when there are large numbers or big samples involved. In, for example, attempting to examine teacher performance by considering pupils' achievement in test or examination situations, the more data the researcher has the easier it will be for the researcher to establish any causal links and make observations about other cases.

Quantitative data presented in correlation studies, social surveys, statistics, or in interaction counts in the classroom have featured heavily in educational research. For many people the larger the sample, the greater the number of people responding to a questionnaire, or the more closely placed the intervals between coding some classroom interaction, the better the subsequent theories or explanations will be. In many people's eyes there is an air of respectability about numbers which increases the more numbers are involved. The reliance upon quantitative data within positivism and the use of the scientific method have drawn many criticisms. In fact this has probably been one of the most contentious areas of the debate on social research in recent years. Let us now examine the main threads of these criticisms.

Criticisms surrounding the use of quantitative data as the exclusive and best source of data for social research has come in two forms. First, researchers have drawn attention to the limitations and problems of research techniques which are designed for the collection of quantitative data. Second, researchers have pointed to the problems involved in relying solely upon objective, quantifiable measures or indices of social phenomena without paying attention to the interpretations and meanings individuals assign to events and situations in a qualitative way. Social surveys can capture a large area or population and allow a descriptive measure of the extent of a particular concern, such as poverty, and are important in establishing the nature of our society as a whole. However, critics have pointed to several problems with social surveys most notably the reliance on fixed or structured questionnaires in such surveys. These questionnaires may not be flexible enough to enable respondents' true feelings or attitudes to come through. People often treat these kinds of instruments with suspicion. Questions may structure responses too much or they may lead the respondent into answering in a particular way thus affecting the accuracy of the survey. Perhaps most important is the overall wording and presentation of a structured questionnaire. Is there ambiguity or vagueness in the questions? Might the presentation of the questions be off-putting to certain repondents? How are questions dealing with sensitive areas worded and presented? The underlying assumption of much survey work and the use of fixed or structured questionnaires is that people not only say what they mean but also do what they say.

Following on from this it is argued that in searching for quantifiable data researchers destroy or ignore the qualitative context out of which all 'data' emerge, that is out of the day-to-day lives of ordinary people in routine everyday situations. Critics of positivism suggest it is as important to look in detail at a small number of cases as it is to look generally at a large number of typical cases. A major division emerges within social science on the quantitative–qualitative axis. While not denying the value and significance of the broad general view developed by quantitative approaches, groups of researchers have stressed the need for a detailed appreciation of both the immediate interactional circumstances of events in the social world and the historical and cultural context out of which they grow. This has led a number of sociologists and anthropologists in particular towards looking in detail at everyday events by using a range of so-called introspective, biographical, subjective, or qualitative research techniques which are aimed at uncovering the actor's point of view from within the social situations they occupy. Rather than collecting quantitative data through quantitative techniques like surveys and structured questionnaires it is argued that social researchers should collect qualitative data by means of techniques which are designed to reveal the actor's perspective. In educational research the debate over quantitative or qualitative data and techniques is reflected in the move over the last two decades, to consider what is going on in particular schools and classrooms.

These criticisms on the reliance upon quantitative data in social research have also been elaborated in the critique of the use of official statistics in sociology. While the points are quite specific the general issue is clear. Official statistics are collected by officials for specific purposes. Individuals may find themselves in situations where, for example, a crime is not reported leading to the event not being recorded. Again researchers have stressed the importance of interpretation, for example, in identifying a sudden death as 'in fact' objectively a suicide, a death by misadventure, unlawful killing, or whatever. The point is clear once more. It is as necessary for the social researcher to qualify through the eyes of the observer. This has led some researchers to question the emphasis which is placed upon generalization in positivistic research in particular but the status of generalizations in social research more widely.

*Generalization*

Generalization refers to the process whereby a particular set of observations or findings can be applied to a much larger set of circumstances or population. A generalization may be said to refer to that kind of statement which seeks to include, under a general term, heading, or class of events, a set of particular cases. This is done in order to highlight certain common themes or aspects of the cases in question and establish connections between phenomena that it is practical to observe directly so that statements may then be made about situations that it is neither possible or practical to observe in their entirety. The fullest realization of the use of generalizations is found in the use by social scientists and historians of the comparative method. Comparison of situations might be said to be at the heart of any kind of systematic inquiry and it is always important for the researcher to be able to compare findings with other research. Similarly it is important for the teacher to compare her experiences and research findings with those of others. The comparative method involves the comparison of data gathered from widely differing societies or cultures in terms of phenomena that are seen to be comparable, for example kinship organization and marriage rules, or types of social organization in general. Social scientists have often sought to discover regular, general patterns of human behaviour by drawing comparisons between many different cultural or societal forms and pointing to the common elements. An integral element of this kind of approach and a central aspect of the platform of the scientific method is the production of high-level generalizations.

The human sciences make widespread use of generalizations and indeed it would appear impossible to do social research without using generalized statements. Imagine educational discussion without reference to 'working-class children', 'middle-class children', 'maladjusted children', 'ethnic minorities', 'slow learners', 'bright kids', and so on? We find people talking quite unproblematically about working-class values and middle-class types. Sociologists routinely refer to class and status groupings to refer to the hierarchical arrangements of vast numbers of individuals in a society. Psychiatrists speak of illness categories like 'psychoses' and 'neuroses' to refer to patterns of behaviour associated with mental illness. These general terms are used after a consideration of particular circumstances to apply to a much larger category of events that are likely to display the same characteristics as the ones originally observed. So we find the literature on early childhood socialization for example replete with phrases like 'working-class child-rearing patterns', or 'middle-class notions of deferred gratification'. These are generalizations; of course generalizations can be used in a 'soft' or a 'hard' fashion.

Generalization is an issue which has received considerable attention in social and education research. Obviously it is central to any notion of teacher research. Social scientists differ on their view of generalization. There are those, influenced by positivistic methodology and the scientific model, who argue that generalization is essential. Those whom we might describe as holding to an anti-positivistic position influenced by interpretative social science say that it is definitely not. Then a whole host of people, occupying a middle position and, as seems to be increasingly the case, making use of a number of different research techniques within the one study, argue that it is sometimes necessary.

The question of generalization and its incorporation as a major goal in the scientific method has proved for many the key question in relation to research by teachers. Given the circumstances and practical constraints placed upon teachers it is questionable whether generalization in the sense in which it is viewed in 'science' could ever be achieved given the reliance by teachers upon individual cases or circumstances, limited numbers of people involved, or even the use of single informants. Yet, if generalization is perceived to be a central platform of the scientific method, is research by teachers and others into education with its characteristic focus upon the small-scale, local and particular, going to be devalued?

Many researchers have moved away from attempting to deliver large-scale generalizations and indeed generalization as such is no longer seen by many as either the ultimate or only goal of social research. As we have seen the attempt to produce ever larger generalizations can result in failing to examine adequately the cultural contexts of social action. There is certainly a tension between concentrating upon large numbers of cases in general and few cases in particular. The ethnographic interpretative model of social research suggests that any move towards generalization must begin from the particular circumstances of individuals and groups. Furthermore, it is highly unlikely that any research the teacher will become involved in could ever be large enough to sustain the kinds of high-level generalizations that are seen to be a crucial part of the scientific method.

In this section we have been examining the predominant model of social research, the scientific method, and the logic which underpins it, positivism. For a number of years a growing dissatisfaction with positivism has been a characteristic of debate in the human sciences. Within educational research this model has been regarded as having a strait-jacket effect on the practice of research. Educational research was to be done by professional academic researchers using tried and tested principles and procedures. For many researchers and teachers alike this model created unnecessary constraints upon what aspects of school and classroom life could be researched and how. The scientific model was increasingly seen as being incapable of capturing the fluidity, spontaneity, and creativity of classroom life. More forceful critics complained that positivism operated with a mechanical, or still worse, a dehumanized view of human beings. It is not surprising that alternative traditions in social research were to emerge. These traditions and reactions to positivism and the scientific method were to send shock waves throughout the entire research community, the effects of which were felt in both educational research and the developing area of teacher school-based research. In Spradley's (1980) terms the explorers became much more noticeable in social research.

## The interpretative ethnographic model of social research

Alternative ways of making sense of social reality have always existed. In contrast to positivism may be placed interpretativism or naturalism. These two terms capture the essence of the ethnographic, qualitative, or interpretative model of social research. This approach to understanding and investigating the social world has argued that the key feature of human social life, that individuals routinely interpret and make sense of their worlds, means that investigation of the social worlds must relate these intepretations to the natural everyday situations in which people live. Social life can be adequately understood only from the point of view of actors themselves. The terms interpretativism and naturalism refer to a particular stance or attitude towards the investigation of the social world. In this section we will examine the basic assumptions of this approach, how it developed, and the mode of social research it has given rise to.

The first and perhaps most important distinction to be drawn between positivist and interpretative research is the emphasis placed by interpretative social researchers on the need to distinguish between the characteristics of the natural world and those of the social world. As we pointed out if there is a qualitative difference between the natural and the social world it follows that the ways of investigating the social world must be very different from the ways of investigating the natural world. For the positivists the best model around was that entailed in the natural scientific paradigm. In contrast interpretative researchers suggest that the humanities, especially social history with its emphasis upon interpretation of the past through what people leave behind them, provides a more suitable base line from which to begin investigation of the social world.

Interpretative researchers also take issue with the model of human beings positivist researchers often seem to work with. Human beings are thinking, feeling, conscious, language- and symbol-using creatures. Interpretative researchers therefore stress the principles of intentionality to grasp the active side of human behaviour. In contrast to the often passive view of individuals reacting to situations or stimuli, interpretative researchers stress that human action is for the most part deliberate and that people do not simply react to events and situations but reflect on this situation and act on this reflection, in a reflective way. Human beings are capable of choice and have the ability to act upon the world and to change it in line with their own needs, aspirations, or perceptions. Social research therefore has to confront directly the way in which individuals' subjective experience is manifested in what they do and say. This in turn reveals one of the major characteristics of the interpretative approach. These researchers argue that by and large much social research neglects the medium through which social reality is expressed and understood. Interpretative researchers therefore take seriously the question of language and meaning and give priority to first unravelling actors' descriptions of events and activities in a qualitative fashion rather than focusing upon observers' descriptions in a quantitative fashion. As a result direct, first-person accounts provided by actors themselves in their own language feature heavily in ethnographic, interpretative research.

These assumptions have some very definite implications for the way in which interpretative researchers go about their work. As a result interpretative research might be said to be deliberately open ended, prepared to change direction or take a developmental view and accept the possibility of using a variety of sources of data since the social world is so complex. Interpretative models of social research will therefore be geared towards faithfully reconstructing the actors' perspectives. This carries with it the suggestion that description will come first and explanation second. Any theories which are developed must be grounded in the actual data the researcher has. This results in interpretative researchers only moving from discussion of individual cases to wider, general situations when they have achieved a close, detailed description and explanation of those individual cases. Finally, interpretative researchers recognize the inevitable involvement of the researchers in this kind of work. Rather than occupying an aloof and objective position interpretative social research stresses the value and inevitability of the researchers becoming involved and developing relationships with the subjects of the research. This leads these researchers to choose more directly participant forms of observation. One of the best ways of developing an appreciation of this research tradition, the model of research design it employs and techniques of data collection it makes use of is to consider the specific perspectives, or schools of research with which it is most usually associated. Three schools or perspectives are associated with the interpretative, ethnographic model of social research, the so-called Chicago School and what became known as symbolic interactionism, phenomenology, and ethnomethodology. We will briefly consider the Chicago School of Sociology and symbolic interactionism in order to draw out the major features of the interpretative, ethnographic model of social research. Phenomenology and ethnomethodology are subsequently discussed in more detail in the course of Part II. This will provide the basis for an account of the principles of ethnographic enquiry and how these relate to school-based research in Chapter 3.

During the 1930s and 1940s the Department of Sociology at the University of Chicago developed a particular style of social research which contrasted markedly with the dominant positivistic and objective models. The emergence of a distinct 'Chicago style' of research was in part a reaction to criticisms of positivism and the scientific model and in part a reaction to changing social conditions. The rapid social changes which were affecting American cities like Chicago and the influx of large numbers of different immigrant groups brought with it greater social complexity and many human problems. These cities were extremely heterogeneous and so large neighbourhoods and areas could be identified. Problems of crime, poor housing, low-paid employment, and poverty were all features of these cities. Sociologists were faced with the problem of describing and explaining social behaviour in these kinds of areas. The Chicago School of Sociology was to take the lead by producing a series of studies of the social life, attitudes, and social organization of individuals and groups in the city. The complexity of social life in the city suggested to these researchers that a model of social research and a series of techniques quite different from those entailed in positivism and the scientific method was needed.

The researchers and students at Chicago in the 1930s were encouraged to 'get their hands dirty' in real research. To go and live in the slums and the ghettos, to hang around street corners, bars, and pool halls, to visit the 'other side of the tracks' as well as talk to officials, examine public records and official statistics. Chicago University is therefore most famous for the development of the technique known as 'participant observation'. This technique is founded on the principle that only by participating and sharing in the lives of the group being investigated can one achieve a real understanding of what is going on. For this reason researchers using the method of participant observation attempted to take on the role of a typical member of the group they were investigating and spend a period of time living and working with them. Although these researchers are best known for their use of participant observation as a principal means of data collection many did in fact make use of unstructured interviewing, official records, and personal documents such as letters. A good example here is the early monumental study of Polish emigration to America by W. I. Thomas and F. Znaniecki.

*The Polish Peasant in Europe and America* (1918–20) marked a watershed in the development of the social sciences in the USA between positivist or objectivist social science on the one hand and interpretative social science on the other. This vast book attempts to chart the patterns and meaning of immigration to the USA by thousands of Polish people. In order to consider the impact of this movement on the lives of the individuals themselves the authors collected a wide range of data that was designed to enable the researchers to gain insight into the actors' definition of the situation. First Thomas and Znaniecki collected over 754 private immigrant letters written in the first person to and from immigrants in the USA. These letters were from people occupying all kinds of positions in the social hierarchy. There were letters from industrial workers, farmers, peasants, and members of the middle class. Second, the authors made use of the archives of a Polish newspaper, material from the Polish Emigrants Protective Society, the Legal Aid Society, and various documents in Poland. Finally *The Polish Peasant in Europe and America* contains one of the first sociological life histories, the autobiographical narrative of a young Polish man by the name of Wladek Wisniewski. What is important about this work is the commitment of the authors to uncovering the actors' perspective, in this case the experiences and feelings of Polish emigrants living and working in the USA by means of the utilization of a vast array of sources of data not usually associated with science or sociology. The work was to have an important if short-lived influence. It does however convey the concerns of an interpretative model of social research as it was beginning to emerge.

While the methodological developments we have been describing were taking place in Chicago some important theoretical and philosophical thinking was taking place which was to lead to possibly one of the most influential perspectives on educational research. 'Symbolic interactionism' is virtually at the other end of the pole from positivism. Symbolic interactionism, as the term suggests, focuses upon human beings' use and interpretation of symbols suggesting that human beings consciously create or construct social life by generating meanings and making interpretations within small social groupings. The basic concerns of symbolic interactionism are with the ways in which individual actors make sense of, analyse, or interpret any given situation. In this sense symbolic interactionists deliberately concern themselves with subjectivity, that is the subjective meanings and experiences of individuals. This approach tends to concentrate on processes rather than structures in social life or the cement which holds the bricks together. This approach is heavily influenced by the work of the American social psychologist George Herbert Mead who suggested that the key ingredient of being a human being was the capacity to reflect upon one's own circumstances. Human beings have a self; they can see themselves reflected in other people's responses and reactions to them. Human beings can think about these reactions and act accordingly. Charles Cooley developed the notion of the 'looking-glass self' to capture this process of seeing oneself reflected in the eyes and actions of others. Symbolic interactionism highlights the ability of individuals to put themselves in the shoes of other people and to see things from this position as well as their own. In this way symbolic interactionism differs from positivism in arguing that human beings respond to situations rather than merely reacting to them.

Herbert Blumer (1969) was one of the key figures in the symbolic interactionist tradition and was responsible for unravelling the sociological research implications of Mead's thought. Social researchers had, he argued, to take on board the fact that social life was indeed constructed out of complex sets of social interactions, which made it necessary to focus upon actors' meanings and motivations as to the cause and effect of events in the social world. Such a concern with the way in which people interpreted and made sense of social action led Blumer to claim that the appropriate methodology for investigating the social world was one that enabled the researcher to observe individuals in their ordinary, everyday, natural social settings and to record their accounts of what it was they were doing. In short, ethnography was the method best suited to achieve this since it allowed for a qualitative focus upon actors' accounts and experiences rather than an objective view through the eyes of an outside observer.

As well as the concept of interaction, research in the symbolic interactionist tradition has generated a number of important concepts which have proved useful for educational researchers. Social action is essentially viewed as a fluid and changing affair, open to negotiation and renegotiation by actors. These actors all have designated roles like husband, doctor, father, and member of a local political party. While roles are important, the symbolic interactionists stress that what is in fact seen to be involved in any particular role is not given but rather made or constructed by the incumbents of the role themselves. Hence, while a definition of the role of teacher can be approached in general terms, 'being a teacher' means vastly different things to different people, all of whom call themselves 'teachers'.

Another important concern of symbolic interactionists which has been influential in some educational research is the way in which individuals manipulate the physical features of their environment. The work of Goffman (1971) is a case in point here. Goffman attempts to analyse the actual encounters, performances, and stages which make up everyday social life. His 'micro-sociology' takes us backstage revealing the ways in which people project an image of themselves to present upstage. Clearly teaching as a performance would be amenable to analysis in these terms. Staffrooms are backstage, the chalk-face of the classroom upstage. Goffman has provided a microscopic focus upon the nature of interaction in everyday life which has resulted in a series of concepts and ideas that can sensitize the researcher towards looking at issues which typically go unrecognized.

The perspective known as symbolic interactionism then holds to some underlying principles about the nature of the social world and the way to investigate it which might be said to be qualitative or idiographic in orientation. An idiographic approach stresses the legitimacy of investigating individual lives, particular cases, or small groups and is only interested if at all in a secondary fashion with factors that go beyond the individual or the group. The concern with generalization therefore gives way to locating the subjects of the research in their own cultural and interactional context emphasising the need to understand the situation. Here we find Spradley's wilderness explorers. Figure 2.3 summarizes the main assumptions underlying the interpretative, ethnographic model of social research.

The perspective known as symbolic interactionism inspired a whole

```
Interpretativism
Humanities base line
Subjectivity
Interpretation
Language and meaning
Development of grounded theory
Idiographic
```

**Figure 2.3** The basis of the interpretative, ethnographic model of social research

generation of sociological studies which took the concept of interaction as their starting-point and which used the techniques of participant observation and ethnography as their principal research strategies. The impact of this perspective was acutely yet excitingly felt in educational research. There was a major move from the late 1960s onwards to locate educational research in the context of the local and particular realities of individual schools and classrooms. For too long, it was argued, the 'black box' of the classroom had gone relatively unexplored. If success and failure was to be explained, the arenas in which learning takes place had first to be thoroughly explored. The effect of symbolic interactionism on educational research was twofold, methodological and theoretical. First, as we have seen, the qualitative and interpretative methodology generated from symbolic interactionism and elsewhere held considerable potential for research in schools and classrooms. Second, the concepts and theories which symbolic interactionists generated and with which they worked proved particularly useful in exploring such fields as the development of school counter-culture, the negative effects of labelling pupils and the way in which learning in schools was defined, redefined, and negotiated in subtle ways by teachers and pupils. As a result, the perspective became quite popular in educational research over a period of time.

Symbolic interactionism was only the first of three perspectives that has contributed to the development of an alternative model of social research to that proposed in the positivistic, scientific model. 'Phenomenology' and 'ethnomethodology', both discussed in more detail in Part II, were respectively concerned to develop an understanding of the structures and frameworks which hold our shared everyday world together and the methods, most notably the use of language, by which members construct, reconstruct, and make sense of their social worlds. The research orientations of these two perspectives build upon the fundamental ideas of symbolic interactionism and this has led some people to regard symbolic interaction, phenomenology, and ethnomethodology together adopting an 'action frame of reference'. An examination of some of the studies and topics which have emerged from this tradition will highlight the ways in which schools and classrooms have been explored using this approach.

The application of participant observation and ethnographic techniques fused with the insights of symbolic interactionism is best seen in two early studies. David Hargreaves's (1967) study of social relations in a secondary school highlighting the implications of streaming and the development of academic subcultures was one of the first to demonstrate the value of participant observation to educational research. A little later Colin Lacey's (1970) study of a grammar school, which grew out of the application of anthropological research techniques to educational problems, demonstrated still further the importance of getting inside the school and collecting first-hand qualitative data. As we shall discover in Chapter 7, the development of a theory about labelling and typing generated by the interactionist sociologists, most notably Howard Becker, enabled researchers like Rist (1970; 1973) to focus on the importance of examining the influence of labelling on school attainment. Recently, phenomenology has inspired educational researchers to think again about what counts as knowledge in schools and to examine the curriculum in more detail (Young 1971; Keddie 1973). Also the central import-ance of language, or more appropriately talk and conversation, highlighted by the ethnomethodologists has resulted in researchers exploring classroom processes by means of a detailed examination of verbatim transcripts of class lessons (French and French 1984). More recently the interpretative, ethno-graphic model of social research, together with a range of qualitative research techniques, has been used to explore such areas as the under achievement of many girls in science subjects, the influence of ethnicity on school partici-pation, teaching styles, school transition, teachers' and pupils' careers, dis-affection from school, and many more areas.

Certainly the interpretative, ethnographic approach to social research has had a great impact on educational research. There has been a slow but gradual movement away from the domination of positivistic research design and methodology towards interpretative, ethnographic, or qualitative research in the study of education. This is clearly seen in the contributions to the *British Educational Research Journal* and in a number of recent volumes of research. This had led many researchers to become polarized between the two traditions we have been outlining here. Paradigms and camps have emerged along the positivist-interpretative divide. Increasingly, however, more researchers are trying to bridge the gap by, for example, considering the role of measurement in ethnography (Pollard 1984a: 33–48; Hammersley 1986b). For the most part, however, the goals and assumptions of the two traditions we have been exploring in this chapter are difficult if not impossible to reconcile. We have therefore not been discussing artificial dichotomies but real differences in the social research community. It is worth finally comparing the two traditions of social research we have been considering and the models of research to which they give rise: see Figure 2.4.

| The Scientific Model | The Interpretative Model |
|---|---|
| Positivism | Interpretativism |
| Natural science base | Humanities base line |
| Objectivity | Subjectivity |
| Causality | Interpretation |
| Quantification | Language and meaning |
| Falsification | Development of grounded theory |
| Nomothetic | Idiographic |
| Generalization | Particular cases |
| Research techniques include: | Research techniques include: |
|   statistical procedures |   participant observation, ethnography |
|   experiment |   life history |
|   social survey |   unstructured interview |
| Tends to be MACRO and QUANTITATIVE | Tends to be MICRO and QUALITATIVE |

**Figure 2.4**  Comparison of opposing traditions for doing social research

In Chapter 3 we will focus more closely upon the principles and procedures of ethnography as a basis for school-based research conducted by the teacher. It is our view that the interpretative, ethnographic model of social research and the methodological tradition it has generated form the most suitable basis for research conducted by most teachers into their own and immediate practice. In this sense interpretative, ethnographic research is best seen as an attitude or frame of mind which embodies a certain orientation towards investigating schools and classrooms. We believe this to be the case for two main reasons.

First, the various critiques and debates within both education and the human sciences over the years has led us to the view that neglect of the immediate, everyday meaningful contexts in which social action takes place can only result in at best partial and at worst, distorted pictures of social reality. Second, we understand many teachers' distrust of much academic research which is seen as being distant and aloof. The techniques of interpretative, ethnographic research help to bridge the gulf between so-called pure, academic research and the everyday realities of teaching. This approach and the techniques which accompany it are clearly amenable to use by teachers themselves, are best suited to the particular needs of the teacher researcher, and are capable of delivering valid knowledge of school and classroom processes. This suggests that interpretative, ethnographic techniques have a special value in school-based research. This approach deliberately reduces the distance between 'researcher' and 'subject'. Indeed the subjects themselves become part of the research and can in fact help the researcher by actually doing the research themselves. Teachers can simultaneously remain teachers and researchers by adopting this approach. Hence we believe that the interpretative, ethnographic model is best suited for the majority of situations the teacher researcher may wish to explore and has a considerable potential for the purposes of reflecting upon professional practice which has been clearly demonstrated. The chapters in Part II of the book therefore unravel the kinds of qualitative techniques the teacher researcher can use.

### Evaluation of the interpretative, ethnographic model of research

As with any research orientation or tradition the interpretative, ethnographic approach to social research is not without its critics. It is not our intention to add yet one more voice to the prolonged positivism–anti-positivism debate within education and the social sciences. We have been concerned to unravel the differences between the two traditions and to provide a rationale for the use of a range of qualitative ethnographic techniques as forming the basis for a piece of school-based research. However, it is only fair to raise some of the doubts and queries that have been levelled against the interpretative, ethnographic tradition. While we will briefly address some of these questions here, the answers ultimately lie within the chapters dealing with the techniques themselves and their use by teacher researchers. There seem to be three main questions and we will provide our responses to them in the form of a dialogue.

*Q But is qualitative research really scientific?*

*A* If being scientific means being systematic, rigorous, and analytical then qualitative research can meet the criteria of being scientific. But qualitative and ethnographic researchers do tend to approach research design, data collection, and analysis in a fundamentally different way from many other social scientists.

*Q If qualitative ethnographic research depends so much on the involvement of the researcher is it possible to remain objective in such research?*

*A* Objectivity is certainly a hotly debated issue in the social sciences. It is of course questionable whether or not objectivity actually applies to school-based research. In attempting to try and emulate the procedures of the natural sciences some social scientists claimed that objectivity was both desirable and possible. Qualitative and ethnographic researchers are much more cautious because they stress the importance of the involvement of the researcher. The involvement of the researcher in qualitative ethnographic research studies are seen by some to be positive values of such research not weakness. However, the researcher must never become so involved that she ceases to be an observer and remains only a participant. Detachment and reflection are important skills for qualitative researchers to develop.

*Q If qualitative ethnographic studies are so particular, localized, and small scale, is it possible to make any generalizations from them?*

*A* The issue of generalization in qualitative research is a problematic one. The problem partly emerges out of a misunderstanding about generalization and partly from an overt concern with generalization as the ultimate and only goal of social research. Generalized statements regarding, say, the effectiveness of open-plan teaching, or the influence of differing teaching styles upon pupils' 'achievements' would require a lot of research in many different schools, something on the scale of the ORACLE project. Teaching styles mean different things to different people; many different viewpoints and situations would therefore need to be examined before any generalizations could be made. First, it is questionable whether or not teachers could engage in a large enough study to make high-level generalizations. Second, most qualitative, ethnographic research in schools and classrooms is not concerned with the production of generalizations in this way. Instead these researchers are more concerned to produce adequate descriptions of educational contexts and analyses which highlight and explain the social processes that shape and influence teaching and learning in schools. The question of generalizability does apply to qualitative ethnographic work in so far as it is important for the teacher researcher to examine whether or not teachers and pupils behave in similar ways to those observed in a cross range of situations. This is important because it allows the researcher to put the actions into a broader more general context. Ethnographers have not always been clear how their descriptions apply across a range of circumstances. Another way in which generalization enters into qualitative research is the way in which ethnographers can move from discussing particular cases to more general patterns or wider sets of circumstances by suggesting that the social processes observed in one situation seem to hold constant and apply to a range of other social settings. Thus general statements about the phenomena can be made because they can be shown to operate across a range of particular situations.

*Q Interpretative ethnographic research relies quite a lot on qualitative data. Are quantitative approaches incompatible with qualitative approaches? Can the researcher use quantitative and qualitative data?*

*A* Many textbooks separate quantitative and qualitative research techniques in part because they tend to be derived from the different traditions of positivism and interpretivism. Textbooks invariably deal with quantitative or qualitative techniques but some try to bridge the gap by dealing with both types, or at least a selection of both types. The reality of much social and educational research is that researchers will make use of a variety of sources of data and will use different kinds of analyses. For example it is perfectly legitimate for the teacher researcher to use school records, examination statistics, DES statistics, and information from longitudinal studies. Similarly, in the course of conducting some ethnographic inquiry in a school the teacher researcher may use a structured questionnaire and attempt some correlation of the results or do some systematic observation in the classroom which will involve counting the number of different types of interaction at time intervals in a particular classroom. There is in this sense no problem with quantitative techniques and sources of data. Provided that the teacher is reasonably statistically literate and capable of following some basic procedures, some important information for school-based inquiry can be developed. The problem with quantitative data is the way in which they are used and what they are used for. Interpretative, ethnographic researchers are concerned to qualify through the eyes of insiders, rather than quantify through the eyes of an observer. Their argument is that quantitative data on school and classroom processes need to be supplemented by contextual details supplied by interpretative qualitative techniques. A good example of the strengths and weaknesses of incorporating qualitative and quantitative sources of data in one study can be found in Pollard's (1984: 33–48) study of teacher and pupils coping strategies where in fact 'measurement' is introduced into an ethnographic study.

## Teachers doing research

So far in this chapter we have been outlining the philosophical, technical, and methodological differences between two major opposing research traditions in the social sciences. We argued that the interpretative, ethnographic tradition was for a number of reasons best suited to school-based research conducted by the teacher. This is only part of the story. All social and educational research, as well as that conducted by the teacher researcher, faces a series of practical and analytical questions and all social research might be said to involve a series of stages. These stages encompass the whole of a research product and help us to see the way in which any piece of social research can be conducted. These stages enable the researcher to unravel some of the complex questions that doing research raises. Figure 2.5 presents these stages.

**Figure 2.5** The research process

What do each of these stages involve for a teacher engaged in school or classroom research? We will examine each of these stages in turn in order to unravel the kinds of questions the teacher researcher will have to address in conducting a piece of school-based research. At the outset of course it is important to recognize that the reasons why a teacher might be doing any piece of research will likely be very different from those of a 'professional' researcher.

## Research design and preparation stage

All research or evaluation begins somewhere. All research is underpinned by some basic assumptions and there are different models or blueprints for research design as we have seen. The researcher will also have a set of questions in mind or broad areas it is hoped to focus upon. Questions conerning the delineation of a topic or problem for investigation, the location of certain sources of data, the choices of data collection procedures and how to analyse them are all initial preparatory questions the researcher needs to think about. However, the teacher researcher will be focusing upon practice, albeit broadly defined. But, as Rob Walker has reminded us, research into educational practice is not as straightforward as it may at first appear and problems do not always present themselves in a ready-made fashion but rather need working and reshaping into a form that is amenable to research (Walker 1985: 46). The key word here would seem to be amenable. Not all of the research problems the teacher may want to focus upon are in fact able to be researched. Futhermore, small-scale school-based research will make demands of time, energy, and resources upon the researcher and these are always in short supply. Teacher research must always have at its heart commitment to a reconsideration of the bases of practice in both a critical and reflective manner.

Three questions emerge at this point. First, the teacher needs to ask herself *why she is undertaking research into this aspect of her own or others' teaching?* Second, *how will the research further understanding of the problem or issue?* And third, *can the problem realistically be researched and if so how?* A further set of questions emerges if the research is part of a collaborative piece of research involving a number of other teacher researchers. Here it will be important to be clear about what the nature of the contributions of the various parties involved will be, how responsibilities are to be shared out, and so on. Once a topic for research is established additional questions emerge. These may be listed and could act as a checklist.

### Research design and preparation stage checklist

1  What sources of data will be used?
2  What problems are likely to emerge in gaining access to these sources of data?

3 How are the data to be collected?
4 Are any ethical issues likely to arise from the research and how might they be overcome?
5 What time scales are involved in the research?
6 How will the findings of the research be disseminated?

Each of these questions will be explored in more detail in the subsequent chapters of the book. They are important vital considerations the teacher researcher will have to make. However, there are some deeper considerations to be borne in mind during the initial research design stage.

In the first part of this chapter we drew out the distinctions between major traditions of research in the social sciences. Spradley's analogy of petroleum engineers and explorers was used to highlight the differences between positivism and the scientific model and the interpretative, ethnographic model. These two approaches, as we pointed out, generate different research designs. Usually research which adopts the positivistic, scientific model approaches the whole issue of research design as illustrated in Figure 2.6.

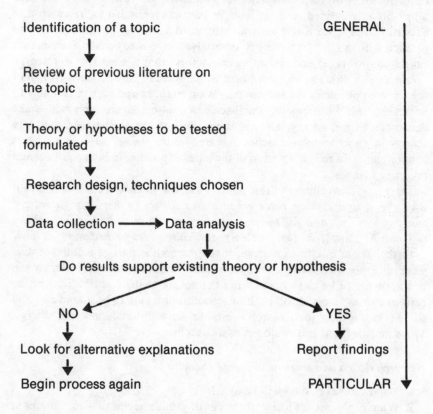

**Figure 2.6** A positivistic scientific research design

It is clear to see how this model operates in a deductive fashion moving from the general to the particular. Theory or hypotheses come first, data collection comes afterwards. A model of research design based upon the interpretative, ethnographic model will look on the surface to be much the same as this but on closer inspection turns out to be quite different: see Figure 2.7.

While there are similarities between these two research designs there are crucial differences. The main difference lies in the way in which any theories or concepts generated in interpretative, ethnographic research tend to come after the data collection phase, not prior to it. This model also highlights the developmental or emergent nature of interpretative research by stressing that the process of analysis operates to a certain extent simultaneously as the data are being collected: a theme we will come back to in Chapter 3. This model works by induction, in other words research moves from the particular to the general. Such a model reflects the interpretative researchers' concentration upon research in 'natural settings' and its avoidance of the rigid controls needed in an 'experimental' quantitative approach. Qualitative techniques

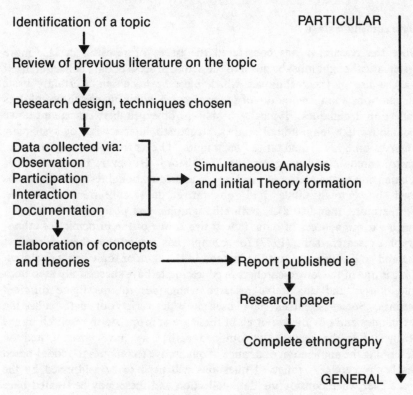

**Figure 2.7** An interpretative ethnographic research design

aim to develop an appreciation of a given situation in which the researcher is bound to be involved while the quantitative techniques aim to minimize researcher effects by establishing a position of social neutrality and objectivity.

Within the qualitative tradition there is a certain disagreement as to whether one should develop theories alongside data collection or to collect the data first and then look for a fit between the data and theories. Those who argue for the latter suggest that by doing the analysis last one avoids as far as possible the contamination of the data by the researcher. We have found from experience that there is positive advantage in developing data collection and analysis side by side as it enables one to try out different explanations of the fit between data and theory as one proceeds. The key question for the qualitative researcher is how it is possible to obtain as authentic an account of school or classroom life as possible without forcing the data into a theory or avoiding the temptation of 'hammering reality into shape'. These issues are explored more fully when we unravel each technique in detail in the chapters in Part II.

## Data collection stage

Once the researcher has considered the issues of research design, more systematic thought must be given to the actual process of data collection itself via the use of the techniques which have been chosen. Certainly basic assumptions about the nature of social research will influence choice of data collection techniques. Typically a split is observed between quantitative techniques like longitudinal studies, structured interviewing or systematic observation, and qualitative techniques like participant observation, unstructured interviewing, or the life history. However, this bears little relationship to the reality of much social and educational research which has used both quantitative and qualitative data collection techniques. Furthermore, many studies, both ethnographic and positivistic, have combined various sources of data; indeed this is one of the principles of ethnographic research. King (1987) for example has argued that there is 'no best method' and we should suit the method to the issue or topic being explored. King is one of the few researchers in education to have successfully used both quantitative and qualitative research techniques to investigate different settings. Social scientists have used a wide variety of data collection techniques and obviously not all of these are appropriate to research by the teacher. For the reasons we outlined earlier we have concentrated on describing the application of a range of qualitative techniques to school-based teacher research. A range of questions will need to be addressed by the researcher when considering data collection and these may be treated once again as a checklist.

*Data collection stage checklist*

1　Has the choice of data collection technique been thoroughly explored?
2　What, if any, is the mix of data collection techniques to be employed?
3　Have any potential problems associated with a particular technique been considered?
4　How flexible are the data collection techniques being used?
5　Is the researcher clear about the relative strengths and weaknesses of any particular technique being used?

The teacher researcher following an interpretative, ethnographic research design and using a range of qualitative techniques will find that 'data collection' will involve three basic processes which constitute the central ingredients of any qualitative research technique. These are observation, interrogation, and documentary and oral data collection. The first process involves listening to and looking at what the people in the research setting itself are doing. The second process involves talking to these subjects about the meanings they attach to their actions. The third process involves the interpretation of meanings from written or oral data. The outcome of all three processes is data collected which will then need to be sifted, analysed, or evaluated. What one is doing here is creating what we can call either first-order accounts or primary sources and then, by means of analysis, second-order accounts or secondary sources. The chapters which follow immediately will detail the most effective ways of doing this for each of the techniques involved.

## Data analysis and evaluation stage

Analysis is what the researcher does with data in order to develop explanations of events so that theories and generalizations about the causes, reasons, and processes of any piece of social behaviour can be developed. Analysis therefore looks for the major properties of any event or set of events. There are very many different kinds of analyses which ultimately depend upon the nature of the particular research design employed and underlying assumptions held. Researchers have used statistical analysis using mathematical techniques, thematic analysis, class analysis, content analysis, conversational analysis, qualitative analysis. The chapters in Part II unravel some of the important tasks the teacher researcher will need to engage in when analysing her materials.

While analysis is important the purpose of teacher school-based research means that the enterprise does not finish with analysis. What the researcher does with the research findings is often inextricably linked with the underlying design of the research which we outlined in stage 1. Teacher research comes from and inevitably returns to professional practice. This means that evaluation and an examination of the practical and policy implications should feature in the analysis stage of any school-based teacher research. Evaluation might therefore be defined as that process which subjects data and the theories developed to some kind of assessment in terms of specific criteria in order to unravel the effectiveness or otherwise, the success or otherwise of particularly arranged activities to achieve certain ends or goals and ultimately to improve the quality of the particular sets of actions involved. The processes of analysis and evaluation take on a particular importance in teacher research.

The teacher researching her own practice is in a different role from an outside researcher in that the positions of observer and subject have to a large degree been merged. It has been argued that this is one of the strengths of the teacher researcher role and helps to overcome the distrust or cynicism many teachers feel towards research. However, one still needs to be clear about the assumptions which underlie the research and check one's own interpretations with other members of staff and other teacher researchers. One of the major criticisms of qualitative approaches is that the assumptions on which the researchers made their selection of data or material to focus upon are not always made explicit. One of the implications is that in studying say an issue such as classroom control, the teacher researcher may need to involve teachers, pupils, parents as well as outside agencies. Finally it is important to recognize in any analysis that the individual classroom is part of a much larger system and it is therefore important to take into account the influence of forces outside the classroom. The checklist below proposes a series of questions about data analysis.

*Data analysis and evaluation stage checklist*

1 Have the aims of the research been achieved?
2 Is the analysis complete; if not, why not?
3 Have the underlying assumptions about key concepts and meanings developed been critically addressed and where necessary been compared with others involved?
4 Has the analysis exhausted as many explanations as possible?
5 Have the data been properly evaluated?
6 What are the implications for practice of the outcomes of the research?
7 How can the results of the research be disseminated?

*Three questions for school-based research*
Three questions are always in the minds of social and educational researchers. The extent to which these questions are applicable to school-based research is debatable. All the same a working knowledge of these questions is important since in many respects they can help the teacher researcher to think more sharply about what she is doing. We will conclude this chapter by briefly and simply defining validity, reliability, and representativeness.

## Validity

Validity refers to the extent to which the materials collected are true and represent an accurate picture of what or who is being studied. The notion of validity therefore suggests that researchers can employ 'validity checks'.

## Reliability

Reliability concerns the extent to which any particular method of data collection is replicable, that is if the research was to be repeated by someone else using a different technique, would the same findings result? The idea of reliability therefore concerns the question of whether or not the data are products of the research technique employed.

## Representativeness

Representativeness surrounds the extent to which the situation, individuals, or groups investigated are typical or representative of the situations, individuals, or group as a whole. Representativeness therefore raises questions about the choice of situations, subjects, and groups.

## Summary

In this chapter we have outlined and discussed the main elements of the positivistic scientific and interpretative ethnographic approaches to social and educational research. We have concentrated upon the underlying assumptions which inform social research and the controversies and debates this has given rise to. Our reasons for suggesting that the interpretative, ethnographic model of social research is best suited for the purposes of school-based research were explained and we concluded by considering what doing research means for teachers themselves. Our account will no doubt upset some and please others. For a long time both social research and educational research have been stuck at the albeit important level of debate between paradigms, perspectives, or schools. Often this has been acrimonious and counter-productive. Far too much debate has centred around the differences in theoretical orientations rather than methodological and substantive issues. Teacher school-based research is inevitably going to be touched by these issues. However, the need to get on with the job is paramount in the case of teacher research. The issues we have been discussing in this chapter have not been resolved, nor will they be in the foreseeable future. The need is for teachers themselves to be aware of these issues and have a sufficiently developed methodological 'know how' in order to generate research into their own practice. Interpretative ethnographic research, we suggest, holds the greatest promise for teachers in this regard. It is now time to get to grips with the means by which teachers can begin to develop knowledge about their own practice by doing research. Part II therefore deals with a range of techniques that may be used by the teacher in some school-based research. We move therefore from questions of research design to data collection and analysis.

## Suggested further reading

Those readers unfamiliar with the background to contemporary debates on the nature of the human sciences might consider R. G. Anderson, J. A. Hughes and W. W. Sharrock (1986) *Philosophy and the Human Sciences*, London: Croom Helm, which has the rare quality of dealing with some extremely complex issues in a clear, straightforward way. In addition a number of dictionairies of education and the social sciences are appearing which contain entries on particular methodological issues or individual techniques which are worth consulting. The application of the qualitative or interpretative approach to educational research is treated extensively in R. Bogdan and S. Biklen (1982) *Qualitative Research for Education: An Introduction to Theory and Research,* Boston, Mass: Allyn & Bacon. The concept of teacher research is explored in an interesting article by E. Cope and J. Gray (1979) 'Teachers as researchers: some experiences of an alternative paradigm', *British Educational Research Journal* 5: 237–51. We still find the writings of Lawrence Stenhouse a source of interest; a useful start is L. Stenhouse (1975) *An Introduction to Curriculum Research and Development,* London: Heinemann, since he has been so influential in the development of the notion of the teacher as researcher. Useful assessments of Stenhouse's contribution can be found in the *British Educational Research Journal* 9, 1 (1983). D. Hustler, T. Cassidy and T. Cuff (eds) (1987) *Action Research in Classrooms and Schools,* London: Allen & Unwin, includes contributions from teachers on their own 'action research' in schools. J. Nixon (ed.) (1981) *A Teacher's Guide to Action Research,* London: Grant McIntyre, also contains some useful suggestions and examples. A collection of classic studies in classroom research can be found in M. Hammersley (ed.) (1986) *Case Studies in Classroom Research,* Milton Keynes: Open University Press. The case study method as used in psychology education and the human sciences in general is explored at length by D. B. Bromley (1986) *The Case Study Method in Psychology and Related Disciplines,* London: Wiley. A general guide to the whole area of teacher research which is worth consulting is W. R. Borg (1981) *Applying Educational Research: A Practical Guide for Teachers,* New York: Longman.

# Qualitative research techniques and the teacher

## Introduction

Part II of the book concentrates on the organization and use of a range of qualitative research techniques in school-based research. We aim to provide a clear understanding of both the rationale and organization underlying a series of qualitative research techniques, so that the prospective researcher is aware of the skills and knowledge required in order to make use of them in any piece of school-based research. As well as outlining the methodological aspects of these techniques we also offer a preliminary discussion of the ways in which the data collected by means of these techniques can be analysed. We see a range of qualitative research techniques as sharing a common orientation to social and educational research in general: this may be described as ethnography. Ethnography and fieldwork provide the framework within which the individual research techniques we examine can be placed. Thus Part II of the book begins by considering the nature of fieldwork and ethnography.

Ethnography provides a research framework that allows for the description of the routine, everyday, unquestioned, and taken-for-granted aspects of school and classroom life. Central to this approach is observation, going, and looking. The ethnographic model of the research process offers a unique opportunity for teachers, trading on their own knowledge and involvement in their own settings, to investigate the processes of teaching and learning. As such the following chapters will hopefully convey some of the excitement of 'doing research' and demonstrate how professional practice can be considerably enhanced by looking at school and classroom processes using the research techniques we outline here.

Our choice of individual research techniques to focus upon in detail has been guided by the particular circumstances of classrom teachers. We have concentrated on describing the elements of those techniques which ordinary teachers can most readily use and which are sufficiently flexible to adapt to the school-based context of teacher research. Interviewing however is such a central research technique that no book on research methodology can be allowed to ignore it. Clearly there are a number of different types of interview and interviewing strategy. We focus upon unstructured interviewing and conversations in more detail since we believe that these are likely to be of most value to the teacher. Chapter 5 outlines the importance of a time or historical dimension in school-based research by detailing the issues involved in collecting and using documentary sources in the context of school-based research. Chapter 6 recognizes the centrality of classroom interaction by outlining the major ways in which researchers have gone about investigating the classroom and suggests ways in which the teacher researcher might begin research on classroom interaction. By way of conclusion to this part of the book Chapter 7 provides a case study of the ways in which the spatial dimensions of teaching and learning may be investigated in order to highlight the value and use of ethnographic research for teachers.

Throughout the chapters in Part II we have made reference to various studies and research findings not so much for their substantive content but for the techniques and methodology employed. Interested readers can follow up these studies at a later point. The further reading sections at the end of each chapter provide suggestions for readers to follow up. While Chapters 4 to 7 may be usefully read in any order, Chapter 3 provides the major background information and orientation to this part of the book; as such we suggest that it should be read first.

Chapter three

# Ethnography, fieldwork, and the teacher

**Introduction**

A young graduate student in his late 20s makes his way through the rain and industrial grime of a northern city, en route to begin research in an inner-city open-plan primary school. On arrival the school resembles the inside of an aircraft hanger. The researcher feels a tap on his leg, 'Hi, I'm Geoffrey, they think I'm thick me but I'm not'. Geoffrey's introduction is as quick as his departure, for on turning, the researcher finds Geoffrey running off and a middle-aged short man approaching him. 'Did you get lost?' he enquires. It transpired that the researcher had mistakenly entered the building via the playground doors and not through the 'official' entry point, which led into the foyer with the head and his secretary's offices adjoining it (Hitchcock 1980).

Somewhere in Brixton, London, an American researcher sits in a coffee bar speaking to a group of young Afro-Caribbeans about their experience of school. He says little, nods sympathetically now and again, answers the questions they ask of him, occasionally scribbling down some notes. Later he writes up those notes and files them under various headings and ponders on some questions he might want to ask his friends tomorrow (Cottle 1978).

Elsewhere in a Midlands town a sociologist is getting to know the culture, language, ideas, attitudes, and expectations of a group of 'lads' who constitute a school counter-culture. He discovers that the lads are 'learning to labour' (Willis 1977). Meanwhile another researcher is charting the day of a school principal (Wolcott 1973) and yet another researcher is observing teachers and children in an infant school (King 1978). All these people have one thing in common: they are all engaged in *ethnographic fieldwork*.

The terms fieldwork and ethnography are often used interchangeably in social research. However, fieldwork usually refers to the means by which the product, the ethnographic description of a group, organization, culture, or set of practices, comes into being. Such a bewildering array of activities have been conducted under the heading of ethnography that it makes it a little difficult to say exactly what ethnography is. While it may be difficult to describe in anything other than general terms what fieldwork and ethnography consist of, it can safely be said that the use of these approaches

51

was in part a response to dissatisfaction with positivistic, quantitative approaches and in part a result of modern anthropology's encounters with and attempts to understand others very different from ourselves. In general terms fieldwork is the primary means by which most anthropological information has been obtained. It involves the prolonged, intensive, and direct involvement of the researcher in the lives and activities of the group in question. This 'going and seeing' and living with the 'natives' was the hallmark of the emergence of scientific anthropology. The aim of these researchers was to share in the experiences of those being studied in as natural a fashion as possible in order to understand better how these people viewed and made sense of their worlds. Observation and participant observation became the key means by which this was achieved. As Malinowski (1922: 25), one of the first social scientists to use the technique of ethnography, has put it, the goal of ethnography 'is to grasp the native point of view, his relation to his life, to realise his vision of his world'.

It is clear that certain requirements would have to be met in these situations. First, in societies or cultures very different from the researchers' own, a new language needs to be learnt, a reason for being there in the first place would have to be established, and a working relationship with the people themselves developed. Of course as anthropology moves from the distant and exotic to our own industrial societies some problems diminish yet, as we shall see, other problems emerge.

One of the difficulties of talking about 'ethnography' is that it is often used in conjunction with other terms like participant observation, qualitative methodology, case study, and to a certain extent, action research. As such it is difficult to define precisely, it is better instead to focus upon the kinds of features which are characteristic of ethnography. Perhaps one of the most striking features about ethnographic research is its utilization of a wide range of sources of data. From observation and interviewing to the use of documents and photographs, ethnographers are concerned as much with the ordinary, routine, mundane aspects of a group or organization's life as they are with the extraordinary. For the most part ethnographers tend to spend a long time looking at a small group of units for analysis; in other words they tend to focus upon the *micro* level of human interaction and social processes rather than concentrating upon the larger picture, macro or social structural level of institutions, social classes, whole cultures, or societies. It is therefore the aim of this chapter to provide teachers with the basic and general principles of fieldwork and ethnographic research in particular as these pertain to the teaching and learning context.

A working definition of ethnography may now therefore be defined, though in broad terms only. It is possible to distil a summary of the characteristics of ethnography. Ethnography involves

1 the production of descriptive cultural knowledge of a group;

2 the description of activities in relation to a particular cultural context from the point of view of the members of that group themselves;

3 the production of a list of features constitutive of membership in a group or culture;

4 the description and analysis of patterns of social interaction;

5 the provision as far as possible of 'insider accounts'

6 the development of theory

Thus an ethnography in fact becomes the realization of the fieldwork experiences and encounters, formalizing as it does the overt or covert involvement of the researcher in a particular setting and the information obtained resulting in a written report or document, the 'ethnography'. Fieldwork and ethnography therefore are certainly fairly basic modes of research. Ethnography is about portraying people and we use the term here to refer jointly to a particular style of social research, accepting that there are important variations in this and to the products of that research. Originally ethnography and fieldwork were the key tools of the anthropologist studying a non-western society, quickly though these anthropological approaches were seen to be of value in studying the ethnically diverse, complex industrial societies of Britain and North America. When anthropologists turned their attention towards educational experiences of ethnic minority groupings it was only natural that the tools of fieldwork, ethnography, the use of informants and cultural description were to become important in developing a distinct anthropology of education in North America. Yet the foundations for doing this were laid down some considerable time ago when Malinowski, complete with his tent, pioneered the fieldwork method in his study of the Trobriand islanders in the Pacific.

While the major impetus in the development of fieldwork and ethnographic techniques has come from social and cultural anthropology, sociology too has played its part, though educational research has come to appreciate the value of ethnographic techniques only fairly recently. As we saw in Chapter 2, the school or approach to sociology associated with the University of Chicago pioneered the use of participant observation in the study of industrial locations and produced some fine ethnographies during the period between the two world wars. People like Robert Park and Ernest Burgess encouraged their staff and students to develop participant observation, observing and participating in the lives of those social groups who lived right under their noses, on their own doorstep in Chicago, but who, for many reasons, had been ignored by social scientists. The Chicago approach is a landmark in the history of empirical social research yet for our purposes is important in another way. What these researchers did was to combine participant observation and forms of observation with a whole range of other sources of data and techniques. They constructed life histories, interviewed people, and made use of official records and documentary sources like newspapers, diaries, and letters. Thomas and Znaniecki, for example, in their monumental study of Polish emigration to America, *The Polish Peasant in Europe and America* (1918–20), made use of over 700 letters. This is why we have collected the various qualitative techniques discussed in this part of the book together for they all ought to be seen as part of the wider ethnographic approach. The teacher researcher will always have to locate the interview, the life history, the field notes, observations, and the documents collected within the social and cultural context of which they are a part.

The extent to which the teacher will use all or some of these techniques within an ethnographic study of an aspect of schooling will of course vary with the nature of the study. The question of which particular technique to use is less important than the need to remember that schools, classrooms, and staffrooms are located in a particular time and place. Ethnography gets us to pay attention to culture, to neighbourhood, to children and staff's backgrounds, to class, status, ethnicity, and gender, to the minutiae of everyday interaction and to the particular contextual meanings and significance of events and activities of the school and classroom to members themselves. As such educational ethnography incorporates a broadly humanistic approach to investigating the social world of the school. But what is it that ethnographers do?

## What do ethnographers do when they do ethnography?

From the study of ethnographic accounts and the experiences of one of the authors it is possible to build up a picture, or more appropriately a collage, of the kinds of ordinary activities that ethnographers engage in when they are involved in ethnography. Ethnographers look, listen, ask questions, take part, learn the language, learn and record any specialized use of language or argot, make inferences from what people say, locate informants, develop relationships, become friends, and experience different ways of life. Typically ethnographers will observe ceremonies, collect and trace family trees (genealogies), observe meetings, record daily events, watch children and adults play, keep diaries and write letters home and of course countless other things besides. In order to put this picture into sharper focus let us briefly consider Wolcott's description of his work in Ed Bell's school.

In developing his study of an American school administrator or principal Wolcott developed a range of methods to facilitate his understanding of Ed Bell's work and which enabled data to be gathered on a number of aspects of the school. He outlines six sources of information which supplemented his direct observations. He collected routine distributions of notices, copies of school records, reports and correspondence, he took notes at 60-second intervals for blocks of two hours relating to the interactions and activities of the principal, he obtained impressions of school life from fifth- and sixth-grade pupils, used a tape recorder, and designed, distributed, and analysed a staff questionnaire at the end of the school year (Wolcott 1973: 8–18). It is interesting to note that Chapter 2 of Wolcott's ethnography is entitled 'A day in the life' which provides a rich and detailed account of what a typical day in the life of a school principal is actually like. Clearly here, as in school-based research, more generally the research will act as the key instrument or funnel through which data are obtained in the research.

It is clear to see from this description and others that the ethnographer becomes involved in a range of activities and it is not always possible to specify in any detail beforehand what to consider. What the ethnographer does in the field is for the most part dictated by the nature of the social organization of the field itself, the influence of such key variables as the age, ethnicity, gender, and status of the researcher and the nature of the composition of the group being studied. The above description conveys the process whereby the researcher attempts to immerse herself in the flood and stream of happenings in the setting. An initial feeling experienced by the beginning ethnographer is the desire always to be where the 'action' is. Once the 'action' ceases to become new, but instead routine, ordinary, and taken for granted, it has ceased in that sense to become strange, then the ethnographer is truly immersed in the culture and it is time to leave. As W. F. Whyte observed in his classic participant observation study of an American Boston Italian slum neighbourhood, he began as a participant observer and ended up as a non-observing participator (Whyte 1955).

Here we arrive at that special and unique point the teacher researcher is placed in. Teachers, unless they look at other schools and other classrooms, are usually already participants in the worlds they wish to describe and uncover by means of fieldwork and ethnography. Even when they do research in other schools they are considerably tuned in to the world of schools and classrooms. We will examine the implications of this observation shortly. Enough has been said however to give an initial flavour of what fieldwork and ethnography is all about in general terms. Let us now consider in more detail a breakdown of what might be involved in doing ethnography in educational settings.

### Steps, stages, and tasks in doing fieldwork and ethnography in educational settings

It is important for the teacher researcher to develop an appreciation of the skills, steps, stages, and tasks involved in the conduct of ethnographic inquiry. Certain skills need to be spelled out and from experience, certain things seem to be best done before others. It is helpful therefore to see the fieldwork and ethnographic process broken down into seven elements although there are often overlaps between these stages: see Figure 3.1.

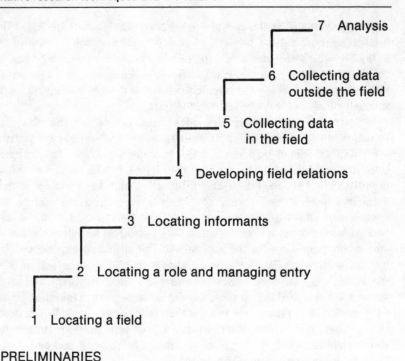

7  Analysis

6  Collecting data
   outside the field

5  Collecting data
   in the field

4  Developing field relations

3  Locating informants

2  Locating a role and managing entry

1  Locating a field

PRELIMINARIES

**Figure 3.1**  Steps and stages in doing fieldwork and ethnography in educational settings

*Preliminaries*

There are incredible strains in conducting any kind of fieldwork. For the most part these stem from the fact that the researcher is the main vehicle of the research. What the researcher sees, hears, and becomes involved in constitutes much of the data in ethnographic research. It is clear to see therefore how the personal dimension of the fieldwork experience is of considerable significance. A number of writers have provided both sobering and amusing accounts of the fieldwork experience; some of the best of these are contained in Powdermaker (1966), Frielich (1970), and Wax (1971). Fieldwork and ethnography, perhaps more than any other research technique, involve the researcher in a direct and often fairly intense relationship with people and events. No matter how modified these approaches become in the hands of the teacher this personal dimension of the fieldwork equation needs some attention as an important preliminary issue. Emotions, values, attitudes, and expectations will all play a part in any fieldwork situation. When the researcher is a familiar participant in the setting, as is often likely to be the case with teachers, all of these issues can become compounded.

None of these problems and difficulties is insurmountable. For the majority of situations the teacher is engaged in researching, what is required is the development of an attitude or a frame of mind to this kind of research. All in all the personal skills which are conducive to successful completion of field research, as we shall see, turn out to be not unlike those required for the achievement of normal successful social interaction, for example appearing interested and friendly, sympathetic and willing to listen to others, refraining from appearing dogmatic and overbearing. However, this does not conversely mean that teachers conducting research must hide their intentions or beliefs. The point is quite simple. The more the researchers' views, attitudes, and opinions enter into the research situation, the less of the actors' perspectives and ideas will be revealed. These are all undoubtedly matters of degree and the resolution of these problems will depend upon the nature of the research and the setting in question. The point must be stressed however that ethnographic field research is not simply only a matter of following a set of technical instructions, but also involves a personal dimension also. Teachers in particular need to spend some time thinking through this aspect of their research as an important preliminary issue.

It is useful to conceive of doing ethnography in a steps and stages fashion. The most important issue to address to begin with is the actual location of a field of inquiry.

## Locating a field

When researchers speak about the 'field' they are referring to the immediate physical and social boundaries surrounding their chosen research area. Obviously a field in this sense can be quite extensive. It is important for the researcher to locate and delineate the boundaries of the particular field in question. The field for the teacher might be all those situations directly connected with teaching and learning in a particular school. The field will involve a range of activities and typical categories of persons and individuals. It is unlikely that the teacher researcher is ever going to be able to cover all of the field she sees as being central to her project. It is important therefore to be able to see the field as a whole and to establish its boundaries and decide on what can and cannot be looked at in the project. Furthermore by doing this the teacher can develop a fair idea of what data and information outside the immediate field might need to be collected. While the field can be extended or narrowed as the research progresses so that new information can be incorporated, or fresh lines of thought developed, the location of a field in a general way will help the researcher to clarify reasonably well the nature of the issues to be covered and areas and people involved. A useful way of approaching this task is to try and visually represent the field by means of a diagram. This is the point at which important practical decisions about both the size and composition of the field itself will be made. Such an exercise should help the teacher to appreciate more clearly what the focus of the research is, and indeed could become. This process will involve the teacher in identifying key persona, key topics, and key sources of data. Once such an exercise has been completed the teacher will have a more realistic appreciation of what areas to concentrate on, how to do this, and how this meets the initial aims of the project in question. However, an often forgotten dimension to this process of locating a field is that potential problems, difficulties of access and so on can be at least anticipated by the researcher in advance of the research proper.

*Locating a role and managing entry*

All social research is governed by questions of access to people, information, and settings. Once access is obtained, actually entering the field and establishing a role for the researcher are two further central elements in ethnographic work. There are differences in the nature of these problems between the teacher conducting an ethnographic inquiry into some aspect of the process of schooling and say the anthropologist working within a non-western society, or the sociologist producing an ethnography of urban heroin addicts. Our anthropologist has first to learn a different language and possibly a number of dialects. The sociologist is investigating illegal activities amongst desperate people. The problem of access, managing entry, and developing a role for the researcher in these two scenarios is rather different from those faced by the teacher researcher starting ethnographic work in an educational context already known. However, while there are many differences between educational ethnographic research and ethnography in other settings there are many similarities.

The researcher cannot enter a scene unannounced and begin to conduct interviews. All researchers have to plan and prepare their work carefully; part of this preparation involves securing access and permission to enter the scene being investigated if this is required and once in the scene (1) establishing a reason for being there and (2) developing a role, a persona so that people know who the researcher is, what the researcher is doing there, and if necessary why! It follows that a fixed set of guidelines on these matters cannot easily be laid down since situations and circumstances will vary. Furthermore the character of the researcher will vary also. However, the teacher embarking on fieldwork and ethnographic inquiry is subject to many of the same sorts of access, entry, and role problems other fieldworkers face. But as far as the teacher researcher is concerned the differences depend to a great extent upon whether or not the researcher is doing fieldwork in her own classroom or her own school, or whether she is doing research in another school or classroom unknown or less familiar to her.

While some of the difficulties fade away when the teacher is conducting fieldwork in her own setting, others are thereby created. Familiarity is simultaneously an advantage and a disadvantage. The teacher knows the school, the staff, and children; she has a reputation and an 'official' role as for example a music teacher, top infants teacher, head of science, deputy head, or head. She has worked in the school perhaps for a number of years; she is established as someone with particular characteristics. The researcher already has an abundant store of important information about the school, its organization, and the children inside her head. The problem of course is that this all-too-familiar setting is very often largely taken for granted. Hence the teacher engaged in ethnographic research in familiar settings has the problem of rendering the familiar strange in order to avoid missing or taking for granted crucial aspects of the situation or topic being explored. While much ethnographic work is *overt,* that is visible, know about, and recognized as such by the subjects, for example when interviewing or clearly observing them, in contrast much ethnographic work is done and data gathered by *covert* means, that is when the researcher is simultaneously engaged or participating in the setting yet unknown to the other people in that setting, is observing, watching, listening to them, and making a mental record of the actions and conversations that ensue. All of these matters will involve role adjustments. The teacher might have to step out of her role as a teacher in order to facilitate observation. Her involvement might have to increase or decrease in certain activities. All in all though there are considerable advantages where access, entry, and the establishment of a role are concerned if the teacher is doing fieldwork in her own school. None the less it is always important to establish what it is the researcher is doing with the appropriate member of the school management and where necessary gain permission and more importantly support. It should also be noted that it is courteous to let people know at least in part what you are doing. This of course can help to facilitate and foster good field relations, an area we shall discuss shortly.

In contrast, the teacher – perhaps as part of an INSET, DES, or other course, or conducting self-supported research, engaged in fieldwork in a school or school-related setting other than her own – faces different problems of access, entry, and role. First of all permission will have to be granted and here, depending upon the nature of the circumstances, Walker's advice is worth considering.

> To gain access to the school, you need first to approach the Local
> Education Authority; to gain access to the staff, you need to approach the
> head; to gain access to the pupils, you need to approach the staff. Each
> fieldwork contact is thus sponsored by someone in authority over those
> you wish to study and relationships between 'sponsors' and researchers
> can not be broken if the research is to continue.
>
> (Walker 1980: 49)

The extent to which each of these things is necessary can be ascertained only by the teacher and common sense should prevail. What is certainly a lot more delicate is the actual process of entry and the development of a role with a group of teachers and pupils who are relatively unknown to the researcher. This situation is becoming increasingly common with school interchanges of staff, short courses involving teachers visiting other schools, and so on. A 'softly, softly' approach is usually the best line to take. Often entry and the development of a role can be facilitated by the help of a key member of the school. Many ethnographers and participant observers have gained entry into a setting with the help of a key informant. The most famous example here is Doc who was responsible for initiating W. F. Whyte into street-corner society so that Whyte could produce his classic account of an Italian American slum neighbourhood (Whyte 1955). Hitchcock's entry into the world of Cedars Junior, an urban open-plan primary school, was facilitated by Liz, a long-standing college friend who taught in the school (Hitchcock 1980; 1983b) and developed a role that was not unlike that of a student teacher on teaching practice. Another problem facing the teacher who is not familiar with a particular school is the negotiation of gatekeepers. All organizations and institutions have gatekeepers whose function it is to vet personnel entering the buildings, making sure they see only what they are supposed to see.

There is an important sense in which these problems can be resolved only in the course of the research. We must not however forget that the issues surrounding access, entry, and roles themselves cast important light on to the social organization of the setting itself and may in turn be regarded as an important source of data on the setting in question, as Burgess's account of gaining access to Bishop McGregor School and its Newson department demonstrates (Burgess 1984a: 40–5).

## Locating informants

The production of adequate ethnographic accounts has centred around the extent to which the ethnographer can offer a description of the features constitutive of membership in the group, culture, or institution being studied, together with a description and analysis of what happens in that setting, the knowledge, abilities, and ways of interacting characterisitic of the group. This has been achieved by anthropologists and sociologists and more recently educational researchers, by the use of 'informants': people who were knowledgeable about their society, culture, or the activity in question. Hence for a long time the idea that not just anybody will do as an informant was the accepted notion. Researchers were encouraged in the methods and techniques handbooks to search and make use of what Back described many years ago as 'the well-informed informant' (Back 1955: 30–3), someone who knew the setting under investigation well and would be able to provide the ethnographers with the correct information needed. In many cases ethnographers have relied upon a few or even single 'key informants' in constructing their accounts. The ambiguous nature of what might constitute a culturally competent individual, and thereby someone who might be regarded as good key informant material, was initially not questioned. The elicitation of accounts, narratives, and other information from key informants is a hallmark of ethnographic research. But how does the teacher researcher identify which accounts are more important than others; which are more truthful than others? The question of the location and selection of informants by teacher researchers is best seen in terms first of the technical issues raised, second in terms of the practical aspects, and finally in terms of the distinction between adults and children as informants.

Researchers often speak about the two connected themes of informant reliability and response validity; these in turn surround the issues of the truth and accuracy of informants' accounts and the extent to which the accounts are not natural but derive from the nature of the research encounter itself and are thereby influenced by it. A distinction is sometimes further drawn between 'internal validity', that is the extent to which the researchers' presence and choice of informant affects the kinds of data that are subsequently generated and 'external validity', the extent to which the data and materials obtained by the fieldworker and the analyses developed can be applied to other school and classroom situations. However, ethnographers tend to be much less concerned with the generalizability of their findings than other researchers. All these issues are what we might describe as technical issues in ethnographic and field research. They are the kinds of issues that might be attended to in the design of the research in the first instance.

These technical issues often seem to suggest that there are solutions to the problems of informant selection provided one simply follows technical procedures. The practical and everyday reality of schools and classrooms poses special problems surrounding the selection and location of informants for teachers doing fieldwork and ethnography. For example, not everyone in the school will be seen by all members of the school themselves to be valid, reliable, and competent commentators and sources of information on the school itself. Political and status issues are likely to emerge here. For example, is 'competence' in these terms equitable with status, length of stay in school, seniority, and the like? Teachers need to be wary of developing a too mechanistic view of the selection of informants. While we are not suggesting that everybody's voice has equal influence or power, we are saying that it is important to recognize the existence of as many voices as possible. An important principle emerges here. Fieldworkers quickly discover, in contrast to the advice of technical manuals, that the field itself dictates and demonstrates the relative 'worth', 'significance', 'validity', and 'competence' of its various component voices. Teachers need to attend to this feature as a serious and crucial aspect of their research. Perhaps there is nothing to be done about the fact that the nature of the field and its organization dictates in a large measure whom the researcher can take as an informant. It is none the less an important comment on the nature of the setting itself which in turn may be treated as important data on that setting. Furthermore the age, sex, status, and possibly subject specialism of the teacher doing the research is clearly likely to influence her choice of and encounters with informants.

In much social research, especially sociology, subjects for the research are usually chosen by means of some form of 'random sampling' in order to ensure their representativeness and typicality. This is not the case in ethnography. The selection of informants in ethnography, unlike the subjects for a postal questionnaire for example, are chosen more by luck and dictated by the nature of the field itself and many ethnographers of schools and classrooms like those working in other settings have relied upon key informants. Key informants are those people with whom the researcher focuses upon as a key source of data on the setting. They are spoken to by the researcher more often than others in the setting. In more cases than not the key informants used by the teacher researcher in educational settings are often neither typical nor representative, but are instead people whom the researcher feels are integral to the scenes and situations being investigated. The teacher will frequently use informants who by their position, role, status, or gender are not representative of the scene as a whole. This does not mean that they are of no use as a source of data. The question of the selection and use of key informants is not so much one of their typicality and representativeness, but rather with placing what any informant says into the wider picture, which necessarily includes other perspectives, contextual description, and the researchers' own observations. Furthermore, teachers in the course of conducting a particular piece of research will collect data and obtain information from a variety of sources, not simply key informants. Again what is important is for the teacher to be clear on what informant selection strategies were employed and why. In other words, what was the basis upon which certain informants were chosen?

There are however a series of practical issues that the teacher needs to attend to regarding informants. These might be regarded as a checklist for the research design stages, as well as during the fieldwork itself.

1 Has a range of viewpoints been covered by the informants used?
2 Are different positions, roles, levels, and status groupings being represented by the informants used?
3 Has the informants' behaviour and talk been monitored by the researcher across a range of situations so that the importance of context can be established?
4 Do the informants used have specialized subject or general subject/area knowledge, occupy central or marginal positions?
5 Has the influence of the researcher's own age, sex, class, ethnicity, and status been considered in (a) the informant selection procedure and (b) researcher/teacher, informant/teacher relationships?
6 Since schools, like many other institutions, are frequently very hier-

archical, has the selection of informants given due weight to the existence of unequal voices?

Teachers will need to recognize the essentially practical and *ad hoc* nature of the use of informants, together with the broader analytic and technical consequences of whom they gain much of their information from. Can informants be friends? Can you ask ethnographic questions of those with whom you teach? The use of the term 'informant' itself is perhaps too simplistic and mechanical to convey the real nature of the involvement between a teacher and a fellow colleague known for some time. After all the technical and scientific talk in the world it is still easier to get on with some people than others. On the other hand, some informants may not give the fieldworker information for fear of boring them with the commonplace. These are all eminently practical matters: their resolution hinges to a large extent upon the fieldworker's own interpersonal relationships and the question of informants then blurs considerably with issues of field relations more generally which we consider next. However, the question of children or pupils constituting key informants raises important questions that we might briefly discuss first.

*Children as informants*

We consider some of the questions surrounding pupils' accounts in Chapter 6 when we examine the classroom as a social environment and focus upon classroom talk and interaction. The idea of children as informants raises methodological issues as well as moral and ethical ones. On the surface there is really no problem in using children as informants provided all the usual reasonable precautions one would take regarding other informants are taken. The whole issue would seem to surround taking children seriously. In many ways the use of pupils as key informants is simply a further extension of portraying the actor's perspective and as such any study which did not pay reference to children's views and interactions of pupils' perspectives could be found to be lacking.

A number of researchers are now focusing upon pupils' viewpoints or 'pupil strategies' (Woods 1980b). Pollard (1987: 95–118) for example discusses some of the processes involved in trying to collect information on middle-school children's perspectives, while Beynon (1984: 121–44) shows how a focus upon pupils as 'data gatherers' enabled Beynon to see how, when starting secondary school, boys' endeavours in 'sussing out' the teacher were a crucial apsect of their school experience. These strategies allowed the children to 'locate' the teacher, develop expectations, and maintain their own peer-group organization.

Using children and pupils as informants raises a number of problems. Despite the obvious differences in status, sensitive ethnographers have been able to develop good ethnographic descriptions of child culture and life in school. The prospective researcher might consider the ways in which the following researchers have resolved some of these problems and the kinds of data and analyses they have been able to produce: Ball (1985); Corsaro (1981: 117–46); Davies (1982); Shostak (1982: 175–85).

## Developing field relations

Once the fieldworker has located the field, managed entry, and located key informants the process of developing field relationships becomes crucial to the successful completion of the study. The development of good field relations becomes all the more important if doing fieldwork in someone else's classroom or school, or with a group previously unknown to the researcher. She must build up some degree of confidence, trust, and rapport with the subjects. Indeed one classic textbook on the topic describes participant observation and ethnographic technique as consisting of 'lore on establishing and maintaining good relationships in the field' (McCall and Simmons 1968: 28).

It is always worth remembering that people do not have to accept you, co-operate with you, or help you. Discretion, sensitivity, and common sense are therefore paramount here. Schools, like most other organizations, thrive on gossip, hearsay, innuendo, and so on. The researcher will need to cut a path through this, recognizing its importance and being sensitive towards the implications and consequences. Writing down what somebody says in a notebook in front of them might on some occasions be perceived as an invasion of privacy, or overly formal, while on other occasions it would not be seen as being out of place. We will discuss writing field notes later but it is important to bear in mind that how the researcher conducts herself in the field, including how and where she writes field notes, will certainly influence the researcher – staff relationships and consequently the nature of the data collected. Some ethnographers have, as an attempt to get around this problem, moved to a secluded or private place like a cloakroom simply to jot down broad headings and verbatim comments, to be 'written up' later after leaving the field.

Perhaps the most difficult area for the teacher researcher to handle in conducting fieldwork and doing ethnography is her own feelings, emotions, and attitudes. Teachers often hold strong views; the researcher herself is likely to have very definite views. Some of these views have perhaps generated the desire to conduct the research in the first place. However, the teacher researcher must never lose sight of the ultimate goal of such endeavours: the description, elaboration, and analysis of the actor's perspective and worlds. Undoubtedly the teacher will be confronted with perspectives and opinions that are diametrically opposed to her own and if certain people are not going to be alienated from the research a way of handling these interactions will have to be developed.

Many of these problems are considerably reduced when the teacher is conducting fieldwork in familiar settings. First and perhaps most importantly, the teacher has a good common-sense knowledge of the interpersonal relationships of the staff in school; allegiances, friendships, and major lines of disagreement are known to the teacher as researcher by virtue of her own practical involvement in the setting. Here the teacher researcher must trade on this 'insider knowledge'. In this sense teaching and ethnography have much in common for teachers themselves have continually to make sense of, interpret, and describe the settings in which they find themselves. They are themselves *also* participating and observing in the course of their routine work. All of this gives the teacher researcher conducting fieldwork in familiar settings many advantages. However, the problem of the familiar is that it can all too often become taken for granted. Even in familiar settings the fieldworker has continually to be open to everything going on around her. Suffice to say that while some problems in the development of field relations tend to fade into the background if the school or classroom being investigated is familiar, certainly others arise. The situation may be diagrammatically represented, as shown in Figure 3.2.

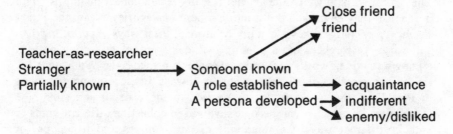

**Figure 3.2** The teacher as ethnographer in familiar (classroom) settings

The length and character of the project being undertaken will certainly influence the development of field relations when the teacher engages in fieldwork in unfamiliar settings. However with the increasing amount of school and classroom exchanges now taking place, especially on short courses, in-service work and longer DES-funded courses, teachers concerned to develop qualitative research techniques are likely to find themselves in relatively unfamiliar schools and classrooms. Figure 3.2 demonstrates the kinds of transformations in what really amounts to definitions of the situations as the teacher researcher moves from a stranger to one or other category of the range of possible relationships available as a result of becoming known. This is how one fieldworker summarized the character and development of field relations in the course of doing fieldwork in an urban open-plan primary school in Northern England.

The characteristic features of the fieldworker's relationships with staff in Cedars Junior may be summarized in the following manner:

(1) The relationships tended to emerge over a period of time.
(2) The relationships were to a large extent the product of contextual or situational features.
(3) The relationships began by being reasonably fluid and became more stable.
(4) Relationships *can* and *do* change.

(Hitchcock 1980: 100)

The development of good field relations is an integral feature of the processes of fieldwork and ethnography. The ways in which the teacher will handle these issues depend on the field itself, the nature of the research, and the characteristics of the researcher. What is not in doubt is the importance of developing trust, rapport, and confidence. Field relations do emerge over time and they will of course change.

### Collecting data in the field

The typical ways in which the teacher researcher can collect qualitative data in the field may be broken down into a series of categories. Again the extent to which any study makes use of one or more of these ways of collecting data will vary. Researchers often combine various ways of collecting data in ethnography. Fieldwork in educational contexts provides the opportunity for the teacher to collect data in quite a variety of ways. In the remaining chapters in Part II of the book we try to unravel in more detail some of these techniques. The teacher can become involved in collecting different kinds of data in different ways. Combinations of data sources and techniques of collecting data are a feature of many educational ethnographies. Amongst the major sources of data and means of collecting data in ethnography we find participant observation and observation, making field notes, and keeping a field journal or diary, unstructured interviewing and conversations, documentary sources and collecting life histories, collecting evidence of specialized language use or argot, making inventories, drawing maps, plans, and diagrams, using still photography and video cameras. In the remaining chapters of this part of the book we will concentrate upon interviewing, collecting and using documentary materials, and focus upon classroom interaction as important aspects of school-based teacher research. In this section we will confine our comments on data collection in the field to the process of making and using field notes, keeping a field journal or diary, collecting argot, making inventories, and still photography.

### Field notes

Field notes may be regarded as the basic raw data out of which the researcher fashions or moulds the ethnography. In many cases the ethnographer's journal, diary, or field notes hardly ever see the light of day in their original state in the finished report. Selections of verbatim transcripts of conversation, anecdotes recounted in the field, or sections from diaries by way of illustration are the usual ways in which these 'raw' materials find their way into the 'polished' finished report.

The teacher making notes is engaged in an important exercise for she is not simply recording events and producing data, but is also simultaneously engaged in the first stages of preliminary analysis out of which ideas and lines of inquiry can develop. While note-taking is a very basic activity, it is none the less an important activity. It is vital that the teacher researcher develops a careful and systematic approach to note-taking. Note-taking, writing up, and organizing field notes are quite exciting if painstaking and time-consuming activities.

Notes should be taken by the teacher from the very beginning of the research project. It must be remembered that the notes and records of observations have been lifted from a particular context and are only a partial record. In order to try and get round this the teacher can endeavour to provide some background information on the context of the sequences described in the field notes. More often than not these field notes will be supplemented by other data collected by the teacher. Given the importance of field notes it is preferable that the teacher endeavours to set a particular time aside after a day in the school or classroom in order to write up the field notes. While there certainly are different types of field notes we describe a typical pattern the teacher researcher might follow.

First, in the school or classroom itself shorthand, quickly scribbled temporary notes, or jottings concerning the events and activities observed are written down by the teacher in the field at a suitable time and place. Abbreviations or personalized systems of referring to individual staff, pupils, areas, or activities are likely to be generated. Key words or key phrases are frequently jotted down; short quotes are remembered and noted as accurately as possible. In a busy school or classroom situation where the teacher researcher is also likely to be involved in teaching, these notes are likely to be very rough and probably intelligible only to the researcher.

Second, the rough and often indecipherable initial notes taken by the teacher in the field will have to be translated into something more easily readable and much more permanent since these records are going to be read and re-read at a later date. These temporary notes can in fact act as memory jerkers for the creation of longer, more permanent notes. In the production of this set of more detailed elaborate and permanent field notes certain basic procedures need to be followed.

1 Write on one side only, normally of A4 size paper.
2 Number each page of the permanent notes consecutively.
3 Start a new page for each new day of the research.

4 The notes must be prefaced by the date, location, or context of the observations and brief biographical information on the main informants referred to (these need only be written once).

5 It is usually preferable to write any verbatim quotations in a different colour pen if in long hand, or underlined so as they stand out from the main body of the notes if typed.

6 Finally it is absolutely *essential* that at least one copy of the original permanent notes is made in order both to guard against loss or damage and to make the process of analysis and writing up easier. The length and detail of these permanent notes will be dependent upon the nature and context of the research. However, the most typical experience is for the researcher to write long and detailed notes at the start of the research, while everything is fresh and new, and for these notes slowly to shrink towards the end of the fieldwork or period of observation.

Third, in ethnographic fieldwork the process of initial analysis, classification, and organization of the data very often takes place while the researcher is still involved in the field. While writing up and organizing the permanent field notes the teacher will quickly develop her own observations and ideas or hunches. This marks the beginning of the process of analysis. The teacher can use a margin to add any comments, questions, or ideas, or if these are likely to be much longer than a couple of sentences the reverse side of the paper to which these comments refer may be used. Once well into the fieldwork or periods of observation this is the point at which themes, patterns, or recurring features may be noted. This is also the point at which the teacher can assess the amounts of material collected on a particular topic and whether or not some activities are described in more detail than others, or indeed if there are any gaps of major significance.

Fourth, as a result of the first three processes described above it is possible for the teacher to consider whether or not any specialized field notes on particular themes, topics, or substantive areas will need to be made in addition to the general field notes contained in the permanent record. Here the teacher may wish to construct a checklist or an *aide-mémoire* on the particular topic or area to be looked at in detail in order to focus attention more sharply.

Finally, sorting, categorizing and coding of data are essential aspects of the analytical processes involved in doing qualitative ethnographic research. Once the fieldwork or observation period is completed the teacher may begin these central and crucial tasks.

These are the major stages of field note collection and preparation. It is important that the teacher takes these issues seriously since for most purposes the field notes will form the major basis for many school-based research projects. The teacher needs therefore to be systematic and methodical in all aspects of producing field notes.

The completed field notes of a particular piece of educational research will provide the teacher with a general chronological story, narrative, or picture of the events being considered. The important time dimension provided by the chronological character of the record allows the teacher to appreciate the order in which materials were collected and observations made. This can of course be very important if for example the teacher is observing and monitoring a child's educational career through a period of time. The teacher will also need to spend some time thinking and responding to the actual circumstances of note-taking itself. The overt or covert nature of making the initial temporary notes is a matter for the discretion of the teacher and the nature of the circumstances encountered. It is usually possible to make brief scribbled notes in a fairly unobtrusive fashion. But the teacher needs to take care and let common sense prevail on this issue.

In general the teacher has to provide descriptions of ordinary as well as extraordinary events. Informants' words should be recorded as accurately as possible with no emendation or alteration by the researcher. The teacher can focus on a particular unit of observation, for example a staff meeting, a lesson, or other activity and produce fairly detailed notes on this or detailed portraits of individual staff or children can be constructed from the field notes involving those individuals. The possibilities of making field notes and the uses to which they can be put are great.

## The field journal or diary

If the teacher has the time it is well worth considering keeping a separate field journal or diary, especially if the research is going to be carried out over a number of months. The natures of these journals or diaries vary greatly and many famous social scientists have kept their own private intimate diaries; some researchers have even written letters from the field. The personal and private nature of these field journals or diaries needs to be distinguished from the professional nature of the field notes. The value of keeping a journal or diary is as much emotional as it is technical or analytical. The journal or diary allows the researcher to let off steam, to complain, or to moan. They enable some of the pressures which are inevitably placed upon the teacher in such work to be taken off. But the significance of keeping a journal or diary is not only the emotional security it may afford, but also the opportunity for the teacher researcher to reflect on the research, to step back and look again at the scenes in order to generate new ideas and theoretical directions. The fieldwork journal or diary is the place where the researcher, in conversation with herself, can record hopes, fears, confusion, and enlightenment. It is the place where the personal side of the fieldwork equation can be recorded. These kinds of journals or diaries need to be distinguished from other kinds of field notes.

## Inventories

When anthropologists first encounter an alien group whom they intend to live with and observe, one of the standard tasks they carry out is the production of inventories or cultural inventories, that is a listing of the various aspects or domains of the culture, and the categories of person, activity, and artefacts found within that culture. These kinds of inventories add depth to cultural descriptions and may be used by the teacher researcher in the course of an ethnographic study. If for example the classroom is the main unit of analysis the layout, objects, furniture, as well as the groups of children can be listed and noted. The photographing of schools and classrooms can also be used to help construct an inventory and description of a particular school or classroom.

## Layouts, maps, plans, diagrams

A further way of both collecting and presenting data is for the teacher to make use of any official plans of the school building that she has access to, or to construct her own. Since school layout and the arrangement of furniture and seating are indeed important interactional features of teaching and learning, the teacher can construct classroom plans, or maps and diagrams of particular areas. When the teacher researcher is concerned to discover aspects of the spatial organization of schools or classrooms these plans can offer an important visual representation of the themes the teacher is exploring. Indeed, a number of researchers have made extensive use of these sorts of maps or plans in educational research. We discuss this area in more detail in Chapter 7.

## Argot

Social scientists often note that in most organizations and institutions a distinction exists between the formal or official rules and goals of the organization and the informal and unofficial rules of the organization. As well as the official language of an organization there will exist an informal specialized language, a slang, shorthand vocabulary, or argot used by the members themselves. Schools and classrooms are no exception here. The existence and importance of the use of a specialized language has been demonstrated by many ethnographers and sociologists doing research in work-places, including factories, schools, and hospitals, and amongst numerous deviant and criminal groups. It is essential to develop a working knowledge of the language and specialized terms employed by members in the field. An initial task for the teacher here would be to sift the field notes or even produce from the field notes a glossary of the specialized terms or argot employed by either teachers or pupils. However, this is just a first stage.

Learning the argot is not the same as knowing and being able to use the argot in socially and interactionally approved and defined ways in the setting under investigation. This specialized argot is best seen in terms of the staff's perceived likely outcomes of involvement with the children concerned.

In many ways the talk of teachers and pupils and their utilization of specialized language conveys the ethos and climate of the culture of the school. This is therefore a rich source of imagery on all sorts of aspects of school and classroom life. Many researchers have paid attention to the specialized language or argot used and developed by the pupils themselves in a focus upon 'pupil culture'. For example Willis (1977) tried to capture the attitudes of the lads in his study of a school counter-culture by using as far as possible their own words, while Measor and Woods (1983: 57–76) and Woods (1980b) both pay special attention to pupils' own views as expressed in their talk and specialized terms. In attempting to understand the meanings and interpretations of teachers and pupils, the researcher has a number of techniques at her disposal and a focus upon and analysis of argot in schools and classrooms offers a rich potential.

## Still photography

Anthropologists and sociologists have made use of photographs and photography in their research for a long time. Photographs provide an extra source of data and new and fresh angles on the settings being researched. Photography may be seen as a perfectly natural extension of qualitative research since photographs can provide a rich source of descriptive data on a setting providing a sense of the location and the environment. However, those who have made use of photographs do this within the broader context of supporting ethnographically derived data. Photography as a tool in educational research does present an exciting potential yet there are difficulties and problems that need to be borne in mind. Photographs fall into two categories: those photographs already in existence and those that are specifically taken by the teacher.

First, the teacher researcher might come across old photographs of the school and school-related activities that might be of value to the research. If for example the research has a documentary or historical focus photographs will almost certainly be of significance. School-solicited photographs – photographs of the school released to the press and local groups – often present the image of the school which its members might seek to promote. Other photographs might be found in libraries, newspapers, or magazines. Photographs of major school events and class portraits can be used to identify people and changes. Photographs can in this sense be used as documentary evidence. However, the teacher must always ask who took the photograph, for what purpose, and what audience it was intended for? These are the kinds of questions that must be asked of any documentary source as we point out in

Chapter 5 when we discuss documentary sources in detail. Used with caution and supplemented by other sources of data the teacher can, depending upon the focus of the research, make creative use of these kinds of photographs.

Second, the teacher can take her own photographs of the school, classroom, playground, or related activities. These photographs will be taken for particular purposes; for example they may be used in the consideration of the use of space, classroom organization patterns, or the influence of school design. The presence of a camera, like a tape recorder, may influence people's reactions and it is best to try and avoid 'staged' photographs, aiming instead for as much of a natural pose as possible. One of the ways around the problem of many people's reluctance to be photographed is to get them to take the photograph. The teacher can ask another teacher to take photographs of, say, classroom activities, or indeed anything that the teacher finds significant; this has the advantage of offsetting any potential researcher bias in taking the photographs.

## Collecting data outside the field

It may seem odd at this point to suggest that the teacher might want to collect even more data. One of the characteristic features of qualitative research and ethnographic fieldwork in particular is that often vast amounts of rich, highly descriptive data can quickly be amassed. Indeed, one of the problems the teacher will have to face is knowing when to stop! A range of data from outside the school or classroom can be collected and referred to in the course of the research project. Instantly government and particularly DES statistics come to mind, but official reports like for example those of Warnock or Swann, as well as examination board reports, are all important potential sources of data. Most of these sources are readily available in libraries, but some schools now hold copies of major reports.

On other occasions, data from agencies outside the school will have to be consulted by the teacher. These agencies themselves will present the teacher with an important source of data. Certainly it is difficult to imagine how the teacher engaged in researching aspects of teaching and learning where ethnicity is a crucial variable cannot become involved in outside school activities, especially in neighbourhood, community, and family contexts. The teacher may indeed find herself with two quite distinct types of field in which she has to become involved in order to uncover aspects of a single problem or issue. Obviously if the teacher finds it necessary to become involved with members of an ethnic community and the parents of Asian or West Indian children, then locating a role and managing entry, locating informants, developing relationships, and collecting data in this new field will become very different from the ways in which these steps and stages have been handled inside the school and classroom. In some cases when collecting data outside the field the researcher may have only brief formal encounters with people or officials. In these cases the emphasis given to the data derived from these encounters must be set against their fleeting or brief character. It is virtually inevitable that the researcher is likely to go beyond the immediate field at some point or other in search of data. This must be recognized and the issues unravelled.

## Analysis

Analysis may be described as the attempt to organize, account for, and provide explanations of data so that some kind of sense may be made of it. The researcher moves from a description of what is the case to an explanation of why that is the case. This is usually perceived to be one of the most daunting aspects of research, but as we have pointed out the teacher has already been engaged in initial forms of analysis while collecting data in the field. For example, the teacher has reviewed her field notes in the process of rewriting the temporary field notes into permanent ones and will have begun to see themes and patterns emerging. This process can also suggest new lines of inquiry for the researcher. Up until this point, however, these activities have been largely informal or piecemeal, and usually conducted on an *ad hoc* basis.

There are, as we noted in Chapter 2, different kinds of analysis that result from the adoption of one or other model of research design and view of the research process. Usually social scientists draw a distinction between quantitative and qualitative analysis and it is worth briefly contrasting the two styles of analysis again at this point. Quantitative analysis principally involves the measurement of the amount, extent, incidence, or patterning of particular events so as to draw some general findings. In contrast, as we saw in Chapter 2, qualitative analysis, underpinned as it is by a commitment to explain individual actions in terms of actor's definitions and interpretations of the situation, focuses primarily on identifying the meanings of social situations and the organization of the activities in question. We will now concentrate upon unravelling the kinds of analyses the teacher researcher adopting an ethnographic approach is likely to engage in.

Once the teacher has completed the fieldwork, conducted all the interviews or observations, and generally has the data required, the formidable task of sorting and organizing begins. 'Data analysis' and 'writing up' the research therefore refer to the process whereby this mass of data, in whatever shape, is scrutinized, coded, or sorted, so that the teacher's own appreciation and understanding of the problem investigated may be furthered and this type of analysis may be conveyed to other professionals. The point of analysis for researchers using a qualitative approach is not so much with testing a preformulated theory or hypothesis, but rather with generating ideas from the data. All we wish to do at this point is to provide a basic knowledge of the ways in which analysis might be approached by the teacher researcher.

An important distinction needs to be borne in mind by the teacher when thinking about analysis. There is a difference between analysis that is done in the field and analysis that is done after the fieldwork is completed. This is sometimes referred to as informal and formal analysis. The teacher has already done a lot of analysis in the field itself. Once the fieldwork is completed and all the data have been collected more formal kinds of analyses can begin.

The initial task of analysis in qualitative ethnographic research is the organization, sorting, and coding of the data together with the development of some kind of system for the retrieval of information on particular topics from the mass of data. Here the keywords for the researcher are patience and care, for time spent at this point will certainly help to develop analytical skills. The initial operation is not unlike that which the researcher has perhaps already been doing in the field, that is reading through the notes and materials in order to see what features and issues consistently crop up, what topics appear more than others, and discovering what the researcher has little data on. The process will reveal certain themes, patterns, and categories of events and activities. In order to give an idea of what this process involves we can examine the way in which this kind of analysis developed in the ethnographic study of one school.

In the course of an ethnographic study of an inner-city open-plan primary school the researcher had collected over 300 pages of A4–size field notes (Hitchcock 1980). During the initial stages of the analysis of these materials the researcher was able to isolate a series of key topics and units of meaning which tended to feature regularly in the field notes. These were extracted, sorted, and indexed in the following way:

Richard and Geoffrey
problem children
explanations of failure
dealing with trouble
attitudes to parents
categorizing kids
clubnight
school holidays
staff relations
attitudes to open plan
using space
building boundaries
parental involvement
relationship between school and outside agencies
socializing the researcher

These general headings or categories can be written on to the top of a postcard and should include reference to the page number of the field notes on which reference to these topics appears. From the original general categories the teacher needs to move towards unravelling families of activities, or a series of codes under which groupings of categories can be placed. Using the same set of field notes as above this procedure would result in the following:

Teacher's Definition of the Situation Code

attitudes to children
attitudes to parents
attitudes to open plan
relationship with other staff

Relationships Code

staff–researcher interactions
head–staff interactions
Mrs Smith and the staff
relationship between infant and junior staff
parent–parent relationships
parent–teacher relationships
school–outside agency relationships
the local social worker
the educational psychologist
home–school liaison workers

Activity Code

coffee-time
staff meeting
dinner-time
wet playtimes
clubnight
sports day
the school holidays

Special Event Codes

selection of children for the holiday
dealing with Richard and Geoffrey
stealing on school trips
involvement of parents

Physical Context Code

home-base
enclosed home-base
Fletcher maths area
wet areas

furniture arrangement
plan of school
plan of home-bases
plan of enclosed home-bases
staffroom
plan of staffroom
foyer
playground layout

Social and Organizational Processes Code

dealing with the researcher
friends and enemies
dealing with space
roles and allegiances
dealing with trouble

While these codes are not exhaustive they cover quite a lot of the materials contained in the field notes. The codes refer to basic aspects of social life in school. Teacher definition codes refer to the attitudes, values, and expectations held by teachers in Cedars Junior towards the issues and events that confront them. Relationships code refers to the more formal sets of social relationships, lines of communication and interaction patterns in the school and between the school and outside agencies. Activity code focuses upon the kinds of routine, mundane, everyday occurrences in school, while the special events code highlights the extraordinary events that promoted discussion and debate. Physical context code encompasses the physical architectural aspect of the school, furniture, objects, and artefacts and the way these are used by teachers and pupils. Finally the social and organizational processes code brings together many of the more informal aspects of the relationships code. Here informal patterns of communication, friendship networks, social roles and teachers and pupils' responses to the issues, such as the nature of the school, trouble, disruption, and so on could be included. Some researchers would extract certain topics from these main codes and cut out the relevant sections referring to these areas in their field notes and other materials and place them in individual files.

Given the large amounts of material usually generated by ethnographic fieldwork it would be impracticable and time consuming to have to sift through all of the field notes and materials to get at one example. Here the researcher will need to construct some kind of index to the materials collected and ideas and concepts generated in the course of the research. Indexing can indeed be as simple or as complex as one likes. What needs to be remembered is that the production of an index is not the goal in itself. The index is simply a means to an end, a way of enabling the researcher to retrieve and find data, references, or materials quickly. It is possible to produce more than one index depending upon the nature and size of the materials and the focus of the research. Lofland (1971:118) has spoken about the use of 'mundane' indexes, which simply include for example names of people, teachers, pupils, everyday events in school, or locations, referring to the page number which contains mention of them in the notes on the one hand, and to 'analytical' indexes which are used to group together references on particular topics or issues in the field notes. The advent of computer technology has of course made the whole of this process infinitely more sophisticated. However, the teacher engaged in small-scale research needs only to follow the basic principles laid down here in order to facilitate analysis. In the end the aim of analysis is to move from accounts of what people do and say as descriptions of their worlds, to how and why they do what they do and say what they say. We have tried to show how the teacher therefore moves from a description of events and activities to an explanation of them.

## Summary

In this chapter we have provided the teacher with an outline framework of the major features of ethnography as these relate to school-based teacher research. We have argued that fieldwork and doing ethnography in educational settings may be conducted in a systematic fashion by following a series of steps and stages. The main sources of data and ways of collecting data available to the teacher were outlined and the question of the analysis of qualitative materials was briefly introduced. This chapter therefore provides the background to the remaining chapters in Part II. We have considered basic aspects of ethnographic research the teacher researcher will need to orientate towards in conducting small-scale school-based research. Enough has been said in this chapter to give the reader an indication of the rich and exciting potential of ethnography as a research orientation. Many teachers have been critical of educational research for ignoring the everyday realities of their lives and work. Ethnographic research can at least lay claim to taking those realities seriously and in describing and explaining them uncover some of the deeper layers of meaning and interaction that influence and affect teaching and learning in our schools and classrooms.

## Suggested further reading

For those readers unfamiliar with ethnography useful introductions are provided by M. H. Agar, (1986) *Speaking of ethnography*, Qualitative Research Methods Series vol. 2, Beverly Hills, Calif: Sage, and M. Hammersley and P. Atkinson (1983) *Ethnography: Principles and Practice*, London: Tavistock. In addition two books dealing with ethnography in school-based research best read together are M. Hammersley (ed.) (1983) *The Ethnography of Schooling: Methodological Issues*, Driffield: Nafferton

Books, and P. Woods (1986) *Inside Schools: Ethnography in Educational Research*, London: Routledge & Kegan Paul. The latter work has some useful suggestions on possible areas for school-based research and is a very clear and readable advocacy of the ethnographic approach in teacher research. The most comprehensive and valuable collection of writings on fieldwork methodology is R. G. Burgess, (ed.) (1982) *Field Research: A Sourcebook and Field Manual*, London: Allen & Unwin. This is complemented by R. G. Burgess, (ed.) (1984) *Field Methods in the Study of Education*, London: Falmer Press; while R. G. Burgess (1984) *In the Field: An Introduction to Field Research*, London: Allen & Unwin, contains examples drawn from the author's own research in schools. The method of participant observation is explored in J. P. Spradley (1980) *Participant Observation*, New York: Holt, Rinehart & Winston.

# Chapter four

# Interviewing, asking questions, and conversations

## Introduction

In this chapter we provide an introduction to one of the major tools of social research, the interview. Central to the interview is the issue of asking questions and this is often achieved in qualitative research through conversational encounters. We will outline the different kinds of interviews available and show how the teacher researcher might make use of interviews and conversations as a source of data in schools-based research.

Interviews have been used extensively across all the disciplines of the social sciences and in educational research as a key technique of data collection. This has given rise to considerable diversity in the form and style of interviewing as well as the products of such an approach. Researchers have approached the interview in so many different ways that broad types of interview can be pointed to. The differences refer to such matters as the nature of the questions asked, the degree of control over the interview exercised by the interviewer, the numbers of people involved, and the overall position of the interview in the research design itself. Roughly defined interviews might be said to be 'talk to some purpose'. However, as we shall see, this definition does not get us too far. We can point to a range of different interview types which are worth listing; these include:

structured interview
survey interview
counselling interview
diary interview
life history interview
oral history interview
ethnographic interview
informal/unstructured interview
conversations

It is important to add to this diversity the fact that in social and educational research interviews have been directly conducted by the researcher or by a team of trained researchers. Interview materials have been analysed by those directly involved in the research and by those who have only a minimal involvement in the research. Interviews have been conducted with both small and large groups. We are here concerned to develop an appreciation of the basic principles and initial modes of analysis in using interviews and conversations in small-scale school-based research. As such we will concentrate upon the type of interview described as unstructured, semi-structured, or informal.

The chapter contrasts structured interviewing with unstructured interviewing and also considers conversations and the diary interview. The interview as a research technique may be examined in terms of three key aspects which we will focus on in turn: the interview situation, methods of recording interviews, and the analysis of interview and conversational materials. Most of the key issues therefore facing the teacher researcher using the interview in school-based research will be examined, but four basic questions, which affect all types of interviewing, need to be addressed by the teacher at the outset of the research.

1  Why interview?
2  Where do I interview?
3  Whom do I interview?
4  When do I interview?

The teacher researcher needs to work through these questions briefly providing answers to them before embarking on the interviews proper. The answers to these questions will give the teacher a good idea of what type of interview to use and what specific issues might arise in the course of a school-based project making use of interviewing. We will now look at the main differences between so-called structured and unstructured interviewing strategies.

## The structured interview

The structured interview lies close to the questionnaire in both its form and the assumptions underlying its use. This is one of the most widely used types of interview largely because of the wide range of uses to which it may be put both inside and outside the social sciences. For example structured interviews are used in market research, public opinion research, studies of voting behaviour, attitude research, and in a host of other contexts. In social and educational research the structured interview is the type of interview used when a high degree of control over the interview situation is required or seen to be necessary. Researchers who make use of structured interviews usually seek results which can form the basis of generalizations, that is statements about a large number of cases. For this reason structured interviews are very often done with quite large samples of individuals. It is possible to isolate the key features of structured interviews so that they can be compared with other types.

Structured interviews display a number of features in common. However these characteristics take on a greater or lesser significance depending upon the particular research project. Typically they are usually arranged around a prearranged schedule of questions which are usually both short, direct, and capable of immediate (frequently 'yes' or 'no') responses. Often the researcher will have tried out the questions and their order before the major research by means of conducting trial or pilot interviews beforehand. Since one of the main aims of researchers using structured interviews is often to produce generalized statements, fairly large numbers of people are needed. However, constraints of time, energy, and cost often prohibit the use of large numbers. At this point the researcher will make use of a sample.

The sample is a procedure which allows the researcher to select people from a large group to question. This large group is referred to as the 'population' which could be secondary-school teachers, middle-school children, or whoever. Since the researcher cannot interview the whole of this 'population' a representative sample has to be obtained. In order to do this the researcher must find a suitable 'sampling frame', that is a list of all the people in a particular group or category from which the researcher will draw off a sample. There are two main ways in which the researcher can sample a population. These methods are referred to as quota sampling and random sampling. When the researcher uses a quota sample to interview she will be interviewing a specified percentage or quota from the categories of people identified in a population. Here attention is paid to keeping equal numbers of men and women, comparable ages, social backgrounds, and so on of the people forming the sample. In contrast, random sampling which is based upon probability theory refers to the procedure whereby the sample of people to be interviewed is chosen purely randomly from the identified population. The assumption is that the random sampling will thereby reduce any possibility of bias since each individual within the population identified has an equal chance of being chosen to be interviewed. This is of course not as straightforward as it appears. For example, how truly random is a sample of individuals drawn by choosing every fourth entry in the telephone directory? Only as 'random' as those people who have telephones and are in the directory!

Another key feature often associated with the structured interview is that the interview schedule itself is capable of being administered by a person or persons who did not design the questions; frequently, trained interviewers are used. Structured interviews have the advantage of being able to cover wide areas and large numbers of people. They are furthermore cheap to administer. As we noted earlier, the response categories in structured interviews are fairly straightforward, often only involving categories like 'yes' or 'no'. This makes the response easy to analyse. Most of the advice on the operation of the structured interview draws upon the experience of large-scale social surveys. It would of course obviously be difficult to duplicate the circumstances of such surveys in small-scale school-based research. It is interesting to note the kinds of problems these researchers face however. In a handbook (published by HMSO) MacCrossan (1984) offers some general guidelines and advice for interviewers here which might be of interest to the teacher researcher.

MacCrossan offers some comments on the sample, the interview, and the findings. She stresses the need for the sample to be as representative as possible and of obtaining complete interviews with as many members of the sample as possible. The interviewer needs to be able to persuade the interviewees of the importance of the survey, in the hope of ensuring their co-operation. Once the responses have been collected the task of classification and coding of responses begins. This highlights the need for interviews to record answers to questions accurately and as instructed and of 'probing' for full and precise information (MacCrossan 1984: 6). However, while MacCrossan's comments are informative she is referring to situations where the resources for doing the research will be far greater than the teacher researcher has. All the same, teachers can make use of structured interviews and to this end these observations are of value. We will briefly consider some of the issues the teacher researcher will face in setting up a structured interview.

*Setting up a structured interview*

It is possible to construct a set of tasks we would need to undertake in setting up a structured interview. These tasks follow a sequential order and it is best to approach them in this fashion.

1 Note the areas on which information is required.
2 Translate the broad areas into a series of general questions.
3 Construct clear, direct, and unambiguous questions in line with (1) and (2). Initially try to develop questions which are capable of being answered in a straightforward 'yes' and 'no' fashion. Terms such as 'always', 'sometimes', or 'never' can be introduced to grade and extend the responses.
4 Construct a clear and simple layout and presentation of the questions which will enable the interviewer to tick or circle answers easily so as to avoid confusion when collating and analysing responses.

It is important to note that in the context of school-based research the teacher is likely to be doing all of this kind of interviewing herself; she will not have the advantage of a large team to help her. On the other hand hard structured interviews can provide the teacher researcher with a fairly large amount of data in a relatively short period of time. Quite large numbers of teachers or pupils could be interviewed in this way providing important basic data.

However, what the structured interview is unlikely to reveal are the complex and emergent factors which shape the social world of schools and classrooms, because fairly rigid, prearranged questions form the basis of this technique. All the same, even the most highly structured interview is usually a good deal more flexible than the questionnaire since it is still a face-to-face situation and the researcher can usually leave room on the interview schedule for residual categories such as anything else, or expansion. Typically a structured interview is of most value to the teacher researcher when basic straightforward data is needed quickly for purposes of evaluation. This has led researchers to make use of less structured versions of the structured interview.

## The semi-structured interview

The semi-structured interview is a much more flexible version of the structured interview. It is the one which tends to be most favoured by educational researchers since it allows depth to be achieved by providing the opportunity on the part of the interviewer to probe and expand the interviewee's responses. This can be done also by including spaces on the interview schedule for the interviewer to add comments or make notes. In this way some kind of balance between the interviewer and the interviewee can develop which can provide room for negotiation, discussion, and expansion of the interviewee's responses.

In a small-scale school-based research project the teacher can make use of the semi-structured interview, but care does need to be taken in both the construction of the sample, the questions, and the conclusions which may be drawn from the responses. The semi-structured interview is itself quite valuable as a pilot study, that is a short, preliminary, investigative study designed to reveal issues which can be explored in more depth later by means of a variety of techniques. For many researchers operating within the ethnographic framework there are considerable limitations to both structured and semi-structured interviews as a means of data collection in social and educational research. The prospective teacher researcher needs to appreciate what these reservations are.

The major value of structured interviewing was seen to be its systematic approach to data collection. Furthermore, the processes we have outlined suggest that the structured interview can be a fairly objective affair since the formality involved reduces the risk of researcher/interviewer bias or interference. The results of structured interviews could therefore be regarded as objective manifestations of real social situations. The results are more easily analysable and since the structured interview is supposedly 'context independent' and free from the influence of the researcher the data produced could be more reliable. In response to some of these issues a series of criticisms of structured interviewing have developed, principally from within sociology.

One of the most famous criticisms of structured interviews and conventional models of social research design more generally has come from the American sociologist Aaron Cicourel. In Chapter 3 of his book *Method and Measurement in Sociology*, (1967) Cicourel makes some revealing comments about the overall nature of the 'interview complex', that is the relationship and interaction between questions, interviewer, interviewee responses, and response interpretation. For Cicourel the main problem would seem to surround the relationship between what the interview is intended to achieve and what is in fact interactionally done in achieving this. In other words, in the effort to sustain an objective approach to data collection that will reveal valid and reliable data, the structured and indeed semi-structured interview needs to ignore, by-pass, or pay lip service to the socially organized practices which need to be managed in order actually to get the interview completed. The interview has to be dealt with as it happens and for many researchers this observation carries with it the consequence that interviews must be flexible, unstructured, and sensitive to the context of the interaction. Cicourel has put the matter thus:

> The interviewer cannot check out his own responses in detail and follow the testing of a hypotheses during an interview; he is forced to make snap judgements, extended inferences, reveal his views, overlook material and the like and may be able to show how they were made or even why they were made only after the fact. The interviewer cannot escape from the difficulties of everyday life interpretations and actions. The commonsense 'rules' comprise literal hypotheses testing, but they are necessary conditions for eliciting the desired information.

(Cicourel 1967: 100)

Cicourel's comments point to an important series of issues. It cannot be assumed that the interviewer–interviewee relationship or the nature of the interview discourse is unproblematic. Certainly the structured interview is highly appropriate for many research situations. An example drawn from outside the arena of educational research may be used to illustrate some of the problems with formalized structured interviewing and survey interviews which reinforces Cicourel's viewpoint.

In underdeveloped and developing countries it is important for a variety of reasons to establish existing and projected fertility patterns. It is important from the health, welfare, social planning, and educational aspects to be able to describe and predict the size, nature, or composition of a country's population. In underdeveloped and developing countries this is quite vital. Cicourel, a long-standing critic of conventional, positivistic orientations to social research, has questioned the claims to validity upon which many traditional fertility studies and more widely interview surveys depend. In his study of Argentine fertility, Cicourel (1973) argues that there is essentially a betrayal of meaning in such approaches as he demonstrates that standard elicitation and coding procedures of interview materials routinely distort what 'family size', 'birth control', and so on actually mean to the families involved. In other words the 'ethnographic context' of the people's lives does not form the background to either the development and generation of appropriate questions or the culture-specific location of the meaning and interpretation of subsequent answers. Cicourel suggests that there will as a result be inevitable distortion. Hence the picture of 'social reality', 'social structure', 'fertility', or 'education' claimed to be revealed by such interviewing techniques will in fact have a dubious relationship to the worlds which they are supposed to be researching. Furthermore, the neat, packaged, coded tables that result from such work will not show the interpretive and judgemental work the interviewer/researcher puts into the situation in the first place in order to obtain the empirical materials.

Those researchers adopting what might loosely be described as 'unstructured' interviewing techniques share a rather different set of assumptions about the nature of the social world and the subsequent form of social research which broadly encompasses the ethnographic, qualitative, interpretative model of research design we outlined in Chapter 2. These researchers claim that survey and structured interviewing procedures are not commensurate with the nature of the social world. Such approaches, it is argued, are not sensitive enough to the social contexts of the interview itself, the characteristics of the interviewer or interviewee, and the topic under investigation. Neither are they sufficiently flexible enough towards questions of design and wording or sensitive to the problems of recording.

Qualitative researchers point towards the importance of the establishment of rapport, empathy, and understanding between interviewer and interviewee. They point out that it is not always possible to specify in advance what questions are appropriate or even important to any given social grouping prior to involvement with that group. They offer the observation that people do not always say what they mean in so many words, suggesting that social meanings are complex and not unequivocally revealed by a dictionary-like translation of 'responses' to prearranged 'questions' which can then be mechanically 'coded' to reveal patterns for subsequent analysis and generation of theory. Underlying these criticisms are the personal qualities and interactional skills of both the interviewer and respondent. As John Lofland has pointed out in an often-quoted passage,

> I would say that successful interviewing is not unlike carrying on
> unthreatening, self-controlled, supportive, polite and cordial interaction in
> everyday life. If one can do that, one already has the main interpersonal
> skills necessary to interviewing.
>    It is my personal impression, however, that interactants who practice
> these skills (even if they possess them) are not overly numerous in our
> society.

> (Lofland 1971: 90)

We are not claiming that once teachers possess these skills, automatic success at interviewing is guaranteed. For Lofland the situation seems mysteriously one-sided. The characteristics, composition, and interpersonal skills of the respondent in interaction with the interviewer come together to create a particular social situation. This brings us to a second example.

The unstructured or informal interview depends heavily for its success on the relationship that is developed between the interviewer and respondent. Lofland stresses the features needed for successful interviewing as a series of interpersonal skills. It is also crucial for the interviewer to develop a familiarity with the biographical and contextual features of the respondents's life history, outlook, customs, and life-style in order to be able to relate more fully and in a more appreciative way with those being interviewed. This will be especially noticeable when interviewing pupils, where for example Measor (1985) found issues of her own appearance and status as being important factors that were attended to by the pupils she interviewed. These issues and the interpersonal skills Lofland refers to become crucial when attempting to build a relationship and establish rapport with respondents when one is exploring sensitive or delicate areas. In a study of the sexual behaviour of young people, for example, Schofield (1968) found that due to the characteristics of the young people themselves, the nature of the topic being explored and common-sense attitudes, specially trained interviewers were needed to work with the young people involved. Such a task is not easy but there are a number of examples in educational research that testify to the ability of sensitive researchers to develop these skills when engaged in unstructured interviews with pupils. Two good examples are the study by Measor and Woods (1984) of school transition and Willis's (1977) ethnographic account of a school counter-culture. In situations like these where there is likely to be no shared membership and where interviewer and respondent are clearly in an unequal relationship, the question of personal skills and of course ethics looms large. Those relying heavily upon structured interviewing techniques have been criticized therefore for not giving due weight to the fact that the interviews are 'situated activities' and the materials produced 'situated accounts'.

### The unstructured interview

In a sense this title is a misnomer for as Whyte has reminded us 'a genuinely non-directive interviewing approach is simply not appropriate for research' (Whyte 1982: 111). There must still be structure then in an unstructured interview. The key difference between the different interviewing techniques we have been discussing so far might be said to be the degree of negotiation between the interviewer and interviewee. In the unstructured interview scope is allowed for the interviewer to introduce new material into the discussion which had not been thought of beforehand but arose only during the course of the interview. In other words, the unstructured interview allows the interviewer greater scope in asking questions out of sequence and the interviewees of answering questions in their own ways. The aim of the unstructured interview is to provide for a greater and freer flow of information between the researcher and the subject. Even so the researcher using unstructured interviews does not totally abandon any pre-interview work. It is just as important in using the unstructured interview as it is when using the structured interview to consider beforehand the nature of the encounter and the kinds of general areas the researcher wishes to explore. Usually the researcher might work to a rough checklist of ideas or areas she wants to explore in the interview but will be prepared to let the interviewees 'travel' wherever they like.

As a result of the nature of the technique itself and the assumptions underlying its use these researchers employing unstructured interviews as a means of data collection are particularly aware of sources of bias and the range of factors which influence and shape the encounters between the researcher and respondent. These researchers highlight the need to develop rapport or empathy with those being interviewed. Once this is achieved the belief is that deeper, more meaningful information will be obtained. This will enable the interviewer to move backwards and forwards in the interview itself providing the opportunity to clarify points, go over earlier points, and raise fresh questions. It is fair to say that there is an inherently more equal relationship between researcher and subject in the unstructured interview than there tends to be in the structured interview. The overall aim of unstructured interviewing is to create an atmosphere where the individual feels able to relate subjective and often highly personal materials to the researcher. To allow for this some researchers have even gone so far as to encourage the interviewee to take greater responsibility for the interview, both in terms of planning the interview and organizing the questions.

The unstructured interview is now used widely in educational research generally and in teacher research more particularly. It has distinct advantages for the teacher researcher working within a known culture with fellow professionals. For example it can be used in curriculum evaluation, management, and appraisal exercises. Here its value is extensive since it can help throw light on to a number of aspects of both staff and pupils' experience of the school and curriculum change. When comparing structured and unstructured interviews it is clear to see how unstructured interviews offer the teacher researcher much greater flexibility. Indeed the teacher researcher using unstructured interviewing will quickly see how these often merge into a conversation. Conversations are of course a major element in any kind of ethnographic field research. Conversations therefore not only constitute an important source of data, but also might be regarded as a method of research in their own right. Once this happens it is transparent that elements of everyday social interaction will be incorporated into the unstructured interview. It is in this sense that Burgess (1982: 107–9) talks about the unstructured interview as a conversation. Burgess quotes Palmer here who suggests that the unstructured interview

> assumes the appearance of a natural interesting conversation. But to the proficient interviewer it is always a controlled conversation which he guides and bends to the service of his research interest.
>
> (Palmer 1928: 171, cited by Burgess 1982)

In approaching interviewing as a source of data for school-based research a number of matters will have to be considered by the teacher researcher. These might usefully be examined under three broad headings: the interview situation, methods of recording, and the analysis of interview and conversation materials. There will necessarily be overlap between these three aspects but we will consider each in turn.

## The interview situation

The interview is a complex piece of social interaction. It is important for the researcher to be aware of what might be described as the dynamics of the interview situation. The following six areas could again act as checklist for the teacher researcher to consider both before actually conducting the interviews and later when organizing and analysing them.

1 Researcher effects
2 Characteristics of the researcher/interviewer
3 Characteristics of the respondent/interviewee
4 Nature of the researcher–respondent relationship
5 The interview as a speech event
6 Interviews have an ethnographic context

### Researcher effects

One of the advantages of the structured interview might be said to be the greatly reduced possibility of researcher effect or bias by constructing the technique and questions before the actual interview takes place. But as we saw in the example provided by Cicourel, this kind of interviewing may be unwittingly involved in destroying the very meaning of items it is concerned to discover. In an important sense, whatever kind of interview is used the fact that an individual, the researcher or interviewer, is directly involved with another individual means inevitably that the presence of the researcher will have some kind of influence on the finds or data. Many have argued that the more involved the interviewer becomes with the situation the greater will be the potential for researcher effect. The major problem here surrounds the extent to which the interviewer 'leads on' or influences the respondents' responses. Clearly there is little scope for this in a highly structured interview with a prearranged set of questions which must be answered in order. Alternatively there is much scope for this in the unstructured interview format. If for example the teacher and the interviewees are known to each other there may be a degree of reciprocity taking place, that is the respondent may feel that they have to give the researcher the kinds of answers and responses it is assumed the researcher wants. This is especially problematic when conducting interviews with peers as Platt (1981c: 75–91) has pointed out.

When researcher influence and effect are discussed reference is usually made to the personal and biographical characteristics of the researcher. These factors will take on special significance when the teacher is engaged in interviewing in educational contexts. For example some teachers being interviewed may feel that evaluation or criticism is implied. The teacher researcher will need to consider the context of each interview and examine the nature of any of her own values or prejudices which might influence the course of the interview. Teacher researchers as well as the subjects of their research have values, attitudes, political affiliations, and often firmly held opinions on what constitutes 'good teaching'. The teacher researcher can never get rid of these features. The important point however is that she attempts to understand the significance and impact of them.

## Characterisitics of the researcher/interviewer

The main sources of bias and influence upon interviews is generally regarded as being the personal characteristics of the interviewer. Here the key variables of age, gender, class, and ethnicity will all play a crucial role. While we consider the influence of the characteristics of the interviewee shortly it must be remembered that the total situation must be seen in terms of the interaction of the two sets of characteristics.

The age of the teacher researcher will have an influence on the nature of the interactions she has with her subjects. This of course applies to all social research. In specifically age-stratified societies individuals are often excluded from many aspects of the social activities of a group on the grounds of their age. 'Seniority' and 'youth' are factors that do seem to have a particular significance in schools. Teachers' attitudes towards each other are often based upon the age of the respective parties concerned. Age is certainly a dimension the prospective interviewer would need to pay attention to. Lynda Measor for example describes how in her research she paid special attention to her dress and appearance. She felt that she had to dress rather conservatively when interviewing other staff. Consider the implications for the interviewer of the following extracts from Measor's interviews.

Mr King:   Young art teachers, clueless wonders some of them drab girls,

> who came looking as though they were selling off jewellery
> and wiggly hair and long woollen things and skirts that come
> down to their ankles and toenails that could have been
> cleaned.
>
> Mr Tucks: I've never worn teacher uniform, I teach in what I am wearing
> now [cord trousers, casual shirt, no tie, desert boots]. .... often
> criticised by colleagues.
>
> (Measor 1985: 58–9)

Clearly if one happened to be a young art teacher who remotely approximated Mr King's caricature above then the implications for getting interview materials that were not grossly affected by the interviewer's age and appearance are quite remote. Conversely Mr King might have a problem interviewing Mr Tucks. However, while, as Measor suggests, appearance can to a certain degree be manipulated, age cannot. There are obviously other occasions, as Hitchcock (1980) notes, where being young, new, and a novice can have considerable advantages when interviewing older, more 'senior' teachers provided the right style and demeanour is adopted. But even when the 'old hands' come clean and decide to tell it 'like it is' to a younger member of staff, fieldworker/interviewer, the problem remains as to whether or not the data and materials obtained from such encounters are not wholly products of those encounters? They may not be a 'real' indication of what the respondent feels, believes, or thinks but rather an indication of what the respondent feels is appropriate given the relative ages of themselves and the interviewer.

We have concentrated on age as a crucial aspect of the researchers' identity which can influence the course of an interview as it can field research in general. Certainly the gender dimension of an interview is equally crucial. In many cases the teacher researcher might find it easier to interview people of the same sex, though in other cases different researchers might find it easier to interview people of the opposite sex. The same is true of ethnicity. The difference here of course lies in the possibility that the interviewer or interviewee may hold stereotypical views of ethnic minority group members which those members either reject or find degrading. The question of the perceived status of the parties involved will create the foundation on which the teacher researcher must consider the influence of the characteristics of the interviewer.

### Characteristics of the respondent/interviewee

All the factors discussed above apply equally to the respondent. These variables will affect how the subject interprets the topics being discussed and responds to the interviewer. Ultimately it is the way in which these characteristics are worked out in the relationship between interviewer and interviewee. While it is certainly difficult to disentangle these influences the teacher researcher must at least be aware of them.

## Nature of the researcher–respondent relationship

There are a vast number of possible relationships that the teacher researcher might develop with the people being interviewed which are in the main shaped by the knowledge each has of the other, the relative status and standing of the interviewer and subject, the outlooks of each and the degree of friendship between the two. In many cases the teacher will be interviewing people she knows; in some situations the teacher will have only a passing knowledge of the person being interviewed. What is important here are the identities of both interviewer and interviewee. Obviously if the teacher is engaged in unstructured interviews or conversations with pupils then a whole range of special factors have to be taken into account. For the most part teachers are going to be interviewing other teachers, but parents and members of outside agencies and bodies having dealings with the school may also be interviewed in some pieces of research. The teacher researcher will often be researching and conducting interviews with her peers. As Jennifer Platt has argued, this does present some peculiar ethical, technical, and analytical issues (Platt 1981c: 75–91). The teacher researcher interviewing fellow teachers is simultaneously teacher and a researcher. This dichotomy is often very difficult to manage since it requires the teacher to be both an interested party but not so interested as to take matters for granted. Furthermore, the teacher researcher returns to her field after the research is complete. This dichotomy in the research–respondent relationship in school-based research has both ethical and practical consequences and can of course influence the nature of any interviewing which takes place. The researcher, like her subjects, has an identity, a past, a history, a certain reputation. How much of this can be divulged in the interview on the assumption of a reciprocal return of information by the subject? This is further exacerbated when the researcher and subject are of unequal status or standing in the school. How much are both parties prepared to give to each other? This is practical but also ethical in so far as it involves both parties' definition of what the situation is about and how the researcher will use what has been revealed to her.

When interviewing fellow teachers the designation of 'researcher' and 'respondent' and indeed the 'interview' are too highly formalized and the unstructured interview format is an attempt to take this into consideration. For example, we have heard teachers talk about the way in which all manner of information was revealed to them once the interview was seen to be over. The openness and informality of the unstructured interview carries with it the possibility for the redefinition of what may be discussed in the interview by the respondent. However, what are the possibilities of this developing if the respondent is of 'lower' status or standing in the school hierarchy than the researcher? The basic problem surrounds the teacher's role as both researcher and an individual with a self and an identity in the setting under investigation. This suggests that the view of the interview as some kind of unambiguous research instrument is in fact false. The considerations we have been raising here may make such idealized views impossible to realize in practice, that is in the real situations of everyday life.

Probably one of the most well-known examples of the fundamental importance of the effects of interviewer and respondent characteristics on the outcome and results of interviews is provided by the sociolinguist Labov (1969: 1–31). Considered against the background of so-called cultural, linguistic, and deficit models of school failure, Labov has shown that when interviewed in different ways by different interviewers adopting differing roles, the language of black children can be shown to be highly variable. Labov describes the kind of interview situation which produces 'defensive' and 'monosyllabic' behaviour in the child.

> The boy enters a room where there is a large, friendly, white interviewer, who puts on a table in front of him a toy and says:
> 'Tell me everything you can about this'.
>
> (Labov 1973: 26)

He goes on to compare this with a very different kind of interview situation which resulted not in 'monosyllabic' children but children who were capable of using the English language well and who portrayed the extended ability to use the complex and rich ingredients of non-standard negro English.

> In the next interview with Leon we made the following changes in the social situation.
> 1 Clarence [the interviewer] brought along a supply of chipped potatoes, changing the interview into something more in the nature of a party.
> 2 He brought along Leon's best friend, eight-year-old Gregory.
> 3 We reduced the height imbalance by having Clarence get down on the floor of Leon's room, he dropped from six feet, two inches to three feet, six inches.
> 4 Clarence introduced taboo words and taboo topics and proved, to Leon's surprise, that one can say anything into our microphone without any fear of retaliation.
> The result of these changes is a striking difference in the volume and style of speech.
>
> (Labov 1973: 30)

While Labov is talking about the context of adult–child conversation and interviewing, where certain special factors play an important role, the general points have much wider applicability highlighting the need for careful appraisal of the influence of researcher–respondent characteristics and the nature of the ensuing relationship.

### The interview as a speech event

By describing the interview as a 'speech event' we are drawing attention to the communicational and sociolinguistic aspects of its organization and the production of data contained within the interview and conversational materials in terms of what it is that the parties are doing with the words, phrases, and idioms that they are using. These issues become most apparent when the interviewer and respondent use different linguistic styles or dialects within the interview or conversational encounter. Many studies on the multi-cultural context of learning and the education of ethnic minority groupings point to the potential for misunderstanding, miscommunication, and resulting educational problems when teachers and pupils from vastly differing cultural backgrounds having different languages and speech styles meet in the classroom. These difficulties may well spill over into the interview and research situation in general and are not confined to the inter-ethnic or multi-cultural context. The language of the researcher and respondent is closely aligned to their definition of themselves, the encounter and the front, image, or presentation of self they wish to convey. However, there is a major difference between the two personae here. As we have already discussed, field research, ethnography, and qualitative research require a range of social or personal skills on the part of the researcher. The nature of the language of the respondents will vary, so the sociolinguistic context of the interview will change. The nature of the presentation of self by respondents will vary also rendering very different contexts within which the interview takes place. The effect of these differing definitions of the situation and linguistic codes means that the researcher has to take into account the sociolinguistic context of the interview and the allied definitions of the situation and presentation of selves that follow from this. The teacher researcher needs to consider the implications of these observations not just for the interview situation but in the subsequent analysis of the materials.

## Interviews have an ethnographic context

All the points we have been making so far about the interview situation highlight the need to recognize the influence of a variety of social, cultural, institutional, and linguistic factors. Interviewers and respondents have identities. They have perceptions of themselves and of each other. This knowledge of course varies and changes as people become more familiar with each other. There is a past to the encounters and situations the researcher observes. There is therefore always a context to be taken into account. We might describe this as the 'ethnographic context' of the interview, unstructured interview, or conversation. It points also to the need for consideration of the fact that the informal interview, however unstructured, is still an unusual situation for most people to be in.

## Recording interviews

One of the important aspects of the use of any kind of interview is the question of how to record interviews. One major exception is Whyte's (1982) excellent article on interviewing in field research generally. Basically the considerations relate to the type of interview involved and the decision to use one or another method of recording. First of all it is clear to see that some of the problems regarding the recording of interview materials diminish if the interview is heavily structured since the use of pre-coded categories allows the researcher to record answers quickly and easily. Conversely the flexibility and freedom entailed in the unstructured interview present problems as far as recording goes since the answers or responses and questions are likely to be lengthy, complex, and even 'rambling'.

The researcher has to make an early decision on how to record the interview materials though it is of course possible for the teacher to alternate the ways in which the materials are recorded as a relationship develops and as barriers are broken down. The teacher really has three possibilities to consider. She can (1) tape record the whole of the researcher–respondent exchanges, (2) take notes verbatim as the interview is happening, or (3) write up the main features and exchanges of the interview at some point after the interview is completed. Furthermore, recording unstructured interviews is somewhat different in kind from recording structured, formal interviews since the interviewer in unstructured interviewing takes a much more active role in the encounter. This means that it is important not simply to record the respondents' responses but the interviewer's contributions also.

The tape recording of the interview session will produce the most complete record of what was said. However, the researcher must recognize certain consequences of using a tape recorder. The interviewer will have to manage the inevitable formality and structure that the introduction of a tape recorder will bring to the situation. The effects of this will vary depending upon whether the teacher has a long-established relationship with the respondent or in contrast if the relationship is new or fairly superficial. The researcher must never play down the possible effects which the presence of a mechanical recorder can have upon what people say and the way that they say it. Much will depend on the teacher's handling of the situation and the rapport that she has established with the subjects. The teacher researcher will in any case have to obtain the permission of individuals to tape record the interviews and conversations. If this looks as if it might be difficult then the best course of action to follow would be simply to resort to note-taking. A series of practical issues such as placement of the microphone, the problems of interference, and locating the tape recorder in as unobtrusive a fashion as possible all need to be attended to by the interviewer prior to the interview itself (see also Chapter 5 on the oral history interview).

Taking notes during the course of the interview is another option open to the teacher, but this is also not without its disadvantages. Note-taking can introduce as much formality into the interview occasion as can the presence of a tape recorder. The act of note-taking in the course of an interview means that the interviewer may not be able to give sufficient attention to what is being said because she is so busy trying to record it. If a teacher has not been interviewed before she or he may clearly feel self-conscious, something which may be heightened if the interviewer is writing down everything that she says. The teacher researcher will have to 'read' this aspect of the research very carefully. In any case it will be important to record not just the subject's responses but the interviewer's questions also. It is simply not possible to write as fast as someone is talking unless one is using shorthand. One of the ways in which the teacher researcher can take notes in the interview is by making use of a checklist or an *aide-mémoire* as a relatively informal way of organizing the interview which might make the recording process easier. This could involve the researcher writing up the notes on the interviewee's responses next to an appropriate section which the researcher has put down on a sheet of paper before the interview. However, some might argue that this procedure would introduce an unacceptable level of formality into the interview.

Finally it is possible for the teacher researcher to 'write up' the interview and reconstruct the reality of the encounter from memory at a later point. Some teachers we have worked with find this the only appropriate way to handle interviewing their colleagues since interference, anxiety, and self-consciousness can be reduced to acceptable levels only by minimal intrusion of recording techniques. The main problem with writing up the interview after the event is that the whole of this process is retrospective and there will always be the potential of recording features in the written record which were not present in the original encounter. There is the risk therefore of introducing distortions and making errors. MacDonald and Sanger (1982) for example have argued that note-taking and recording are not simply different ways of recording data but actually constitute different ways of going about research. Walker's comments make the difference clear.

> note taking draws the researcher into the interpretation early in the study and in one sense makes the researcher more of a person in the eyes of the subject. Tape recording lends itself to a recessive process by burying it in the editing and selection of extracts from transcripts.
>
> (Walker 1985: 109)

This brings us swiftly on to the complicated and difficult question of the analysis of interview materials.

## Analysing interview and conversational data

Once the teacher has undergone the daunting and frustrating task of transcribing tape-recorded informal interviews, or has sorted out a mass of field notes, or transcribed a series of verbatim conversations, then she will no doubt wonder what next to do with these materials. The analysis and explanation of data is in many ways the culmination of the research project. At this point the teacher will begin to think about explaining, evaluating, and possibly suggesting ways of changing. However, the teacher will have been forming ideas, developing notions, and thinking about the data as it was being collected. The more formal process of 'analysing interview and conversational materials' can occur at any point in the research once the materials become available. It is therefore important to locate these materials in the overall context and aims of the research. Very often the teacher will have not only the products of more than one interview to consider but also possibly transcripts of group interviews. All these features need to be kept in mind in order to place the interview materials in a meaningful context so that any analysis of their content is in fact justified.

### Preliminary issues in the analysis of interview and conversational materials

Many of the issues surrounding the analysis of materials collected by the teacher apply across the board to social research more generally. It is useful to reconsider at this point the questions that were raised about the analysis of ethnographic materials towards the end of Chapter 3. While many teachers will use interviews of the structured or semi-structured variety using precoded questions, others will be using informal, unstructured interviews and conversations. The task of analysing fixed or semi-fixed responses does present an easier prospect than dealing with the results of informal interviews and conversations. As such we will concentrate upon unravelling some guidelines for the qualitative analysis of interview and conversational data. However, even if the teacher researcher is involved in the coding and quantification of fixed responses to structured interview items many of the points we will make below are still relevant.

One initial observation may be made at this stage. After all the time spent collecting data and conducting interviews the teacher researcher is likely to be anxious to get on with 'doing something' with the materials. The danger here is that the teacher researcher might begin to impute things to the data which are not perhaps borne out by more detailed careful analysis. There is no quick easy route to effective analysis. We feel that it is important for the researcher to get a 'feel' of the interview or interviews, conversation or conversations as a whole to being with. Once this is done specific categories and meanings can be generated later avoiding the tendency of the researcher to impose categories on to the materials at an early stage. It is possible to unravel some general guidelines the teacher researcher might follow when approaching the analysis of interviews and conversations.

*Guidelines for the qualitative analysis of interview and conversational materials*

It is fair to say that the organization and conduct of interviewing has received much greater attention than the analysis of interviews. However, there are certainly some examples in the literature which focus upon the analysis of interview materials and the prospective teacher could profitably consider Spradley (1979), Wragg (1984), Hycner (1985), and Powney and Watts (1987) here. We would point to nine related areas in considering the qualitative analysis of interview and conversational materials.

1 Familiarity with the transcript
2 Appreciation of time-limits
3 Description and analysis
4 Isolating general units of meaning
5 Relating general units of meaning to the research focus
6 Patterns and themes extracted
7 Nature of typifications and perceptions
8 Self-revelation and researcher reflection
9 Validity checks, triangulation, re-interviewing, and re-analysis

Familiarity with the transcript

It is important for the teacher researcher to have a thorough familiarity with the interview or conversational materials before attempting to develop any kind of systematic analysis. The processes of reading and re-reading the materials will enable a sense of their coherence as a whole. Where possible if a tape recording of the interview or conversation is available this should be done with both the written transcript and tape recording since this is the best way of gaining an appreciation of the subtle features of tone, pitch, intonation, and other crucial aspects such as pauses, silences, emphasis. Some researchers would want to add descriptions of the paralinguistic and non-verbal dimension to the interview encounter. This process of familiarization then is a fundamental prerequisite to the successful analysis of these kinds of material.

Appreciation of time-limits

What has been suggested above implies that a fair amount of time will be spent on reading and re-reading interview and conversational materials. This presents the teacher with an important practical matter to resolve. Given the restraints facing teacher researchers it is much better to analyse a few interviews well than a large number badly.

Description and analysis

As we have stated elsewhere description and analysis are integrated in qualitative ethnograhic research styles. The researcher moves backwards and forwards between description and explanation. In effect this means developing what the American sociologists Glaser and Strauss (1967) describe as *Grounded Theory*. By grounded theory is meant the production of analysis and explanation which is grounded in the data the researcher collects, since it requires the researcher to move consciously backwards and forwards between the data and the emerging explanations, analyses, and eventually theory. The researcher continually moves around amidst the raw data contained in the field notes, transcripts, or accounts and then back to analyse, synthesize, and formulate what has been found. The researcher can then return once more to the data and descriptions for further evidence, examples, or clarification.

## Isolating general units of meaning

The researcher by this point will be in a position to consider the very general units of meaning, that is the broad themes and issues which recur frequently in the interview or conversation. It is important at this stage to have a number of copies of the interview transcripts or conversations because the researcher will need to make notes and comments in the margins against particular utterances or responses. The general units of meaning refer to the range of issues the respondent refers to and these in turn are related to the overall focus of the research by the researcher. An example will serve to illustrate this process here. If a teacher provides comments or perceptions on a particular curriculum development project, or an examination scheme then general units of meaning may be identified in the transcript which refer to such issues as teachers' perceptions of teaching, attitudes towards the underlying philosophy of the syllabus or project, views on the children involved. The researcher needs to identify, extract, and comment on these general units of meaning.

## Relating general units of meaning to the research focus

Once the teacher has isolated the general units of meaning from the interview or conversation this is the point at which she can hold them up against the research focus, topics, and concerns in order to see whether and to what extent they throw light upon them. It is important to note that the materials themselves are placed against the research focus and not the other way around which might lead to forcing the materials into the researcher's prearranged ideas and hypotheses. This would run counter to the general ethos of 'grounded theory'. It may of course turn out that the materials relate only tangentially to the research focus or are ambiguous. The researcher will then have to re-think the general focus of the research. Since, by definition, unstructured and informal interviews and conversations are fluid, the scope for straying from the relevant issues to other 'relevant' issues is quite large. Whatever the case the teacher is likely to find that there is much in the so diligently collected and transcribed materials which bears very little relation to the task at hand. This ought to be so since everyday life is such that all manner of varied topics are likely to emerge in the course of an interview or conversation.

The extracting of general units of meaning which relate directly to the focus of the research will necessarily involve leaving much out. What does the teacher researcher do with the sections of the interview or conversation she is not using? This is in many ways a presentational matter. Depending upon the research and the audience complete transcripts of the whole of the interviews or conversations used *may* be included by the teacher researcher in the final report. This relates to one of the advantages of ethnographic work on schools and classrooms. By including as much of the data as possible in the report itself the researcher enables the reader to provide alternative readings and analyses of the data and to consider the way in which the teacher researcher arrives at her analysis.

## Patterns and themes extracted

This is the point when the teacher researcher can explore in greater depth the major themes which emerge from the data and the ways in which these relate to the focus of the research in particular. The question of the research focus itself has of course already been established. There is almost a limitless number of topics the teacher researcher might explore. The constraints will surround the time the teacher has to explore these topics and the ways in which she intends to explore them. Most of the issues the teacher researcher chooses to focus upon will come from the immediate classroom, school, or neighbourhood context. Hence the patterns and themes extracted from the interviews and conversations might be seen in relation to these. Those teachers whose research is part of a course of study may well have been exposed to elements of psychology, sociology, or anthropology as well as educational studies. These disciplines have generated their own analytical categories and the teacher researcher might extract patterns or themes in relation to some of these categories.

The patterns and themes extracted may indeed turn out to be very particular and local. It is important however to remember that there is both a particular individual school context of teachers and pupils as well as a cultural, neighbourhood, community, and societal context of those schools and classrooms to consider. Learning is inextricably linked with both of these contexts. Hopefully the patterns and themes extracted and the kinds of analyses made of the interview or conversational materials will throw some light upon the local and particular as well as the wider situations in which we teach and in which our children learn.

## Nature of typifications and perceptions

One of the most influential approaches within the human sciences over the last few years has been that which has been associated with phenomenology.

The philosopher Edmund Husserl is usually associated with 'phenomenology', a philosophical position concerned to describe the phenomena of consciousness, that is the foundations of our common-sense taken-for-granted assumptions about the social world. In order to achieve this Husserl, in his famous phrase, argued that we had to go 'back to the things' themselves. The way to achieve this for Husserl was to adapt the method of 'epoché', or bracketing the phenomena, that is to free ourselves from all presuppositions about the phenomena in order to see what they are made up of. This method of phenomenological reduction refers to suspending our belief in the world and thereby in Garfinkel's phrase, making activities 'anthropologically strange' (Garfinkel 1967). The aim of this approach therefore becomes the abandonment of all our prejudgements and preconceptions of phenomena so that nothing may be taken as given; this would therefore reveal, in Husserl's terms, the essence of the elements of consciousness and thinking themselves.

While all of this may sound typically philosophical, phenomenology, as a philosophical position, and the sociological approaches it has shaped, ethnomethodology and interpretative approaches in the human sciences, have been responsible for mounting major criticisms of conventional, positivistic social science. Furthermore, these approaches have generated fresh ways in which qualitative materials like those derived from ethnography, unstructured interviewing, conversations, and participant observation, may be analysed.

A number of key concepts feature in the work of those social scientists who have been influenced by phenomenology. Consciousness they argue is always consciousness of something, people *intend* actions, that is they play a crucial role in making things happen themselves. We experience the life-world of our 'intuitive environments' as a world we share in common with our fellow human beings. This world then is an inter-subjective world where the other people with whom I come into contact are assumed to make the same kinds of assumptions as I do and that furthermore, if indeed we were to change places with others, they too would see the world as we do in exactly the same way. This confirms the principle of the interchangeability of standpoints. For phenomenologists these features constitute the natural attitude, the ordinary common-sense mundane practical reasoning of everyday life. Human beings, they argue, share an unshakeable faith in the 'facticity' or realness of their everyday world.

Alfred Schutz (1899–1959) is usually regarded as being the key figure in unravelling the sociological implications of phenomenology but it was with the publication of Harold Garfinkel's book *Studies in Ethnomethodology* in 1967 that the direct practical research implications of phenomenology for sociological investigation were worked out. Shutz was concerned to unravel the nature of common-sense thinking, that is the ways in which we routinely and ordinarily make sense of events and activities in the world around us. For Schutz our common-sense understanding of the world is facilitated by our use of language. Language provides us with a store of labels or types which provides for the mutual recognition of objects and events in our world by different people in the same or similar ways. Schutz describes these processes as constituting 'stocks of knowledge' which are in turn dependent upon the process of 'typification'. We understand the actions of others by employing constructs, models, or idealizations of typical courses of action, typical people and typical motives, objects, events, or activities. We obtain these 'ideal types' from our continual experience of the everyday social world. As Schutz puts it, we have a 'cookbook recipe for actions' which relates to our typifications of real-life situations so that typical people can be associated with typical events which are likely to bring about typical consequences. When we go to the bus-stop we expect a bus with a particular number on it to arrive, not the *Starship Enterprise*! This enables us to apply rules of thumb to situations in order to make sense of them and we have 'recipe knowledge' from which we can extract explanations and provide solutions to problematic situations in everyday life so that if someone did arrive at the bus-stop expecting the *Starship Enterprise* to arrive we can describe them as typically 'deluded', 'nuts', 'a weirdo', or the like.

The notion of typification might therefore be useful in analysing interviews and conversational materials. Most obviously teachers have typifications of their children and students based upon their everyday experience of them together with their biographical situations. These typifications also embrace expectations and assumptions about how the types of child or student so identified will behave in certain typical situations. Of course typifications are not confined to individual actors, but groups of actors, classes, subjects, even teaching styles. One of the ways of approaching the analysis of interview materials therefore is through elaborating, unravelling, and explaining these processes of typification.

Consider the following typifications of children, parents, and families contained in materials collected during conversations and unstructured interviews in the course of an ethnographic study of an urban open-plan primary school:

Bill:  You know these kids, I mean for all that's wrong with them they're game for anything you know, they're really keen at sports, full of enthusiasm they give it their all.

Mrs Smith:  What I find with these kids is that they need more than the average security, it's their backgrounds, these high rise flats and things, a big planning mistake you know. You know what I mean.

Anne:  Some of these kids you know get so frustrated and pent up inside if people keep on telling them off the way some people talk to them ... they're human beings after all.

Anne:      I don't know, some of these parents don't seem to care about their kids at all, they send 'em out any old way, you wonder why some of these lot ever bother having families at all.

Elaine:     I don't know, they're crazy, you just can't do anything with these kids in a situation like this, at least I can't it's really getting me down.

Liz:        I mean there's really two kinds of kids in our school it's quite clear really you can tell. There's my yellow group kind these kind of kids are the really, really bad ones, you know the dirty smelly ones, can't do anything, the ones with sore feet, 'Miss I've got sore feet' [laughs]. Birks, and oh Geoff.

G. H.:     What do you mean 'sore feet'?

Liz:        You know sore feet, they put their shoes on the wrong feet.

G. H.:     Really?

Liz:        Yea, but then there's the other kind my red group, they're really good workers, Teresa, Joanna, Martin.

Mr Brown:   The trouble with these kids is if you give 'em a bit of freedom you find they go everywhere and get all of the things out all over the place.

Mr Brown:   You can tell these kinds of kids, the dim ones their trays are always in a mess, look at that [pulls out Linda's tray] you can tell the brighter ones, they don't need much tidying up.

Mr Brown:   You see the kinds of parents we tend to get here often tend to get things wrong and start taking things the wrong way ... you see we've got three types of parents really, the sort of right-wing type, who look in their English books checking the spellings, mind you some of their spellings are nothing to write home about judging by the letters I've seen but that's beside the point, then there's the overprotective ones who can't leave their little ones without saying goodbye, and then there's those who just come to gossip and meet other parents in the morning.

(Hitchcock 1980: 334–6)

Numerous studies have pointed to this important process of typification in the educational world and these studies might be consulted for the ways in which they have focused upon typifications in their analyses of school and classroom processes. One thinks particularly of Rist's early classic study of American kindergarten teachers' expectations of their pupils based upon social class factors (Rist 1970: 411–51), Sharpe and Green's (1975) study of teachers' ideologies in Mapeldene infant school, a so-called progressive school, Hargreaves, Hestor, and Mellor's (1975) study of deviance in secondary schools, and more recently Pollard's (1985a) account of a primary school. These studies point to the potential of focusing upon typifications as a way of analysing the materials contained in interviews and conversations.

## Self-revelation and researcher reflection

The occasion of research often puts individuals into situations that they would not normally find themselves in. Unstructured interviews, no matter how loosely or informally organized, ask individuals to sit down, take stock, and reflect, albeit in as natural and unprovoked a manner as possible, on particular topics. One hopes that there will certainly be moments in the unstructured interview when the degree of rapport and empathy between the teacher researcher and subject or interviewee is such that the respondent may reveal themselves in more detail then ever before. When respondents do become involved in this process of self-revelation, of 'bearing all' to the researcher so to speak, then the researcher needs to be prepared to reflect on the themes exposed. The nature of teaching itself is such that individuals do tend to develop highly organized conceptualizations of who they are and what they are able to achieve. The unstructured interview offers teachers and pupils the opportunity to verbalize and attempt to articulate some of these aspects of their lives. It is important for the researcher to attempt to pick up on these aspects of the interview and, in the light of any other data that has been collected, reflect upon these points.

Teachers' perspectives are by definition complex. They are often revealed only partially and in different ways to different audiences. The teacher will have to be sensitive towards the possible fluctuations in the way in which teachers themselves may try to present or reveal aspects of themselves in the interview. It is important to remember that the subject may be very concerned to present a positive self-image thereby influencing the content and nature of the replies and accounts as we indicated earlier.

Teaching is full of situations which place the individual in difficult and contradictory circumstances. Students of organizations often speak about the differences between the formal organization of an institution like for example a school or factory, and its informal organization. This refers to the distinction between what is supposed to happen in an organization, its rules and official reasons for operating on the one hand, which is often described as formal organization, and the unofficial, unwritten, taken-for-granted and informal organization on the other hand. In teaching, these kinds of differences often find expression in what we describe as the dichotomy between professional themes such as a 'whole school approach', 'integrated day', and so on, and the practical arrangements of ordinary teachers and ordinary pupils routinely trying to make a 'whole school approach' or an 'integrated day' happen. The two often turn out to be somewhat different.

A focus upon these self-revelatory aspects of the interview may help the researcher to see how some of these problems are resolved by the teacher. For example they may help to see how contradictory attitudes to examinations are resolved, or how teachers handle curriculum or syllabus objectives they perceive to be unrealizeable. A close examination of the interview or conversational materials may throw light on these and other complex questions.

## Validity checks, triangulation, re-interviewing, and re-analysis

It is possible and important to develop checks on the data in qualitative research and we will briefly examine how the teacher might do this with interview materials in this section.

First of all, as we stressed earlier in this chapter, familiarity with the actual materials themselves is a vital first step for the teacher. From the wealth of data the teacher has on the setting itself, she will have inside her head a considerable amount of intuitive knowledge which she can bring to bear on the materials in such a way as to identify lack of consistency, potential errors, and comments that are simply untrue. Basically two approaches have been used to validate interview and conversational data. The processes of triangulation and of re-interviewing and re-analysis are the two main options open to the teacher researcher. These procedures apply to other data collection techniques to check on validity and authenticity but they are especially useful for the teacher making use of unstructured interviews in small-scale research.

'Triangulation' refers to the use of more than one method of data collection within a single study. However, a number of other terms have been used to describe this process, for example mixed method, multi-method, or multiple strategies (Burgess 1982: 163–7). As we have seen, almost by definition, field research will be directly involved in some form of triangulation since the field researcher will obtain data from a variety of sources and in a number of different ways. Triangulation encourages this flexibility and can, as in the case of the analysis of interview and conversational materials, add some depth to the analysis and potentially increase the validity of the data and consequently the analyses made of them. While there are clearly advantages of a multi-method approach to data collection for the teacher researcher, not least because she is likely to have at hand a variety of different sources of data, there are also disadvantages and problems. The researcher has always to be careful that the data elicited by means of the different techniques is actually comparable. In other words, there are many different kinds of data and one data source cannot be used unproblematically to validate another source of data. Documentary sources of data are very different from observational sources or accounts. Alternatively the researcher can engage in different types of triangulation.

Denzin, a long-time supporter of triangulation, has argued that it is in fact a basic principle of social research. Denzin (1970) distinguishes between 'within methods' triangulation and 'between methods' triangulation. Within methods triangulation refers to the replication of a study using the same techniques as a way of checking on the reliability of the study and the nature of the theories generated. Between methods triangulation refers to the use of more than one method of data collection within the same study. Given the circumstances the teacher researcher is likely to be faced with, methodological triangulation is likely to be the most readily available method for checking the data.

Once the teacher has organized and read through the unstructured interview materials she can compare these with other sources of data she may have on the situation which may be derived from participant observation or other sources. One of the best examples of the use of this kind of triangulation in educational research can be found in Cicourel *et al.*'s (1974) study of social interaction in both classroom and testing situations in first-grade and kindergarten classrooms in two districts of southern California. This study was designed to show how the 'facts' of a child's competence and abilities were actually subjectively and socially accomplished in the routine ongoing activities of the classroom and testing situations. The authors produced audio and video tape recording from which the analyses were made. The term widely used in these articles is 'indefinite triangulation' and it refers to the ways in which different sources of data were brought to bear upon the same event. What the authors did was to compare the participants' performances in test and classroom situations with data which were gathered through interviews where the teachers were shown the video tape or test answers and asked to explain their actions and reasons. As such a further level of meaning and interpretation is added to the analytical equation. How far this triangulation process can go is of course an interesting question.

Another way in which triangulation can take place with a view to warranting the subsequent analyses of the materials may be found in the 'diary–diary-interview' method as described by Zimmerman and Wieder (1977: 479–99). The diary can be used for a variety of purposes. We have worked with many teachers who, while engaged on research into their own classroom, have kept diaries of events and activities. The teacher could therefore ask the people within her research if they would keep a diary; this diary could be used as a basis for subsequent unstructured interviews. Hence the diary may be used as a question-generating device and as a validity check also.

Zimmerman and Wieder's (1977: 479–99) study of the 'counter-culture' in California is a good example of the ways in which methods and sources of data may be combined in a research project where all the activities engaged in could not be observed by the researchers. As a result the people involved in their study were paid $10 for keeping a diary for seven complete days and were given a Who? What? When? Where? and How? formula to record events in chronological order. The triangulation takes place when subsequently the subjects are interviewed about the accounts and activities recorded in the diary of the seven days of the individual's life. As Zimmerman and Wieder put it

the diarists' statement is used as a way of generating questions for the subsequent diary interview. The diary interview converts the diary – a source of data in its own right – into a question-generating and, hence, data-gathering device.

(Zimmerman and Weider 1977: 489)

Clearly the diary–diary-interview method is one that could be of considerable use in school-based research.

The second major way in which the teacher researcher might attempt to check or validate the interview materials is to go back to the respondent with the complete transcript or a summary of the main themes and emerging categories. Alternatively it may be possible to re-interview the individuals concerned and become engaged in subsequent re-analysis. Both of these courses of action offer the subject the opportunity of adding further information and the researcher the opportunity of checking on what data has been collected. A second interview could be used to focus upon themes and issues which emerged, or those on which the researcher was not clear.

These are some of the ways the teacher researcher might attempt to check and validate the data. One cannot, however, rule out the possibility of intentional error. As we have noted elsewhere, the first task in establishing the accuracy of accounts in the field is to place them in their ethnographic context and consider whether or not they hold up under scrutiny. The procedures we pointed to in Chapter 3 regarding informants' accounts could easily be applied to the subject matter of interviews and conversational materials. In an important sense, of course, even lies can be regarded as an important source of data.

## Summary

In this chapter we have taken a broad view of interviewing as a data-gathering technique and unravelled the different kinds of interviews available. Our concern has been with examining the applicability of different interviewing strategies to the kinds of research situations the teacher researcher may find herself in. We concentrated upon the unstructured interview and conversational materials in more detail. The interviewing process was broken down into three basic elements of the interview situation, methods of recording, and the analysis of interview and conversational materials, and each of these was discussed in turn. The issues raised in this chapter cover most of the eventualities the teacher researcher is likely to come across. However, the unlikely does occur and the interviewer needs to be prepared to respond to unforeseen circumstances. We have also tried to show how, despite constraints of time, energy, and resources the teacher researcher can become reasonably competent in the use of the interview technique and the subsequent analysis of interview and conversational materials.

## Suggested further reading

Interviewing is likely to become one of the most widely used techniques in teacher research and therefore repays careful consideration. A useful overview of interviewing in educational research is provided by J. Powney and M. Watts (1987) *Interviewing in Educational Research,* London: Routledge & Kegan Paul. H. Simons (1981) 'Conversation piece: the practice of interviewing in case study research', in C. Adelman (ed.) *Uttering, Muttering, Collecting, Using and Reporting Talk for Social and Educational Research,* London: Grant McIntyre, deals with some of the issues the teacher researcher using this technique is likely to encounter. More specific accounts dealing with interviewing as a research technique can be found in J. Finch (1984) '"It's great to have someone to talk to": the ethics and politics of interviewing women', in C. Bell and H. Roberts (eds) *Social Research: Politics, Problems and Practices,* London: Routledge & Kegan Paul; M. Fuller (1980) 'Black girls in a London comprehensive', in R. Deem (ed.) *Schooling for Women's Work,* London: Routledge & Kegan Paul; and L. Measor (1985) 'Interviewing: a strategy in qualitative research', in R. G. Burgess (ed.) *Strategies of Educational Research: Qualitative Methods,* Lewes: Falmer Press. Interviewing and observing children presents special problems. The following works all deal with the issues involved here: W. A. Corsaro (1981) 'Entering the child's world: research strategies for field entry and data collection in a pre-school setting', in J. L. Green and C. Wallat (eds) *Ethnography and Language in Educational Settings,* Norwood NJ: Ablex Publishing; B. Davies (1979) 'Children's perceptions of social interaction in school', *Collected Original Resources in Education* 3, 1; and B. Davies (1982) *Life in Classroom and Playground: The Accounts of Primary School Children,* London: Routledge & Kegan Paul.

# Chapter five

# Documentary sources

## Introduction

In the course of their working lives teachers will come into contact with a variety of written texts. Researchers in both education and the social sciences have made extensive use of written texts though the study of these materials is usually seen as being the province of the historian. Written texts take a variety of forms. We can distinguish between official documentation, which refers mainly to government reports including those from the DES, but other sources of official information in the form of statistics or reports, published reports, including commentary upon particular events and persons from a variety of people, while personal accounts refer mainly to individual subjective accounts of experiences, either written down by the individuals themselves or related orally to a researcher. We use the general term 'documentary sources' to refer to these materials in this chapter and will introduce the kinds of documentary sources available to the teacher researcher, the ways in which they can be made use of, and the questions surrounding their collection. The chapter concentrates on the value and problems of personal documentary sources and in particular the life history technique. We then move on to a consideration of other documentary sources of interest to the teacher, paying special attention to the methodological issues raised together with the need to consider the historical context out of which documents emerge.

## Personal documentary sources

These sources have been used extensively across the human sciences over a considerable period of time. Personal documentary sources would include autobiography, biography, letters, diaries, life histories, and perhaps some literature. One might also wish to include the narratives which are often contained in case studies, ethnographies, or oral history projects. Clearly some of these texts exist already and are independent of the researcher. On the other hand certain texts like histories come into being as a direct result of a researcher who collects the narratives, organizes, edits, and arranges them. Using these kinds of data is not without its problems and there have been many criticisms of both the validity of personal documents and the typicality of their authors! Critics have pointed to the highly subjective nature of autobiographies and life histories, while the use of written sources by the researcher might mean the neglect of certain groups like working-class people or women. In contrast, the first advocates of the use of personal documentary sources as data for sociologists, W. I. Thomas and F. Znaniecki, regarded them as *the* source of sociological data *par excellence*. This was as far back as 1918.

Personal documentary sources constitute a largely neglected source of data on the social world of schools and classrooms, especially when compared to the extensive use of the survey technique, structured interviewing, or systematic observation. We suggest that used with care, and in conjunction with other kinds of data, personal documentary sources offer the teacher researcher a number of possibilities. As we have seen, ethnographic accounts of school and classroom processes tend to pinpoint the immediate here and now contemporary quality of the situation, thus possibly lacking historical depth. One of the values of personal documentary sources, especially the life history, could be said to be its ability to represent subjectively meaningful experiences through time. While ethnography and the case study are concerned with what might loosely be described as situational analysis, that is interactions in schools, classrooms, staffrooms, curriculum planning meetings, and so on, personal documentary research is concerned with biography, that is individual experiences, memories, reflections, and interpretations. The situational and the biographical are therefore two sides of the same coin since the situational will be influenced by the biographical and vice versa. A focus upon the biographical can therefore help teacher researchers to appreciate more fully the situational.

The teacher researcher may profitably gain from a consideration of personal documentary sources. The highly personal and subjective character of the data offers insight into many areas traditional sources of data cannot illuminate. The nature of the different investigative techniques used to collect such materials means that they do not impose the researcher's meanings and values on to the situation but rather let the voices of the teachers and pupils themselves come through. However, there are limitations and problems associated with the use of these documents which need to be noted. As we have already seen, the particular circumstances of the individual teacher place limitations and restrictions upon the choice of research technique. Many kinds of personal documents are simply not available in school situations; the time may simply not be available for the teacher researcher to conduct lengthy discussions with subjects. While the teacher researcher is subject to these sorts of constraints whatever research technique she adopts, the collection of personal documentary sources creates some special problems. We will unravel both the potential and the problems entailed in using these kinds of data in school-based research.

*Personal documentary sources and education*

Teachers and others have often complained that the contextual particulars of the routine day-to-day activities of schools have often been ignored by researchers. Much of this research, it was claimed, did not pay attention to either teachers' pedagogical or practical problems. The use of auto-biographical narratives or life histories of particular teachers and pupils when considered alongside certain themes as for example occupational histories, subject histories, or 'deviant' histories can help the researcher to see the ways in which individual experience relates to wider school and societal processes. One of the characteristic features of these personal documents is their ability to convey an individual's experience of the past. The teacher researcher who takes the time to collect, interpret, and analyse a life history for example has the opportunity not only of seeing events in a different way, but also of discovering how apparently unconnected events seem to come together and shape future experience and behaviour. First-hand accounts of children's and pupils' experiences collected by the teacher can throw light on a whole range of issues and demonstrate the value of this kind of research focus. Two examples can be used here to highlight the value of collecting pupils' life stories, accounts, and experiences.

As a result of a series of in-service workshops for ILEA teachers on the investigation of gender issues in the secondary school (Adams and Arnot 1986) one of the areas examined was the impact of parental aspirations and family culture on pupils' lives and values. The teachers were encouraged to focus upon collecting the pupil's first-hand account. The following account provided by a white girl from a traditional working-class area shows how mothers can influence their daughters' feelings of discontent, fantasy, domestic responsibilities, and the pressures to conform to traditional roles and expectations: all factors likely to influence girls' attitudes to school and learning.

> Me in 10 years' time, that's a joke. I'll probably be chained to the cooker with three kids yapping around my ankles. I hope not. I hope I'll be living in the Caribbean with a millionaire husband with servants to wait on me hand and foot. I'd have a Porsche car and perhaps an old Rolls Royce to pop up the shops in. I'd have a new suit every day and my hair in a different style every week.
>
> I'll tell you the truth now as you can gather the above paragraph was only a fantasy. In 10 years' time, I should think I'll be married, I might have some children. I hope to have a nice car, doesn't have to be brand new but at least it will be decent. My husband will have a good job and

we'll regularly go out to the pub or somewhere special. My house will be clean and I shall have nice furniture. My husband will have a car too, so when he goes out I'll still have a car in case I want to go out. I shall also have a job, it doesn't have to be full-time but at least it will be bringing more money into our home. My job will probably just be a part-time shop assistant or work mornings in a factory or warehouse.

If I see myself like that in 10 years' time, what's the point of me being here working like mad, getting as many exam. passes as I can. It doesn't really seem worth coming to school but you only get in trouble if you don't.

My mum and most of the women I know have lives like this. I think that I will be like them because to me a married women with kids has a life like that, as they should enjoy the time with their families.

This is what will happen to me if I don't do anything about it, not that I'm complaining, it's a decent life for someone like me.

(Adams and Arnot 1986 89–90)

Another example is provided by the work of Tom Cottle. In an extensive series of studies Cottle demonstrates the value of what he describes as the 'life study' in describing the lives of urban poor American Blacks and British West Indians (Cottle 1973: 344–60; 1974; 1978). The fruits of this approach can be seen in his short account of a young female American prostitute, Matilda Rutherford (Cottle, 1972: 519–63) and in his description of the lives of West Indians in London (Cottle 1978). Cottle's work is reminiscent of the Chicago urban ethnographers yet has a journalistic feel to it. His work develops out of long-term friendships and interviews as a form of conversation with the subject. These conversations can take place any time, anywhere. Cottle does not use a tape recorder. He believes that it intrudes too much on the naturalness of the situation. Instead he listens, makes notes, and writes up the conversations later. There must be, in his terms, 'mutual recognition', that is a trusting and informal relationship between researcher and researched. Most of Cottle's work has been done in the USA; however, his work on poor West Indian families in London, (Cottle 1978) does deal quite extensively with British West Indians' experience of the education system. These 'life stories' reveal the reality behind the Swann Report but no doubt also the alienation of many West Indian children in our schools. The following extracts from Polly Davies' story show considerable insight.

Every day I walk by this brick wall. You have to go through this little passageway to get to school. There's usually a cat there climbing around. When I see him I tell him, bring me good luck. He usually runs away, which I tell myself is a good sign. Then I tell myself, no matter what anybody tells you, don't be upset, don't be afraid. Sometimes it works, but most of the time it doesn't especially if Jessie isn't with me. It's better when she's with me. I'd rather have someone yell out, 'There goes two nigger girls' than have me be there all by myself. You don't know what they're going to do next when they do it, and it's always happening. You don't know what's the best thing to do either. Like they'll say, 'Hey, you short nigger, what are you – some kind of a pygmy?' That's my own special name because I'm short. Aren't they clever! I never know what to do. Some people say you shout back at them so they won't do it again. But I couldn't get myself to do that. What am I supposed to do when it happens, like, when we're on the playground or on the stairs? Or in the class too? It happens in class too. 'Hey, pygmy, you read the lesson for today?' What am I supposed to do? Jessie says I should keep my mouth shut and tell one of the boys, like, the biggest person I see and tell him, that kid over there called me a pygmy. That's what she says to do because she says if we don't start fighting back they'll never stop doing it to us. Maybe she's right, but I can't see myself going up to some guy and telling him what someone said to me.

(Cottle 1978: 57)

*Some important questions about personal documentary sources*

The teacher researcher needs to think in advance of the possible strengths and weaknesses of using any research technique or source of data. She also needs to bear in mind the way in which the findings of the research can be presented to others and some of the implications for professional practice contained in them. The following might be regarded as a preliminary checklist for the teacher researcher to attend to when using personal documentary sources as a substantial part of a piece of school-based research.

1  What is the nature of the document or documents in question? Are they largely solicited or unsolicited? What consequences follow?
2  Who is the subject and what grounds for subject choice can be given?
3  How are the issues of validity, reliability, and representativeness to be dealt with?
4  What is the nature of researcher involvement in the project?
5  How is the material to be organized, edited, and analysed?
6  How are the research findings to be communicated to other professionals?

These questions by no means exhaust all the issues associated with the use of personal documentary sources in school-based research. They provide the teacher researcher with only a general guide to some of the issues which will have to be dealt with. The 'answers' to these six questions will however form a substantial part of any research involving personal documentary sources. The reader might like to consider the ways in which other researchers notably Goodson (1983) and Woods (1985: 13–26) deal with some of these issues at this point. Let us now focus in more detail on the use of one of these techniques, the life history, in more detail.

## The life history

The earliest attempt to produce full-length accounts of a single person's life in that person's own words is generally considered to be Paul Radin's *Crashing Thunder: The Autobiography of an American Indian* (1920). Thomas and Znaniecki's (1918–20) life history of Wladek Wisniewski is usually regarded as the first sociological life history. The life history is usually collected over a fairly lengthy period of time and often supplemented with other observations and materials or documents pertaining to the individual. The life history is therefore constructed out of the researcher's recording and documentation of what the subject says as a direct result of involvement with that subject. It is a qualitative method designed to provide individuals with the opportunity of telling their own personal stories in their own ways. The life history reconstructs, interprets, and analyses some of the main features, personally important and critical episodes and developments in a single individual's life. The life history is above all an interactive and co-operative technique directly involving the researcher. It creates a story and brings into being, by affording an opportunity and set of circumstances not normally available, a set of reflections upon a past and a present that would otherwise not normally present themselves in such a form. By thus focusing upon internal subjective experiences, memories, reminiscences, and above all 'stories', an appreciation of the complex, detailed, and interrelated aspects of an individual's identity, experiences, culture, and society may be approached.

Teachers using this technique will find that there is a tension between retaining the rich descriptive character of these accounts and allowing time and space for analysis of them. Distinctions between types of life history may help here. It is possible to distinguish between 'retrospective' life histories based upon the reconstruction of a life or aspects of a life from memory dealing with individual's feelings and interpretations about past events now, and 'contemporaneous' life histories focusing upon the description of aspects of an individual's daily life in progress (Langness and Frank 1981; Frank and Vanderburgh 1986: 188). Contemporaneous life histories are possibly likely to draw the researcher more into the discussion and interpretation of materials, though clearly there is often going to be overlap between these two aspects of a life history. While there are different kinds of life histories with varying emphasis there are also clearly different modes of presenting a life history. First, there are 'naturalistic' first-person life histories where most of the actual published life story is in the words of the individual subject, perhaps with a brief introduction by the researcher providing background detail and context and possibly a conclusion. Second, there are thematically edited first-person life histories where the words of the subject are retained intact, but where the researcher has presented them in terms of a series of themes, topics, or headings, usually in a chapter-by-chapter form. Third, there are what might be described as interpreted and edited life stories where the influence of the researcher is most marked since the researcher sifts, distils, edits, and interprets the words of the subject and while retaining the feel and authenticitiy of the subject's words, presents a written version of the life story, sometimes making use of extensive first-person accounts to tie the researcher's text together.

Certainly there are considerable advantages òf using the life history technique in school-based research. The retrospective quality of life histories can provide historical depth. They will also be able to reveal the differing ways in which an individual perceives educational situations. A number of substantive research concerns themselves seem amenable to investigation by means of the life history technique, for example teachers' careers, teachers' and pupils' values and attitudes, and the ways in which the variables of class, gender, and ethnicity can influence the learning process. There is also the possibility that the act of producing a life history itself may have a beneficial impact on the teacher or pupil themselves, helping them to clarify their own ideas. As a result of the flexibility and adaptability of the life history technique it can be used in a variety of situations. Indeed the teacher researcher could quite easily incorporate a series of short life histories into a piece of school-based research which makes use of significantly different types of data. This perhaps is the reason why the life history technique has been used in such diverse fields as education, welfare, medicine, psychology, sociology, and anthropology.

Despite the above advantages the life history technique is not appropriate for every research project the teacher researcher will become engaged in. The teacher researcher will have to base her decision of whether or not to use the life history technique on a number of factors. Individual circumstances, the nature of the project, and practical constraints of time and energy will all feature. Once the decision has been taken to use the life history technique the researcher will need to attend to some preliminary issues, the process of data collection, and finally analysis of the materials. We will consider each of these phases in turn.

*Producing and analysing life histories*

Figure 5.1 shows the main phases and stages through which the teacher researcher using the life history technique might work. This is by no means the definitive way in which all researchers have used the technique but acts only as a guide.

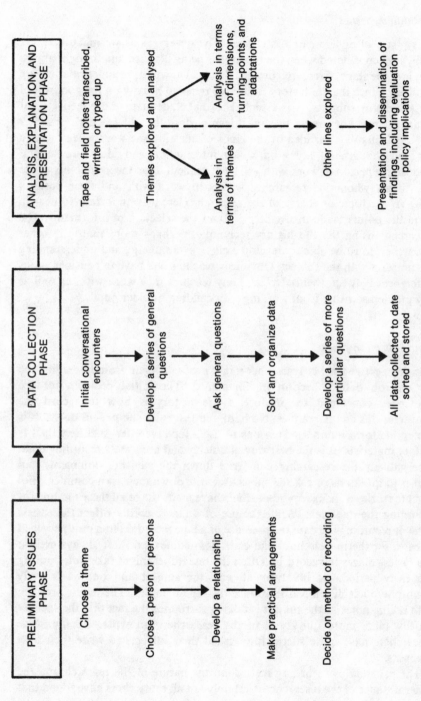

**Figure 5.1** A guide to the production of life histories in educational contexts

PRELIMINARY ISSUES PHASE

Choose a theme

Choose a person or persons

Develop a relationship

Make practical arrangements

Decide on method of recording

DATA COLLECTION PHASE

Initial conversational encounters

Develop a series of general questions

Ask general questions

Sort and organize data

Develop a series of more particular questions

All data collected to date sorted and stored

ANALYSIS, EXPLANATION, AND PRESENTATION PHASE

Tape and field notes transcribed, written, or typed up

Themes explored and analysed

Analysis in terms of dimensions, turning-points, and adaptations

Analysis in terms of themes

Other lines explored

Presentation and dissemination of findings, including evaluation policy implications

*Preliminary issues*

This phase of any research is crucial. The observations we make here are really best considered when the research is being planned and thought about, that is at the stage of research design. Practical as well as technical matters are involved. Since the life history technique relies so heavily on the goodwill of the subject or subjects, it is essential to make adequate and effective prior arrangements. For similar reasons it is important that the teacher researcher has a reasonably clear idea of the kinds of question she wants eventually to ask and the general areas on which information and ideas are sought. Choosing a person to work with will be dependent upon the availability of the individuals whom the researcher wishes to work with and their position *vis-à-vis* the topic or theme of the research. Here it is important to bear in mind the points made in Chapter 3 about the selection of informants. The researcher using the life history technique, perhaps more than any other researcher, must be able to develop a close, sympathetic, and understanding relationship with the subject. Obviously teachers will have to consider status differences between themselves and any teachers they work with, as well as any problems arising from working with children or older pupils.

*Data collection phase*

The prospective teacher researcher might profitably gain from re-reading the sections on data collection in Chapter 3. The initial problem for the researcher concerned to produce a life history is how to record the conversations and narratives. No hard and fast rules can be laid down. It is preferable for a number of reasons to use a tape recorder to collect the life history materials. It is the best way of quickly and accurately recording data. Alternatively the researcher can write down the subject's comments and replies to questions or ask the subject to write down their own commentaries and life stories. Life history researchers have made use of all these methods of recording the materials. While the use of a tape recorder offers the easiest form of recording the data the presence of a tape recorder often puts people ill at ease. Furthermore school and classroom contexts do not always present the easiest places to record in. Often the researcher might take notes during the early periods of involvement with the subject and once a friendly atmosphere has developed introduce the tape recorder. The major problem with taking notes as the subject is talking surrounds the fact that the speaker usually talks more quickly than the researcher can write. Finally some researchers have quite successfully asked their subjects to write their own accounts.

The problem of recording rests upon the nature of the research and the general stance of the researcher. Certainly not all researchers have found that the tape recorder is the solution to all problems. For example Tom Cottle found the tape recorder an unnecessary burden and his comments are worth considering.

> Furthermore, I used no pre-arranged interview schedule. Nor did I concentrate on designing a scientifically determined sample. I made a number of friends, most of whom I met in informal ways, if not purely by accident. I visited schools, housing and employment programs, clinics and hospitals, social service agencies, churches and of course people's homes. As I grew familiar with particular neighbourhoods, meeting people became no problem at all.
>
> As a methodological note, my conversations were not tape-recorded. Like others, I found the tape-recorder to be a cumbersome intrusion in friendship.
>
> (Cottle 1978: 57)

Thus Cottle's informal approach to recording extends to the whole tenor of his research. Some however would regard this as being unsystematic or too informal. Perhaps the only way to assess the success of this approach is to consider the quality of the materials Cottle is able to assemble by using such an approach.

Once the question of how the materials are to be recorded is decided the teacher researcher must begin to think about the general questions to be asked, areas to be covered, and how this is to be achieved. For the most part the teacher researcher is likely to rely upon the kind of extended informal conversation used by researchers like Cottle (1978) and elaborated in more detail by Woods (1985: 13–26). Here the teacher researcher cultivates the art of listening, imposing herself as little as possible into the situation since the more the researcher is to the fore, the less the subject's voice will come through. Any researcher interjections or criticisms must be conducted with care. Empathy, understanding, and the ability to lend a sympathetic ear are all ingredients in the successful production of life histories. One might think that these are qualities teachers would already possess.

The actual conduct of the interview or conversational exchanges themselves will depend upon the extent to which the researcher wants the subject to wander freely from one topic to another or to focus upon particular themes or topics. The number of meetings or conversations involved will vary from project to project and the time available. There will usually be a combination of the subject talking generally and particularly interspaced with the researcher asking general and focused questions. In this way the life history gets built up. Once the involvement with the subject comes to an end many researchers have one final meeting where some of the emergent themes that the researcher is beginning to isolate can be raised, and the subjects' views recorded. Again, as we noted in Chapter 3, while engaging in collecting qualitative materials the researcher is simultaneously engaged in a preliminary analysis of these materials. Many of the themes the researcher might follow up later will appear spontaneously as the data are being collected.

## Analysis, explanation, and presentation

Once the teacher has collected the life history materials and organized them then the task of analysis can begin. However the analysis of life history materials has been conducted in a variety of ways. Some researchers feel that it is simply best to leave the life history materials to stand on their own, while others have edited and analysed the materials in more detail. This points up one of the central tensions in life history research, namely the desire to retain the rich detailed descriptions on the one hand yet to develop some analysis and explanation of the materials on the other. Undoubtedly the many published life histories available and those produced by teachers that we have seen all have their own intrinsic merits. They are all a good read. But the teacher researcher is concerned to try and develop more systematic knowledge and understanding of the factors which influence professional practice and school learning. As such the teacher researcher will want more from the materials, and will consequently have to develop some analysis of them.

Part of the process of analysis will involve the researcher establishing the extent to which the materials are valid, reliable, and representative of the concerns of the project. These issues tend to take on a rather different character for the researcher relying so heavily upon first-person accounts. The researcher needs to establish the truthfulness and accuracy of the accounts so far as she is able. How does the teacher know that people are not telling the researcher lies? How is it possible to establish whether or not the researcher and the subject are engaged in the elaborate creation of a congruent fiction? These are important issues in any research but the use of first-hand subjective accounts bring them to the fore. A major concern of school-based research must be that it goes beyond the 'merely' anecdotal and moves towards accurate as well as authentic accounts of school and classroom processes. Researchers working within the ethnographic tradition have developed ways in which it is possible to check on the validity and accuracy of the qualitative materials. The teacher researcher using the life history technique might consider the following as a short checklist against which they could place the narratives which they have collected.

1 Note the circumstances surrounding the recording and collection of the data.
2 Consider the relationship between researcher and subject.
3 Are there any 'facts' in the accounts which are easily checked on?
4 Compare statements in one section of a life history with statements in another section of the same life history.
5 Compare the statements in one life history with those in other life histories from different people within the same setting.

6 Compare the statements in the life history with data from other sources within the same setting.

7 Compare the statements in the life history with other statements in published life histories of teachers and pupils.

8 If possible get a second opinion on the materials by showing them to colleagues.

While none of these procedures guarantees the absolute accuracy of the materials retained, together they do go some way towards establishing validity. Furthermore this procedure will help the teacher researcher to consider the typicality of comments and the relationship of the materials to the setting as a whole. This process is an important one because reasons are going to be attributed to the accounts and subsequent explanations of them will be offered. This is no easy task, as the case of Vincent Van Gogh's left ear demonstrates. While what is not in doubt is the fact the Van Gogh cut off a portion of his left ear, what is debatable is why he did it. Runyan (1982: 38–41) elaborates thirteen different sets of explanations!

Perhaps the best way to think about the analysis of life history materials drawn from school contexts is to approach them in terms of themes. This kind of approach to analysis is therefore described as thematic analysis and involves the researcher examining the kinds of themes that emerge from the materials regularly, and how they relate to the concerns of the project. The researcher could therefore concentrate upon for example a teacher's occupational history, a particular child's deviant 'career', or the involvement of staff with a subject area or curriculum development project. Some guidelines do exist in the literature and the reader should consult some of the suggested further reading at the end of this chapter. By way of illustration we will briefly consider one way in which life histories may be analysed.

An anthropologist, Mandelbaum (1973), has developed a way of looking at life history materials which may be of use to the teacher researcher. Mandelbaum's solution to the vast and often highly jumbled flood of raw data the life history produces is for the researcher first to organize the materials into some kind of chronological ordering but then to focus upon three aspects. *Dimensions* of life, including the individual's general, social, cultural, and psychological experiences and the subject's subjective world; in other words, how an individual grows up for example, and the attitudes and values surrounding individuals. *Turnings* refer to those turning-points or transitions or changes of status an individual goes through. These turnings occur when the individual takes on new roles or a new status and as a result takes on a new social indentity; it is appropriate therefore to look and ask for key turning-points in a life. Turnings are of course extremely varied, from religious conversion to promotion to a senior teaching post through to marriage or divorce. Finally *adaptations* refer to the ways in which individuals at some point or other in their lives must slightly amend, alter, or change their values, attitudes, and behaviour patterns to accommodate and handle new situations. Mandelbaum's scheme seems to be quite illuminating and it is one which we suggest is particularly appropriate to the educational context. Mandelbaum's scheme was employed in his famous life history of Ghandi.

A problem with any research the teacher develops is what on earth to do with it all once the project is over. This is part of the question of the overall dissemination of research findings and professional practice. We deal with this crucial aspect in Chapter 8. However, the typically large amounts of data that life history and other personal documentary research is likely to generate is such that problems of both the presentation and dissemination of these materials are likely to arise. Here the teacher researcher may inevitably have to become involved in an editing exercise. Some of the issues surrounding dissemination and presentation may become clearer if we consider the kinds of life histories it is possible to produce from work with pupils and teachers. In this section we have simply tried to spell out the main phases through which the teacher will progress when producing life histories in educational contexts, those of preliminary issues, data collection, and analysis, explanation, and presentation.

### Life histories of pupils and teachers

A clear case may be made for the teacher researcher focusing upon the biographies, experiences, and interpretations of pupils and teachers. All educational practices and systems have a history. A focus upon teachers' and pupils' life histories can help to relate individual experience to the wider school, community, or societal context. Individuals' perceptions of the learning environment shape and influence their experience of and involvement in these environments. The teacher researcher is concerned to step back and take a systematic look at her own and others' professional practice. To this end we suggest that some of the following themes may be explored by using the life history technique.

Suggested themes for exploration in pupils' life histories

1 Pupils' experience of previous schools.
2 Pupils' views of subjects.
3 Pupils' attitudes to gender issues.
4 'Disaffected' pupils.
5 Pupils with 'special needs'.
6 Pupils' experience of ethnic minority status.

Suggested themes for exploration in teachers' life histories

1 Teachers' professional training and perception of pupils and subjects.
2 Teachers' career patterns and experience of previous schools.
3 Teachers' involvement in curriculum innovation or development.
4 Teachers' experience of roles and authority.

5 Teachers' attitudes to pupils.
6 Teachers' attitudes to gender issues.
7 Teachers' attitudes to children with learning difficulties.

A focus upon pupils' viewpoints is a relatively recent phenomena. But Blishen (1969), Hammersley and Woods, (eds.) (1976), Woods, (ed.) (1980), and Measor and Woods (1983: 55–76) have all considered ways of investigating pupils' worlds, which face different circumstances. The teacher will have a position in the school, a 'reputation' amongst both staff and pupils. These factors can play quite a determining role in the research process and the teacher researcher will have to consider the ways in which these factors influence matters. Of note here would be such factors as the age of the pupils, their familiarity with the researcher, differences in language usage between pupils and the researcher, and the topics being explored. Perhaps most obvious of course is the question of the truthfulness of pupils' accounts. But as Measor and Woods (1983: 55–76) point out, even pupil myths have a serious and important reality to them. For the most part when working closely with pupils in the construction of life histories the teacher will need to adopt a sympathetic and understanding stance, refrain from imposing her authority and 'definition of the situation'.

While the production of pupils' life histories is not without its difficulties, neither is the production of teachers' life histories. The nature of the relative position and status of researcher is crucial. Again a realization on the part of the teacher researcher that schools are social situations like anywhere else made up of people who get on and don't get on, gossip, hearsay and rumour will serve to sharpen her awareness of the context of the research. The recent teachers' dispute for example created serious rifts in many staffrooms. These are all realities behind teacher research in general.

In an important article Goodson (1983: 129–54) has attempted to demonstrate the importance of collecting and using teachers' life histories. By focusing upon the work of the American educational ethnographer Louis Smith, in particular *The Complexities of an Urban Classroom* (Smith and Geoffrey 1968) and Smith's later research on the same school, Kensington School, *The Anatomy of Educational Innovation* (Smith and Keith 1971), Goodson demonstrates the importance of trying to link the life histories of individuals with the histories of schools as a whole and patterns of educational innovation. Smith's follow-up study was concerned to see what had happened to the original staff and what effect the Kensington experience had had on them. By adopting such an approach and collecting life histories of the heads of the school through retrospective interviews an important picture of the changes the school underwent began to emerge. Smith's problem was to develop a methodology that could deliver descriptions of the major changes and innovations the school went through. His solution was to widen the focus from life histories of the individual heads and their periods of office to the testimonies of other teachers and the wider history of the school district.

Goodson has also gone on to discuss the sorts of materials that can be collected in producing life histories of teachers, in particular their involvement in subjects and curriculum change in *School Subjects and Curriculum Change* (Goodson 1982). The aim of this project was to try to establish the background to the introduction of a new school subject, Environmental Studies. Goodson began by collecting the life histories of the key figures in the promotion of the subject, arguing that in fact the life histories of these teachers became the life history of the subject. It is therefore possible to develop insights into the teachers' changing perception of work set against the background of school organization. Goodson's work demonstrates the importance and value of focusing upon teachers' careers, work experience, and location in a particular socio-cultural milieu through the life history.

Peter Woods has recently discussed the conversational aspects of the life history method (1985: 13–26). Woods reports on research with a sample of fifty secondary school teachers grouped according to age and subject, the aim of which was initially to concentrate upon the ways in which teachers adapted to crises and critical incidents in the course of their careers. The life history was seen as the most appropriate method there, but as a result of the circumstances Woods and those working with him felt it had to be adapted. The point is strongly made that one of the major values of the life history and its reliance upon conversations between teachers and researchers is that it

> contrasts strongly with the more traditional 'researcher-researched' model, where the latter provides the data and the former the interpretation; and yet avoids the limitations of some 'teacher-researcher' approaches. *This life-history approach, we believe, offers real prospects for bridging the divide between education research and the practice of teaching, for strengthening the empirical supports of sociological theory and for communicating sociologically with teachers.*
>
> (Woods 1985: 14; emphasis added)

Certainly the life history technique while generating many problems does provide teachers with an exciting way of obtaining information on their own and others' practice and experience.

## The use of historical approaches and documentary sources

An essential characteristic of much past qualitative educational research, based on ethnographic approaches, was its exploration of the 'here and now' with little regard to the historical context out of which both the actors and the situations studied emerged. Indeed until fairly recently most books on social science methodology contained little or no advice on the value of the historical context or on the use of documentary sources and oral or life history approaches. The aim of this section is to look at the value of the historical context for school-based research and to give practical guidance on the collection and interpretation of documentary and other kinds of written and non-written sources. This will develop the themes looked at earlier in the chapter, especially those relating to the value of life histories as a means of locating the actor in the process of educational change: the value of the historical-synchronic dimension.

First, what do we mean by 'history' in the context of this chapter? We are less concerned here with history as a distinct discipline, or even with the ways in which historical approaches can both deepen and strengthen qualitative research in certain areas of schooling. When we speak of history we are talking about the time dimension of social affairs which has often been missing from much educational research outside the area of the history of education. It has been argued that field researchers are in danger of misinterpreting the present if historical sources on the past are neglected (Pitt 1972).

Starting from the position that both science and history are given to generalizations about reality, it will be argued that while the former aims for generalizations that are predictive and universal, the later might be described as being more retrospective and concerned to summarize experience within the boundaries of time and space. In this sense the enterprise of the historian has much in common with that of the qualitative social scientist in that both are engaged in uncovering those subjective areas which are difficult to quantify. As Stenhouse (1981) pointed out, these subjects are made up of essentially unpredictable elements since human beings are in essence creative and have the capacity to change and be changed over time. One of the main areas of the application of an historical–time dimension in educational research has been in the field of curriculum change and innovation. We will focus upon this area in order to illustrate the value of the time dimension in school-based studies.

Reid has observed that those who think curriculum work is practical rather than technical and consists in the deliberate solution of problems about what to teach, how and to whom, will value the assistance that history can give (Reid 1986: 159–66). To Reid it is the concreteness of history, its placing of action within a context and its concentration on the particular which makes it so useful. History supplies practical contexts against which such evaluation can take place. Goodson, (1985) and others working in the field of curriculum change have done much to show the importance of the historical context. For Goodson there are three clear levels of the contemporary curriculum which are amenable to historical study. These are:

1 the individual level
2 the group or collective level
3 the relational level

The relational level explores the interrelations and permutations that can exist between groups and individuals, and individuals with other individuals. Of course often these levels overlap. His own study (Goodson 1985) of the development of rural studies from the 1920s, with its mixture of life histories and curriculum history, is a useful starting-point for researchers wishing to understand this approach. This approach owes much to the recent growth of interest in 'oral history' and one which mixes oral sources with written materials. It is important at this point to be clear that these researchers like Goodson reject any notion of the primacy or superiority of written as against oral data in historical or other research. Documentary data, as we described it earlier, includes both written and oral sources. Oral data is one type of historical source among many and has its own strengths and limitations. In the next part of this section we will consider the ways in which teacher researchers can deal with both written and oral data in research.

## What is a documentary source?

Once a written source has been created, for whatever reason, it becomes a 'potential' historical fact and therefore documentary data. For example minutes of a school committee meeting, or guidelines issued by a school to parents are forms of documentary evidence. In reality the researcher is both a user of existing sources and the creator of new ones since she too will be engaged in the process of writing down information gained from participant observation, or making field notes. Everything is potentially a significant 'document' and this prompted Stenhouse to argue for the creation of an archive of raw data of school-based research. The further one goes back into the past the more one has to rely upon existing documentary sources. However, most research done by teachers is likely to draw upon written and oral sources of the more recent past, as was the case with Goodson's work. Using Hexter's formulation, the researcher both seeks out and interprets raw data and then creates a second 'interpreted' record, one which is open to public scrutiny (Hexter 1972).

## How to locate and establish the authenticity of written sources

We need to start from the position that the historical record is inevitably bound to be partial in that a complete record of past events, however recent, is impossible. This highlights the importance of having a familiarity with, and access to, as wide a range of written and non-written sources as possible on the topic being investigated. It brings into focus the essentially interpretive role of the researcher in this work since the researcher's collection and choice of materials becomes so crucial. There might be said to be five main traditions which have utilized documentary sources in their work: historical studies, literary studies, quantitative context analyses, ethnographic studies, and personal documentary research (Platt 1981a; 1981b). While all the above share common problems and solutions the following sections are written from within the historical tradition and will therefore use its terminology.

Historians have usefully divided their sources (data) into two main categories: those that are classed as primary and those that are secondary.

*A primary source* is one which has come into being during the actual period of the past the historian researcher is studying.

*A secondary source* is the interpretation written, usually much later, by the historian researcher.

There is a series of initial stages and tasks which the teacher researcher will need to work through in using documentary sources and these may be listed.

1  Find out the principal primary and secondary sources for the period and topic you are researching.
2  Find out where these sources are housed and/or how they can be obtained, what permission if any is needed to consult them, and how best to use them.
3  What journals are relevant to this topic and what past and current research might need to be consulted.
4  The teacher researcher needs to read around the area, not only compiling a bibliography for a preliminary review of literature, but also familiarizing herself with the special terminology and approaches used.

An actual example illustrates the range and nature of documents the teacher researcher might become involved with in using documentary sources.

Research topic  The impact of new curriculum initiatives on school morale and organizational change in a secondary school

Documents used can be external and internal.

*External documents* Acts of Parliament, Parliamentary debates and committee minutes, Government Green and White Papers, DES Policy Statements, Examination Board Reports and Policy Statements, Local Education Authority Policy Statements, MSC and Training Board Policy Statements and other documents, various syllabuses, newspaper reports, Trade Union and Professional Association Policy documents and the documents/reports of other interested bodies, e.g. employers.

*Internal documents* School Committee/staff meeting minutes, school policy documents, course outlines/syllabuses, field notes, diaries, interview transcriptions, INSET reports/case studies, life history narratives.

The more recent one's period of study, the greater may be the problem of availability and access to documentary sources. This was the case with Saran's action research on Burnham, the teachers' pay and conditions negotiating machinery, since the Second World War (Saran 1985). The particular problem here was access to unpublished material and this necessitated a considerable amount of letter writing to key figures in various organizations to obtain access. These are precisely the kinds of problems that face all users of documentary records and indeed all fieldworkers, namely access, availability, and the scope of materials involved. Things that one may have wished to interpret may not have been written down in any form at all. Documents are destroyed, either intentionally or unintentionally, and it is clear that the loss of data is not uniform across the range of sources. Saran found a number of problems.

> By contrast, the management side of Burnham kept no regular minutes of its ordinary meetings during the era of Alexander's secretaryship (1944–1977), though the archives contained occasional typed minutes, as well as a book of easily decipherable shorthand notes of Management Panel meetings covering several years in the 1950s.
>
> (Saran 1985: 219)

Thus it is clear to see the problems of relying on single documentary sources. Saran's work provides a good guide to the historian's craft of reconstructing the recent past and in using the matching evidence for comparative purposes. Saran made use of journals, newspapers, personal documents and cited one particular instance, *Teachers in Turmoil* (Burke, V. 1971), which provided an account of some of these events written by a 'well-informed observer'. Saran suggests that matching and comparing a wide range of documents is an essential aspect of the researchers' craft. In some instances 'sampling' of documents will also be a task that the researcher has to engage in (Platt 1981a; 1981b). If the researcher turns towards the historian she will find plenty of sound and solid advice on these problems with documentary sources.

To begin with historians have established a number of strategies in order to determine the authenticity of a particular document or set of documents. The following is a list of questions historians and others have developed which should initially be asked of any document being used for research purposes.

1 What kind of source is it? Primary or secondary? What classification might it come under? Is it an official or unofficial document? Is it a central or local government document? If the document is a personal document was it specifically solicited by the researcher or unsolicited?
2 What person, persons, or group were responsible for creating the document? What interests, biases, or prejudices might therefore be likely to be contained in the document?
3 How and for what reasons did the source come into being in the first place? For what audience was it intended?
4 To what extent were the person or persons who produced the document in a position to provide first-hand detailed information about the situation being studied?
5 Every effort must be made to ensure that the source is interpreted in the

context of its time. The document has to be understood in the way that the writer's contemporaries would have understood it. One has to realize that few sources are written with the historian or the social scientist in mind.

6  One has to understand any technical difficulties relating to the source. These could include language, technical names, and processes or handwriting (see for example Marwick 1977).

7  Finally, the researcher needs to ask the question of what 'genre', if any, the document belongs to and if so, in what way is the document influenced by the conventions of form and expression applying to that genre of which it is a part. In other words how, and in what ways, was the document intended to be read at the time of its production? Again the question of context and audience is crucial (Platt 1981a).

These are the initial kinds of questions the researcher needs to address in establishing the authenticity, credibility, and kinds of interpretations it is justifiable to make of the document or documents in question. The researcher then begins the task of analysis, drawing out inferences, relating themes to other findings and, as far as the teacher is concerned, establishing the implications of the documents for teaching, learning, and understanding educational environments. In order to consider some of these next stages let us examine how an historian and a sociologist respectively might approach this.

Some historians have used the terms 'witting' and 'unwitting' testimony to describe this next stage. Arthur Marwick takes the example of a Medieval King's Council.

'Witting testimony' is the information which the person who originally compiled the document intended it to convey. If it is a King's council, that formal record of the debate is the witting testimony. If it is a law defining the relationship between the nobles and peasants, these relationships are the witting testimony of the document. But the first document may, unwittingly, tell us something about the way in which Council debates were conducted; perhaps something about the relationship between councillors and the King. ... Similarly with the second document the law will tell the historian that it was fully assumed at the time that there would be a clear distinction between nobles and peasants; again contemporaries would take this for granted, but it could be valuable information for this historian.

(Marwick 1977: 67)

In contrast, sociologists frequently speak about the problems of 'inference' and 'proof'. In ethnographic work the researcher has to demonstrate how the conclusions she comes to have been inferred from the verbal materials, transformed into field notes, collected during the course of a particular observation study, or in doing informal interviewing. In inferring things about actors' perspectives for example, Becker and Geer (1960) have argued that it is unwise to rely solely upon solicited information since the presence of the researcher might have a considerable effect. The problem of inference takes on a special character for the researcher using documentary sources. It is useful for the teacher researcher to consider the kinds of inferences which can be made that Jennifer Platt points to. Platt argues that there are three kinds of inferences to be drawn from documentary sources. First, inferences from the content of the documents about the beliefs and motivations of the people who produced them. Second, inferences about the real indentifiable state of affairs lying behind the production of the document. Third, inferences from the document to the characteristics of its audience. Each of these kinds of inferences could be worked through in materials drawn from a school-based project.

While one needs to interpret the document as contemporaries would, this should not blind one to the value of present-day interpretations and theoretical considerations. While it is true that history may only answer the questions we ask of it, it is also true that we do not necesarily get the answers we expect. Certainly the researcher will come across contradictions and gaps in the documentary sources. These may not be regarded as simply weaknesses, but can provide the impetus for further research and the teacher could follow some of these areas up. Saran for example has made the point that minutes of meetings, while allowing the researcher to 'peep behind the curtain' only show the 'tip of an iceberg' (Saran 1985: 220). The teacher researcher need not be over-awed by official and semi-official sources, or the wide range of what might be described as a document. Historical sources come in all shapes and sizes. Alison Andrew, in her study of nineteenth-century working-class views on education, found useful evidence in, amongst other places, newspapers, trade union records, bishops' visitations, factory inspectors' reports and riot depositions (Andrew 1985). Documentary sources offer teachers a gold-mine of information and with some care can be made to reveal much.

## Oral evidence, oral history, and the teacher

Simply stated, oral history might be said to be the study and investigation of the past by means of personal recollections, memories, evocations, or life stories, where the individuals talk about their experiences, life-styles, attitudes, and values to a researcher. The data so produced become oral evidence. It is clear that in this sense oral evidence and oral history approaches might be involved in participant observation and ethnographic work generally as well as life history research. These endeavours however are not usually characterized as oral history. What characterizes oral history and oral evidence is indeed the spoken character of the data. Oral history, then, deals specifically with what people say about the past as they have experienced and seen it. Variations of sources of data may be combined with oral evidence in the same study. Using oral evidence and oral history requires the researcher to take a particular stance to the collection and interpretation of data.

One can look at oral data on at least two levels: that of the historically transmitted transcript of oral evidence and that of the oral historical interview. The former is found in, for example, the published or unpublished documents of numerous official or semi-official bodies, including British Parliamentary Royal Commissions, or a case study conference dealing with a pupil in school. The oral history interview is solicited by the researcher, taking the form of a face-to-face encounter with an individual in the here and now. The main problem with oral evidence surrounds the need to recognize the orality of its generation. In other words, the researcher has to find some way of expressing the spoken nature of the words in the first place, complete with intonation, pitch, gesture and the like, since these features are likely to bear upon the way the testimony was intended and hence will influence what interpretations may be made of it. This may in part be overcome by using the original tape recording of the written transcript as well as the transcript itself. Every care should be taken not only over the production of the interview transcripts, but also in describing the nature of the interaction between the subject and researcher. The problems are further compounded by the fact that the teacher might make use of both 'researcher-solicited' and 'researcher-unsolicited' oral evidence. There will be quite major differences between oral sources produced in a context not under any form of control by the researcher and those circumstances where the researcher does have some control. Especially important are, for example, the power relationships between the subjects involved.

Oral sources are therefore very different in kind from the other documentary sources discussed in this chapter. Since teachers are likely to acquire oral data from interviews the special character of those interviews and the skills needed are worth discussing. While the interview technique employed by oral historians has a number of similarities with other interviewing methods used in the social sciences and the issues we discussed in Chapter 4, some special features do need highlighting.

*The oral history interview*

The researcher is fortunate with regards to oral history methodology since *The Handbook of Oral History: Recording Life Stories* by Stephen Humphries (1984) offers some excellent advice, sound guidelines, and important references and materials. Humphries offers five straightforward simple 'dos' and 'don'ts' for interviewing, that if followed are likely to result in a reasonably successful interview.

Do make an interview checklist (containing essential biographical and
career details)

Do be friendly and reassuring

Do be clear

Do show interest

Do use questionnaires flexibly and imaginatively

Don't talk too much

Don't interrupt

Don't impose your views

Don't contradict or argue

Don't rush away as soon as the interview is over

(After Humphries 1984: 19–22)

These are practical, interactional, and technical matters. Interviewing, with its
concentration on the past and the personal, throws some of these issues into
sharp relief. In addition the teacher researcher should attempt to find out as
much about the interviewee prior to the interview and be prepared for more
than one or two interviewing sessions. Again the researcher must never
attempt to stick to a prearranged set of questions rigidly. The best and most
effective oral history interviews are those that allow the interviewee to drift
backwards and forwards through time and space allowing the individual's
subjective experience to come through to the surface. This of course requires
the researcher to be sensitive, understanding the skills in handling
interpersonal communication. While a well-ordered series of questions may
be what the researcher needs, the best interviews are those where the
interviewer listens in to what the interviewee is saying. It is always possible to
pick up points to be followed up at a later interview. In other words while a
structured interview conducted from a pre-set questionnaire may be what the
researcher feels she needs, it is more likely that an unstructured interview or
series of such interviews will produce the best results. In a real sense oral
history is incomplete in that no one can exhaust the entire historical memory
of a subject. One can fill in other details by resorting to documentary and
other sources, as Ivor Goodson did in his work on curriculum change, by
putting oral history alongside a documentary history of the period under
study.

A final point on oral history interviews is worth making. It is likely that the
subjects initially may be as apprehensive as the researcher and will probably
want to provide information they think the researcher wants. One way of
overcoming this is to talk as little as possible and to watch for any gaps,
hesitations, or avoidance of certain topics in the conversation.

*Transcribing an oral history interview and preparing an authentic account*

The transcription stage of any piece of qualitative research will put extra
demands upon the teacher researcher. It is in many ways the most exacting

part of the process of using oral materials. Transcribing generally, as we note in Chapter 6, is far from easy. A half-an-hour's tape may take anything up to two hours to transcribe. Transcribing is time-consuming and demands concentration and this should be planned for at the research design phase. Teachers need to recognize that after all the data have been collected, putting them into a form that is handleable and presentable is just as important an aspect of the research process. Many otherwise good projects have been spoilt by badly presented or transcribed materials. Transcribing the oral history interview is a rather special case. As we have indicated it is important for the researchers to keep both an oral and a written record of the interview.

There are many transcription systems that may by employed, or teachers could create their own systems. The point is to be consistent, following the system all the way through the transcript. Models for transcribing oral evidence have drawn upon a number of traditions, historical, ethnographic and sociolinguistic. First, there are technical problems surrounding what the researcher can actually hear; a good pair of headphones is really essential here. They have the added advantage of cutting out any background noise that could distract the transcriber and here a tape recorder with easy playback facilities is very helpful. It is usually best to prepare the initial transcript in written form. This can be checked and corrected before a final version is prepared. As transcription symbols and systems can vary, depending upon the detail the researcher wishes to convey, so too can the *kind* of transcript. Usually these transcripts can be either complete, unedited transcriptions or edited transcriptions. Some researchers involve their subjects in the transcription process itself and this is a possibility that seems open to teachers given the likelihood of their proximity to their subjects. The decision to work with a transcript that includes everything the researcher and subject say, or to work with an edited version only, is a matter of personal preference. The main problem, however, is how to capture the spoken word in the written form. Inevitably something is going to be lost, but the retention of the tape can offset this. Speech and writing are vastly different. While information, pitch, gesture, and so on are hard to recreate in the written transcript, the researcher can add contextual remarks and comments on certain portions of the transcript. If the transcript keeps to the order of the spoken words, no grammatical corrections are made and the temptation to tidy up the transcript is resisted, then the rhythms and form of the dialogue can be fairly accurately recreated. If there are any cuts made in the transcript it is usual practice to let the reader know this by leaving a dotted line.

The practice of data triangulation, that is the use of more than one set of data (see Denzin 1970), or multiple or mixed strategies (see Douglas 1976) is one way in which the transcript can be further authenticated and validated. In the case of the oral history interview, the transcript can be sent back to the interviewee for comment and the interviewee's comments treated as a further source of data on the occasion of the interview, the subjects discussed and the way they are presented in the transcript. These comments will of course constitute yet another source of data and are often useful in both providing further information not already obtained and triggering new lines of inquiry for the researcher.

The value of oral evidence and oral history approaches can be seen in their ability to add the ever-crucial historical depth to individuals' subjective experience. In this sense it has clear advantages over other sources. Again, as we saw with the life history or life story approach, oral history delivers the subjective world of actors for analysis in ways that other research finds difficult to achieve.

## Summary

In this chapter we have outlined the nature of documentary sources and the ways in which the teacher might collect and analyse them. We have stressed the importance of key technical and methodological issues in collecting and using life histories, oral history, and other documents. We feel that these materials represent an important and rich source of data for the prospective teacher researcher to tap. However, there are problems and issues to which the researcher using documentary sources must attend. Despite this the problems of documentary sources are no greater and no less than other sources of data. They are in many ways a good deal more exciting.

## Suggested further reading

The best accounts of personal documentary research and oral history respectively are K. Plummer (1983) *Documents of Life: An Introduction to the Problems and Literature of a Humanistic Method,* London: Allen & Unwin, and the pioneering and still best introduction by P. Thompson (1978) *The Voice of the Past: Oral History,* Opus Books, Oxford University Press. The problems and possibilities of the life history technique are addressed in a comprehensive article by A. Faraday and K. Plummer (1979) 'Doing life histories', *Sociological Review* 27, 4: 73–98. While D. Gittins (1979) 'Oral history, reliability and recollection', in L. Moss and H. Goldstein (eds) *The Recall Method in Social Surveys,* Studies in Education 9, University of London Institute of Education, confronts some peculiar problems of oral evidence. Increasingly the use of life history approaches and the collection of other documentary sources are featuring in educational research. A good start here is S. J. Ball and I. F. Goodson (eds) (1985) *Teachers' Lives and Careers,* Lewes: Falmer Press.

# Chapter six

# Interaction in schools and classrooms

## Introduction

Schools and classrooms are complex social environments. They consist of different groups of people interacting with each other in various ways. The individuals who make up these groups all have their own identities, perceptions, and values. Teaching and learning will naturally be affected by these features. The most obvious situations where the influence of these factors can be observed is in the interactions and communication patterns between teachers and pupils and pupils with pupils.

Over the years a large body of research into this area has been carried out. Much research has focused upon the verbal interchanges between teachers and pupils including such issues as the influence of styles of teacher talk on learning. Other research has focused upon the ways in which a child's culture and neighbourhood or family background shapes communication and interaction in the classroom. The common denominator in all of this research is that what teachers and pupils actually say and do becomes the major focus of attention. This growing body of classroom research seeks to uncover the 'black box' of the classroom in order to discover the factors which shape and influence pupils' experiences of school and classroom life. In this chapter we will introduce the teacher researcher to some of the main themes in this research and try to show how the teacher researcher can develop her own research into classroom interaction.

The expansion of research in the area of classroom studies over the last twenty years has meant that many different topics of research and ways of exploring those topics has emerged. Teachers have often been sceptical of the findings of much of this research. While some of this scepticism is justified much we believe is misguided. It is important for classroom teachers to treat research findings with caution. We therefore try to provide the teacher with a clear overview of the main traditions in classroom research so that she can adequately assess some of the claims being made and consider in a more critical fashion the nature of the research in question. We will stress that many classroom studies are not unambiguous or unequivocal. Quite a lot of classroom research is tentative and exploratory. Classroom research cannot tell teachers how to teach but what it can do is to alert them to some of the subtle and complex processes of interaction that directly shape and influence learning. What 'research' here can do is to describe the circumstances, background, and parties involved in the interactions which routinely take place in schools and classrooms. Furthermore it can begin to unravel the complexities of communication in the classroom. We therefore aim to do two things in this chapter:

1  Provide a general overview of the main trends, approaches and strategies in classroom research, and
2  Provide the teacher researcher with a basic insight into the mechanics and processes of research into classroom talk and interaction.

The teacher researcher may quite legitimately use some of the techniques employed by so-called professional researchers. However, in many cases this will have to be modified or adapted to suit individual circumstances. The teacher researcher can also focus upon the same kinds of topics as research in the past has focused upon yet may also introduce her own areas of interest. In the following pages we will explore the nature of classroom research and point to some of the implications of this for the prospective teacher researcher. The chapter concludes with a practical guide to observing, recording, and investigating classroom talk and interaction.

## Interaction analysis and systematic observation

No one who has observed a classroom lesson will underestimate the complexity of even the most apparently clearly organized lessons. Any attempts to consider the nature of classroom interaction must be aware of both the diversity and complexity of the processes involved. Interaction analysis and systematic observation were two attempts to produce objective and systematic accounts of what happens in classrooms. In the USA the name of Ned Flanders is associated with the development of interaction analysis while Galton, Simon, and Croll (1980) are seen as epitomizing the use of systematic observation in their work in Britain.

Interaction analysis as a technique used to investigate classroom interaction grew up out of a concern with the improvement of classroom teaching. Many different schedules have been devised but all of them tend to involve a trained observer recording certain features of teacher or pupil talk in accordance with a prearranged schedule so that numerical counts or 'tallies' could be made of certain features of classroom talk in terms of a set of pre-coded categories. This results in 'ratings' of teaching style, the climate of the classroom, and the 'quality' of the teaching. This information could be used to improve teacher education and hence develop more effective teaching. Simon and Boyer's work (1967, 1970, 1975) *Mirrors for Behaviour* charts the variety of schemes and schedules used to do this kind of research. The overriding concern seems to be with the quantification, in statistical terms, of elements of classroom verbal interaction and in turn the need to sharpen and refine constantly the research instruments themselves. As such interaction analysis and systematic observation are observer-oriented efforts to quantify classroom interactions. The best-known example of interaction analysis is contained in Ned Flanders' coding scheme known as FIAC, the Flanders' Interaction Analysis Categories (Flanders 1970).

Flanders was concerned with improving classroom teaching and his approach and findings were to be incorporated into the training programmes of student teachers in the USA. He was concerned to identify two constrasting modes or styles of teaching which he describes as direct and indirect. His system involves the identification of analysis of talk in the classroom in terms of the coding and categorizing of utterances according to ten pre-arranged categories. This enables the researcher to characterize any kind of communicative event in the classroom. Flanders' categories are divided up into *teacher talk,* which can be either direct or indirect, *pupil talk,* and *silence.* There are seven categories for teacher talk, two for pupil talk, and one for silence. The system is displayed in Figure 6.1.

The system requires a trained observer to place each three-second period of a total observation 'episode' into the category which it best represents. Each classroom behavioural episode can then be represented by a sequence of category numbers which can, in turn, later be used to construct a matrix enabling scores to be calculated of, for example, such features as the type, amount, and direction of teacher or pupil talk. Ratios could therefore be calculated from this.

Interaction analysis was one of the first attempts to look systematically at classroom interaction. However, while the approach is one which can be used by the teacher researcher it has received considerable criticism. The researcher is assumed to be objective and neutral and capable of maintaining a significant degree of detachment from the subjects of the research. An emphasis upon the measurement of classroom verbal interactions in terms of the prearranged categories results in quantifiable data. These two features of the FIAC and similar systems has resulted in some strong criticism. All the same there was a clear argument here.

The use of trained observers and an 'uncontaminated' coding scheme ensures, it is argued, a measure of objectivity and neutrality reducing the possibility of any researcher effect or bias. The use of pre-coded categories and counts or tallies lends itself to statistical treatment and analysis. The ability to cover large numbers of situations enables interaction analysis and systematic observation to develop generalizations and in the long run to make suggestions regarding effective teaching. These observations provide the most important sources of criticism and have led to much acrimonious and sometimes unhelpful criticism. People speak of 'Flandering' around, mechanical models, and atomizing classrooms. The major criticisms can be found in Hamilton and Delamont (1974: 1–15), Walker and Adelman (1975: 73–6), Delamont (1976), McIntyre and MacLeod (1978: 111–29) and McIntyre (1980: 3–30). We will condense some of these criticisms and add a few of our own in order not simply to be negative, but to suggest some basic principles for the investigation of classroom talk and interaction.

| Teacher Talk | Response | 1. *Accepts feeling.* Accepts and clarifies an attitude or the feeling tone of a pupil in a non-threatening manner. Feelings may be positive or negative. Predicting and recalling feelings are included. |
| | | 2. *Praises or encourages.* Praises or encourages pupil action or behavior. Jokes that release tension, but not at the expense of another individual; nodding head, or saying "Um hm?" or "go on" are included. |
| | | 3. *Accepts or uses ideas of pupils.* Clarifying, building, or developing ideas suggested by a pupil. Teacher extensions of pupil ideas are included but as the teacher brings more of his own ideas into play, shift to category five. |
| | Initiation | 4. *Asks questions.* Asking a question about content or procedure, based on teacher ideas, with the intent that a pupil will answer. |
| | | 5. *Lecturing.* Giving facts or opinions about content or procedures; expressing *his own* ideas, giving *his own* explanation, or citing an authority other than a pupil. |
| | | 6 *Giving directions.* Directions, commands, or orders to which a pupil is expected to comply. |
| | | 7. *Criticizing or justifying authority.* Statements intended to change pupil behavior from nonacceptable to acceptable pattern; bawling someone out; stating why the teacher is doing what he is doing; extreme self-reference. |

| | | |
|---|---|---|
| Pupil Talk | Response | 8. *Pupil-talk - response.* Talk by pupils in response to teacher. Teacher initiates the contact or solicits pupil statement or structures the situation. Freedom to express own ideas is limited. |
| | Initiation | 9. *Pupil-talk - initiation.* Talk by pupils which they initiate. Expressing own ideas; initiating a new topic; freedom to develop opinions and a line of thought, like asking thoughtful questions; going beyond the existing structure. |
| Silence | | 10 *Silence or confusion.* Pauses, short periods of silence and periods of confusion in which communication cannot be understood by the observer. |

**Figure 6.1** Flanders' Interaction Analysis Categories* (FIAC)

Source: Flanders (1970: 34).
Note: *There is *no* scale implied by these numbers. Each number is classificatory; it designates a particular kind of communication event. To write these numbers down during observation is to enumerate, not to judge a position on a scale.

## Context and meaning

Classrooms are complex social situations. The meanings of events which take place within them are not always clearly and automatically self-evident. Classrooms and lessons have a history. The teachers and pupils make constant reference to the social context of the lesson and the identities of the participants. It is impossible to appreciate fully what is happening in classrooms and hence adequately to describe and explain what is happening without paying attention to this context. By a concentration upon observable behaviour and in effect taking it at 'face value', interaction analysis can become involved in by-passing the viewpoints and intentions of the teachers and pupils themselves.

Walker and Adelman (1975) provide a good example of the importance of context. They describe a lesson where one of the students shouted out 'strawberries, strawberries' after another member of the class had been told off by the class teacher for not doing his homework properly. This promoted much laughter amongst the members of the class. The only problem was that the researcher was unable to understand the joke. It was only some time later that the researcher discovered that the meaning of 'strawberries' was dependent upon the teacher's previous witty comment, 'Your work is like strawberries, good as far as it goes, but it doesn't last nearly long enough!'

*Problems associated with the use of pre-coded categories*

As we have seen, interaction analysis focuses upon that which can in effect be categorized and coded, that is measured. The FIAC system can produce large quantities of data on teacher–pupil talk in any individual classroom. A series of issues arise from the use of pre-coded categories. The major question surrounds the identification of a particular category like, for example, 'lecturing' or 'giving directions' (FIAC). How are these categories decided in the first place and what is their location in the data on classroom processes? The categories developed by interaction analysis researchers are constructed on the basis of the researchers' own pre-judgements. The problem is one of the relationship of these categories to the realities of the classroom.

*Quantification and the neglect of the qualitative*

It is clear to see that interaction and much systematic observation research is engaged in quantification by the observer as opposed to qualification through the participant. The debate here surrounds the value of non-participant observation alone as a valuable research technique in researching classroom processes.

*Problems associated with using the Flanders system in informal classrooms*

From what has been said about the actual procedures of interaction analysis and using schedules like FIAC it is evident that many settings will not instantly lend themselves to observation in these terms. If teaching and learning are simply seen in terms of the communication of information by the teacher and the reception of this by the pupils, then systems like FIAC will be able to cope reasonably well with what is perceived to be going on. However, if the teaching and learning situation is viewed more in terms of relationships and interpersonal communication, or pupil/student-centred learning then rigid pre-coded observation schedules are at the very best going to miss out on capturing the true nature of the interactions, or at worst they will simply distort them. Such an approach will be unable to capture the particular, the idiosyncratic, and the local aspects of life in individual schools and classrooms. Hamilton and Delamont have succinctly formulated this problem of interaction analysis.

> in the interests of 'objectivity', many interaction analysis research studies feel compelled to survey large numbers of classrooms. It is argued (correctly) that small samples may fail to provide statements relevant to the population at large. However, such an approach (even if it can achieve true randomness) may fail to treat local perturbations or unusual effects as significant. Indeed, despite their potential significance for the classroom or classrooms to which they apply, atypical results are seldom

studied in detail. They are treated as 'noise', ironed out as 'blurred averages' and lost to discussion.

(Hamilton and Delamont 1974: 5)

In attempting to maintain objectivity the surface elements of classroom interaction are examined while the deeper 'hidden' or, as Smith and Geoffrey (1968) describe them, the 'silent languages' of the classroom remain virtually unexamined.

In summary these criticisms of interaction analysis suggest that while the approach may offer some insight into the general patterns of communication in the classroom, there are considerable problems. These problems may be summed up in the idea that interaction analysis relies upon the outside observer's frame of reference and interpretations and not the inside frames of reference and interpretations of the teachers and pupils concerned.

## Systematic observation in the United Kingdom: the ORACLE project

The ORACLE project or the *Observational Research and Classroom Learning Evaluation Project* conducted over a five-year period was concerned to evaluate the nature of primary classroom teaching in the wake of the *Plowden Report's* (1967) findings and recommendations. Galton, Simon, and Croll (1980) *Inside the Primary Classroom,* and Galton and Simon (1980) *Progress and Performance in the Primary School,* deal respectively with the general analysis of pupils' and teachers' activity and different patterns of teacher and pupil behaviour, and with the supposed effects of these patterns on pupil progress.

The ORACLE research team employed a number of different tests, but the main method of observing teachers and pupils in classrooms was through the use of observation schedules which involved the researchers' recording at 25-second intervals what was happening in the classroom in terms of the categories of their prearranged observation schedule. The observation systems used were designed for 'live coding' by trained researchers in the classroom setting equipped with their pre-coded schedules. The ORACLE project had therefore to make use of trained researchers who had experience of primary teaching.

A short examination of the main instrument employed by the ORACLE researchers, that is *The Pupil and Teacher Record: A technique for observing the activities of junior school teachers and their pupils in informal lessons* (devised by Deane Boydell and revised by Anne Jasman) will highlight both the strengths and weaknesses of systematic classroom observation as a way of making sense of classroom interactions and their consequences for learning.

*The observation categories of the teacher record* (see Figure 6.2) is part of the manual mentioned above designed for use by the members of the ORACLE research team. The detail reflects the need for all of the researchers

| | | |
|---|---|---|
| | Task | Q1 recalling facts |
| | | Q2 offering ideas, solutions (closed) |
| | | Q3 offering ideas, solutions (open) |
| Questions | | |
| | Task supervision | Q4 referring to task supervision |
| | Routine | Q5 referring to routine matters |
| | Task | S1 of facts |
| | | S2 of ideas, problems |
| | Task supervision | S3 telling child what to do |
| | | S4 praising work or effort |
| Statements | | S5 feedback on work or effort |
| | Routine | S6 providing information, directions |
| | | S7 providing feedback |
| | | S8 of critical control |
| | | S9 of small talk |
| | 'Silent' interaction, i.e. interaction other than by question or statement | Gesturing Showing Marking Waiting Story Reading |
| Silence* | | Not observed Not coded |
| | No interaction between teacher and any pupil in the class | Adult interaction Visiting pupil Not interacting Out of room |
| | Audience | Class, group of individuals |
| | Composition | Identification or pupils involved |
| | Activity | E.g. Creative writing, practical maths etc. |

**Figure 6.2** The observation categories of the teacher record

*Source*: Galton, Simon, and Croll (1980: 17)
*Note*: * While it was recognised that the term 'Silence' was in some instances a misnomer, its use for everyday purposes was preferred to the cumbersome term *silence or interaction other than by question or statement*.

to use the manual and the categories contained within it in the same way. If this is not done of course the validity of the instrument is immediately questioned. If we consider in more detail the observation and coding of teachers' questions we can see how the ORACLE team developed a highly complex scheme for classifying teachers' questions and they went to great lengths in order to establish that the observers were all coding the teachers' questions in the same way.

The manual identifies five different types of question, and provides numerous examples and definitions on what constitutes each of these types of question. But as Scarth and Hammersley (1986) have argued, there are simply enormous problems involved in differentiating between the different kinds of question. How is the observer going to distinguish between Q1–type questions 'recalling facts', and Q5–type questions 'referring to routine matters'? Furthermore, how are the fine-grained distinctions between Q2– type questions (closed) and Q3–type questions (open) to be drawn, not after a long period of thought and consideration, but at 25-second intervals? These general problems in fact relate to the pre-specified nature of the coding categories. The real problem surrounds how these categories in fact emerged in the first place. If it is not known what the teachers and pupils in fact meant, how can the observer be absolutely sure that a question or utterance fits one category or another? Barrow puts the issue this way:

> The point is that judgements of this kind require a thorough overall grasp
> of the lesson and its place in the wider context of class life, a thorough
> awareness of the state of mind of the children in question, and a thorough
> conceptualisation of cognitive content, none of which is catered for in the
> ORACLE approach.
>
> (Barrow 1984: 185)

Researchers have pointed to the importance of paralinguistic features such as facial expressions, eye movements, glances, expressions, and so on in interpersonal communication. The meaning and significance of utterances, questions, and answers is in part dependent upon the paralinguistic and contextual clues and features accompanying them. It is highly unlikely that these aspects could be attended to by the ORACLE observers. This suggests that there may indeed be fundamental problems with the validity of the observation categories of the Teacher Record as a research instrument.

What emerges as the main problem of the Teacher Record observation schedule is the relationship between the observer's decision to code a teacher's question in a particular category and the teacher's and pupils' perceptions of and orientation towards the utterances in particular ways. This question therefore refers to the validity of the findings based upon the Teacher Record. When we ask about the validity of data and findings, as we pointed out in Chapter 2, we are referring to the extent to which such data and subsequent findings present true and accurate pictures of the events they claim to be describing. Is the observer actually capable of making accurate judgements and correct interpretations of utterances in the space of 25 seconds? This, in turn, leads on to the question of reliability.

We defined reliability in terms of the issue of replicability in Chapter 2. When researchers speak about the reliability of research findings they are referring to the extent to which agreement between different researchers, or in this case observers, using the same instrument or schedule, do in fact observe or code the events in substantially the same way. In the event of a piece of research being repeated would the same findings result from the work of another researcher using the same methods to research the situation? This is especially important for work like that of the ORACLE project because so many different observers were used, their findings being subsequently amalgamated together.

### Some implications for the teacher

Systematic observation schedules like those used by the ORACLE team are highly complicated. While we share many of the criticisms of ORACLE outlined above it is certainly possible for the teacher, bearing these comments in mind, to adapt or make use of systems like these as part of some classroom research. Alternatively the teacher could use the FIAC system or the ORACLE schedule for coding teachers' questions as one of a number of techniques of data collection employed in a single study. The results could be used as a way of orientating the teacher researcher to a set of topics for further investigation. The teacher researcher need not stick with either of these schemes as a number are now available.

It is often difficult to assess the value and applicability of these schemes and so the teacher researcher might wish to consult the checklist worked out by Boehm and Weinberg (1977: 58–9) focusing upon the appropriateness of particular observation systems in terms of questions like observer reliability, sampling, representativeness, and the practicality of using a particular system for certain situations. There is also the possibility of the teacher developing her own systematic observation system or coding schedule to suit her own purposes. We have worked with teachers who have successfully used observation and coding schemes to consider such diverse topics as aggressive talk in the classroom, gender imbalances, sexist or racist talk, evaluating aspects of children's project/topic work and musical skills. Both systematic observation and ethnography begin from the same starting line, *observation*, but the way in which that observation is conducted, what is observed, and the findings arrived at, involve these two approaches running in very different races.

Research into educational processes has been conducted from a variety of standpoints and research into classroom interaction has made use of the whole range of social science disciplines including social psychology, sociology, social anthropology, and sociolinguistics. In a lot of research there has been overlap between the disciplines, that is much research has tended to be of an interdisciplinary nature. A number of researchers have been more concerned with the problem under investigation rather than any disciplinary allegiances. It is however worth briefly outlining the major elements of the disciplines which have contributed to educational research and which form the basis of much investigation into school and classroom processes. We will provide a series of short, thumbnail sketches at this point which the prospective teacher researcher might wish to follow up at a later date. In Chapter 5 we outlined the value and importance of a historical perspective; here we will define the major features of linguistics, sociolinguistics, social anthropology, and sociology.

## Some important social science disciplines defined

Traditionally *linguistics* has been concerned with the structures of language, with the sets of relationship between words, syntax, or within words, morphology, or with grammars. Typically, traditional linguists have concerned themselves with the structure of language in isolation from many other factors and usually building frameworks of knowledge without reference to other disciplines. *Sociolinguistics* on the other hand, simply defined, focuses upon the use of language in social contexts and upon the relationships between language, talk, and society, and between language, culture, community, and neighbourhood. Conceived in this way, sociolinguistics and what has sometimes been described as the sociology of language, invites and makes use of insights, concepts, methodologies, and theories from other disciplines. Sociolinguistic research therefore concentrates upon the social relationships implied in and influenced by language use in social contexts and highlights the abilities of the speaker (communicative competence) and the influence and affects of the social environments surrounding the speaker (speech community).

*Social anthropology* has developed in a number of different directions since Bronislaw Malinowski first set up his tent in the Trobriand Islands. The key ingredients of social anthropology have remained fairly constant. Social anthropology seeks to provide in-depth knowledge of the ways of life of a particular group in terms of the culture of that group. In doing this anthropologists unravel belief systems, religion, rituals, language patterns, kinship systems, economic and political organization, and gender divisions. This has been achieved by extensive use of the principles of ethnographic research. Lengthy periods of participation and involvement in the setting under investigation itself have come to be a characteristic feature of social anthropology.

While the current diversity displayed in sociological research may suggest that a non-controversial definition of sociology would be difficult, a

143

minimum definition can be approached. Sociology concentrates upon the development of explanations of human behaviour in terms of the structures, institutions, and organizations of modern societies. Sociologists focus upon the social processes and dynamics of groups within industrial societies by considering the ways in which 'key variables' like social class, ethnicity, gender, and age affect both individuals' lives and shape the nature of the wider society.

Classroom research has made use of all of these disciplines. The remaining traditions of classroom research we wish to examine now make greater use of anthropology, sociolinguistics, and sociology.

## The ethnography of communication and anthropological approaches

Anthropological approaches to school and classroom life have made use of ethnographic research and participant observation. The research we shall consider in this tradition focuses upon the socio-cultural level of analysis, that is the ways in which neighbourhood, community, family ethnicity, and culture shape and influence the interaction of teachers and pupils as well as pupils with other pupils in school and classroom contexts. Language is here seen in terms of the social, cultural, and interactional aspects which underpin its use in all social settings. What has been described as the ethnography of communication and anthropological approaches more generally view the classroom as being composed of a series of communicative events which are influenced by the cultural and social processes which surround both the school and classroom. Hence family, community, tradition, class, ethnicity, and gender all feature in the research on schools and classrooms in this tradition.

The ethnography of communication aims to 'examine the situations and uses, the patterns and functions of speaking as an activity in its own right' (Frake 1962: 101). Four key figures are associated with the development of this approach in North America: Charles Frake, Dell Hymes, John Gumperz, and William Labov. Developments in the ethnography of communication and the inclusion of anthropological perspectives in research into classroom talk and interaction open up a wide range of possibilities, especially in terms of the relationship between language, culture, and classroom behaviour. It is against the background of urban school failure and underachievement of children from particular ethnic backgrounds in the USA that some of the most important studies from an anthropological perspective have been generated. The focus allows for consideration of the way in which such factors as ethnic identity, home and family background, dialect and bilingualism shape and influence a child's learning.

Two studies highlight the interrelationship of language, culture, and the classroom, those by Murray and Rosalie Wax (1971) and Susan Phillips (1972). Both these studies deal with native American children and examine the involvement and participation of the children in the classrooms using anthropological insights.

The anthropologists Murray and Rosalie Wax were involved with the study of native American Indian families for a long period of time. Their focus upon the educational experiences of American Indians and reservation education is well documented (see for example Dumont and Wax 1969: 217–26 on Cherokee society and the classroom). Their examination of some of the underlying assumptions of the Sioux Indians on the Pine Ridge Reservation held by white educators highlights the need to see educational failure in interactional and intercultural terms as opposed to being simply and mistakenly a matter of the cultural or linguistic deprivation of lower-class or ethnic minority groupings.

Wax and Wax (1971) describe the background to their study of the educational system of an Indian reservation in terms of culture clash and reactions to cultural differences. Their study tried to involve all parties to the educational process, pupils, parents, administrators, and teachers. They found that the white teachers were operating with a 'vacuum ideology' regarding the abilities and achievements of the Indian children. The teachers saw the children as in many respects lacking or deficient. It was claimed that their parents did not read them stories or take sufficient interest in them. This indicated to the teachers that school failure was located in the child's culture. As Wax and Wax have put it,

> It places upon the Indian home and the parents the responsibility for the lack of scholastic achievement of the child. Since the child is entering the school with an empty head, then surely it is a triumph he is taught anything whatsoever. Moreover, the ideology justifies almost any activity within the school as 'educational' (just as it derogates any communal activity outside the school): *for if the child is presumed deficient in almost every realm of experience, then the task of the educator can properly encompass anything and everything.* Finally, the ideology justifies the educators in their social and cultural isolation from the lives of the parents of their students; if the child actually had a culture including knowledge and values, then the educators ought properly to learn about these and build upon them, but if, on entering school, he is merely a vacuum, then what need to give attention to his home and community?
>
> (Wax and Wax 1971: 129)

A misunderstanding about the relationship between culture and education on the part of the white educators on many of the reservation schools results in the continued low achievement of Indian children. Wax and Wax therefore raise issues concerning what is in fact being learnt in many of these schools, and the value of incorporating elements of Indian culture into the school curriculum and classroom setting. If the Indian children are described by people as being apathetic, uninterested, or passive, this has as much to do

145

with the socio-economic position these children find themselves in and the teachers' perceptions of them as it has to do with their culture.

Similar situations have been documented for ethnic minorities in this country as well as for black children in America. For example Shirley Brice-Heath (1982) contrasts the kinds of questioning and question situations the children of Tracton, a southern USA urban black neighbourhood, experienced in the home with the kinds of questions they were routinely faced with at school. Again the low achievement rates of these children are explained in terms of the operation of cultural differences. A focus upon the relationship between home life and family patterns and school and classroom organization is the starting-point for those who see the major differences in the two sets of experiences as providing the potential for interference, hostility, and barriers to learning.

This line is taken up by Phillips (1972) in her comparative study of an all-Indian class and a non-Indian class on the Warm Springs Indian reservation in central Oregon. Many of the teachers reported that the children were generally very reluctant to talk and participate in the classroom. In comparing the nature and degree of involvement in classroom lessons of reservation-reared Indian children and non-Indian children, Phillips draws attention to the nature and organization of the classroom lessons themselves. What Phillips discovered was that the Indian children tended to become more involved in the lessons, participating more freely in them, when situations which required the children to present themselves publicly, as it were, as individuals to the rest of the class, were absent. These and similar situations gave teachers the opportunity to correct children and generally to control and direct their performances which conversely resulted in lower degrees of participation and involvement on the part of the Indian children in the classroom. Phillips relates these apparent preferences on the part of the children to the way in which they experience relationships more generally on the reservation and in the home. In other words, where there is a 'congruence' between the sociolinguistic styles and social relationships of both the school and the reservation then the children tended to perform better and develop greater levels of verbal interactional participation. Conversely, Phillips argues that the generally poor levels of achievement by many Indian children is directly related to the predominance of classroom organization which effectively puts the Indian children in uncomfortable and alien situations; typically those are the situations and circumstances associated with conventional and formal classrooms!

Phillips's study is a good example of the way in which an anthropological and sociolinguistic approach can provide a deeper appreciation of the nature and explanation of participation and involvement in classroom learning. Her idea of 'participation structures' is a useful one. She uses this concept to describe the broad and complex range of factors such as attitudes, values, mutual rights, and obligations which ultimately influence relationships, perceptions, and ways of behaving that spill over into and affect the learning environment. It is an idea that the teacher researcher, as well as the average class teacher, might profitably consider since many of the studies conducted in the British context support her general findings. The total relationship of home, neighbourhood, school, and wider social and cultural contexts undoubtedly plays a crucial role in influencing and affecting learning. Perhaps this is nowhere more evident than in the multicultural context. Many teachers will have to face the ways in which ethnic minority children's participation and performance in school is influenced by family, neighbourhood, and cultural factors as well as linguistic factors. This of course could act as the focus of a piece of school-based research and hence the studies by Wax and Wax, Shirley Brice-Heath, and Susan Phillips will be worth considering.

### Sociolinguistic approaches

Sociolinguists ask the question, 'Who says what to whom, when and where?' Over recent years many sociolinguists have turned their attention to the classroom context. These researchers therefore recognize and try to respond to the fact that language is diversified and that linguistic forms and speech patterns exhibit huge variation. One of the general aims of sociolinguistics is therefore to unravel some of the patterns within this diversity and variation. The ways in which social factors influence the development of language patterns, dialects, and so on, as well as the factors affecting particular speakers are areas that sociolinguists research. Following Hymes (1962: 15–53) we outline a series of key factors which affect the diversity of language by focusing upon the dimensions of sender, receiver, and setting. We also add some further dimensions of our own.

1 *Sender* the identity, status, or position of a speaker is often seen most clearly in what might be described as social class, dialects, or accents. The social stratification system of any society places individuals in different positions, the language used by any speaker will reflect this.
2 *Receiver* the social characteristics of the receiver, the person who is being spoken to, will clearly influence the speech style used by the sender. This is most obvious in such situations as adult–baby or adult–child conversation. It is also clearly expressed in various categories of official to inmate talk, for example prison warders to prisoners. Whenever a social hierarchy or a status hierarchy exists the social characteristics and identity of the receiver is a crucial variable.
3 *Setting* the context of the setting in which communication takes place is clearly oriented towards by speakers and participants themselves as being a crucial determining factor in language use and will influence the style of talk.

In addition to these factors, we would add the following which are likely to be of central importance in the classroom.

4 *Age* the age of the children and the age of the teachers provides an important dimension to classroom verbal interaction.

5 *Class* an individual's social class is generally regarded as being defined by socio-economic or occupational position. Social class therefore provides people with a frame of reference, an outlook, and typical sets of experiences. But social class is a relational concept in that many factors come together to generate the experiences and outlooks usually associated with a particular class position. The relationship between social class, family background, and educational achievement is well documented. Bernstein was one of the first researchers to consider the influence of linguistic codes presumed to be associated with social-class background on educational performance. Class variables enter the classroom sociolinguistic context in both subtle and overt ways. Bernstein for example argued that many children from middle-class backgrounds were able to make use of the same linguistic code which is characteristic of the school situation and turn it to their own advantage.

6 *Gender* in the same way that attitudes to the social class of both speaker and hearer influence the nature of verbal communication and interaction, gender adds yet one more dimension. Gender may be said to refer to the socially constructed and structured perceptions and expectations associated with female and male roles and behaviour. Gender will therefore affect communication in a number of ways from rights of access to talk, to changes in tone, style, and vocabulary used.

These are some of the more obvious factors which affect verbal interaction. The important point however is that these factors combine and interact with each other and in fact provide talk and communication with its unique characteristics. Sociolinguists looking at schools and classrooms have concentrated upon the functions that language performs as a way of unravelling this complexity and diversity.

Nowadays sociolinguists tend to concentrate upon three major ideas, namely communicative competence, speech community and the relationship between language and social networks. The notion of social networks including kinship, friendship, and work and peer group relationships have been discussed by a number of sociolinguists. The notion of communicative competence includes a range of concerns containing the appropriateness or correctness of an individual's speech in particular circumstances and the ability of an individual to manipulate the situation linguistically to his or her own advantage and to change speech styles effectively from situation to situation. Speech community on the other hand refers to the larger groupings of individuals who are said to share a linguistic outlook in common: that is they adhere to the same underlying set of linguistic rules, norms, and values.

The two concepts of 'communicative competence' and 'speech community' are intimately linked since the individual's communicative competence cannot be seen without reference to the various 'speech communities' of which the individual is a part.

## Sociolinguistics and education

Sociolinguists have had a long involvement with research in educational settings and provided very many important insights into the organization of classroom verbal interaction. The kind of work which sociolinguists have carried out in classrooms has covered a wide range of topics. The importance of an appreciation of the sociolinguistic dimensions of classroom talk should now be clear. There are clearly a number of policy-related areas that sociolinguistic research has made an impact upon and certainly has much to offer. For example the question of bilingualism and bilingual schools, mother tongue teaching, teaching standard English to speakers of non-standard English, the organization of classroom talk and in particular teacher talk itself, have all been examined using a sociolinguistic perspective.

Talk in the classroom, however, displays some important individual characteristics. Classroom talk is in many ways very different from other kinds of talk. Typically much classroom talk is organized around the completion of tasks or activities. Possibly one of its most distinguishing characteristics is the way in which one category of speaker, the teacher, attempts to control and direct that talk. Sociolinguistic analyses may be developed by the teacher researcher in any of these areas. The data will constitute audio, and in some cases video, tape recordings of classroom lessons. The teacher researcher can focus upon the characteristics of teacher talk, pupil talk, the nature of the conversational sequences. In this way, sociolinguistic analyses can focus upon the way in which talk is oriented towards particular parties, that is how are teachers' utterances or questions heard by pupils as demonstrated in the contextual features of the transcripts, and conversely how do teachers hear and respond to pupils' contributions to the lesson? For example arrival times, quiet times, and group work in infant and junior classrooms all display particular sociolinguistic characteristics which are worthy of exploration. Indeed much learning is going on in infant schools during 'arrival time'. Similarly discussion work and formal 'chalk and talk' lessons in secondary schools exhibit particular features. Lessons are opened, are started, are developed, and are brought to a close.

These are just a few of the lines of development a sociolinguistic approach to classroom talk and interaction suggests for research. The prospective researcher might begin by considering some of the more well-known studies by Bernstein (1972; 1974), Barnes (1969; 1971), and Sinclair and Coulthard (1975).

Clearly sociolinguistic approaches have done much to open up the complexity of verbal communication in the classroom. The prospective researcher will find the insights of sociolinguistic studies and the use of close observational techniques of considerable value in considering the relationship between language and learning.

Recently the boundary between traditional linguistic and sociolinguistic approaches on the one hand and more general ethnographic approaches on the other has become increasingly blurred. There are a number of important points of contact between a lot of sociolinguistic and ethnographic research in educational settings. Both are concerned with what participants are doing in making sense of each others' utterances and both approaches look at patterns and regularities in classroom talk. However, ethnographic approaches tend to widen the focus of interest to include a much broader range of factors that may influence what goes on between the teacher and the pupils in the classroom. Ethnographers tend to suggest that the 'classroom' is not the only unit of analysis. Some of these differences will become clearer as we consider in more detail what has come to be known as the 'ethnography of schooling '.

## The ethnography of schooling

In this section we will outline some of the ways in which ethnography has been used to examine the social processes in classroom talk, communication, and participation. Like sociolinguistic approaches the ethnography of schooling displays considerable diversity. What ties ethnographic studies of schooling together is their attention to detail. Close detailed descriptions of everyday events provide the starting-point for ethnography. As we saw in Chapter 3, ethnographers become involved in the setting under investigation and collect data from a variety of sources in a number of different ways. This orientation has meant that ethnographers interested in classroom interaction and social processes in school have made use of techniques such as audio and video tape recordings of classroom lessons, unstructured interviews, and participant observations in the setting itself. The ethnographers' concern with a central concept in the human sciences, culture, directs ethnographic researchers towards describing and analysing what it is individuals and groups of individuals share in common, what it is that helps to produce meaning and stability in their lives. It is a focus upon culture which gives the ethnography of schooling its distinctive flavour.

An examination of the kinds of research in schools and classrooms carried on under the general heading of the ethnography of schooling shows the range of topics which have been explored. Figure 6.3 highlights these areas. The teacher researcher can of course focus upon any of these areas as a basis for some school-based research. These areas have all featured prominently in the literature on the ethnography of schools and classrooms.

In order to consider both the contribution of the ethnography of schooling and the implications for the teacher researcher we will examine three areas:

this viewpoint 'deviants' have to be seen in relation to the group, culture, and eventually the wider society of which they are a part. Deviance could therefore be described and understood as involving a series of social processes. These are worth considering since they might provide some key concepts the teacher researcher might wish to relate to any data which she has collected.

All teachers are aware of the ways in which certain children carry with them particular 'reputations'. This is especially true of the transition of pupils from one school to another. Researchers would want to ask questions about the origin of the reputation and the grounds upon which the child's reputation is said to be founded. For example, are teachers actually reacting to a child's behaviour, or to what they expect of the child and what the reputation seems to suggest? The other side of the coin is accounted for in the use of such concepts as identity, self-image, or self-concept. These concepts draw our attention to the subjective experiences and attitudes of those labelled in terms of the pictures of the individual which are offered by any particular label. Many pupils may in fact find it easier to live up to what is involved in any label than to behave in alternative ways. Labels often have a stigmatizing effect; they set people apart and create suspicion around the person labelled. At worst, stigma leads to ostracism and separate treatment. Once an individual is labelled in a particular way and if that label carried with it negative connotations, the person may be forced into seeking subcultural support from others in similar situations. It is in these subcultures that the so-called deviant may indeed gain a positive self-image and identity. Labelling in this sense may have the effect of actually developing and further reinforcing the behaviour in question since the stereotyping of individuals necessarily only focuses upon certain aspects of an individual to highlight and not the whole of the individual's characteristics.

These concepts and ideas ought to be seen as having a sensitizing role. They can sensitize the researcher towards looking at situations in fresh ways. Much educational research has made valuable use of these terms and they offer the teacher researcher an important set of ideas. School failure and classroom deviance might therefore be seen as being learnt or indeed an actual accomplishment. The educational 'life chances' of pupils are seen as being related to these factors as well as those of individual characterisitics, social class background, ethnicity, and gender.

Early studies in sociology of education like those of Hargreaves (1967) and Lacey (1970) using participant observation techniques both made reference to the importance of teachers' attitudes and expectations. Hargreaves maintained that in the secondary school he observed a distinction could be drawn between an 'academic' subculture and a 'delinquescent' subculture which was clearly related to the streaming system in operation. There were progressively more pupils in the delinquescent anti-academic subculture as one moved down the streams. Some time later Hargreaves, Hestor, and

Mellor (1975) went on to focus upon teachers' typifications of pupils in terms of conformity or non-conformity to classroom rules. These researchers developed ethnographic interviewing techniques for use with samples of secondary-school teachers in order to try and explicate the common-sense knowledge the teachers used in order to link behaviour of the pupils to rules, and therby define certain acts as deviant. The most impressive feature of this research is the way in which the researchers are able to develop a model of the stages through which the teacher's typification moved. From their research they argue that

> given the apparent absence of conceptual distinctions in members' accounts of rules, it was possible for us to organise the rules in school in terms of the threefold classification which we shall call *institutional, situational* and personal rules.
>
> (Hargreaves *et al.* 1975: 34)

Institutional rules were typically the 'rules' of the school, situational rules apply to the particular situations, namely the classroom, while personal rules were those relating to the idiosyncrasies of particular teachers. This study throws light upon the processes whereby rules are made, interpreted, and applied in school settings and within different phases or 'stages' of a lesson.

Hargreaves *et al.* concentrated upon the teachers' expectations and definitions. Another important piece of research was that done by Ray C.Rist (1970: 411–51) again using ethnographic techniques. He followed the progress of a group of kindergarten children in an elementary school of a black neighbourhood in St Louis as they moved into the first and second grades. His main concern was with the ways in which the teacher's differentiation of the children into fast and slow learners and on to specific tables appeared to be the result of a series of non-educational criteria such as the teacher's social-class-based assessment and typifications of the children.

Rist's focus upon teachers' expectations of the children and the subsequent social organization of classroom interactions demonstrates the power of the so-called self-fulfilling prophecy. He found that the teachers were using roughly constructed 'types' in order to consider the kinds of features it was deemed any particular child needed in order to succeed. He found that the teachers made very quick assessments of the children during initial early encounters with them. Eventually these assessments became formalized into specific patterns of interaction between the teacher and pupils taking on the character of a rigid caste-like system. The divisions between the groups of children were further reflected in both the seating arrangements in the classroom and the kinds of scores the children were achieving. Thus by the second grade

> No matter how well a child in the lower reading groups might have read, he was destined to remain in the same reading group. This is, in a sense,

another manifestation of the self-fulfilling prophecy in that a 'slow learner' has no option but to continue to be a slow learner, regardless of performance or potential.

(Rist 1970: 435)

These social as opposed to educational distinctions are given considerable symbolic force since the highest reading group of children in the second grade were given the name 'Tigers', while the middle group were described as 'Cardinals', and those assigned a first-grade reading level were know as the 'Clowns'. Many of these issues are taken up in more detail in Rist's book, the subtitle of which is *'A Factory for Failure'* (1973).

The focus upon teacher expectations, the consequences of developing low self-images in children, and the processes of labelling in schools did much to alert student teachers and those already in the profession to some of the problems involved. This is a good example of the way in which 'research' has direct consequences for classroom practice and to the importance of seeing the classroom as a complex social environment.

## Micro-ethnography and the work of McDermott

In this chapter we have been concentrating upon the verbal aspects of classroom communication and interaction. The routine everyday processes of classroom life are also made up of the vastly complex and subtle aspects of non-verbal behaviour or the paralinguistic features which are often taken for granted, yet none the less actually maintain what is being said. Movements, facial expressions, glances, and so on as well as posture and bodily movements all influence the nature of interaction in small groups and certainly may shape and influence teachers' evaluations or perceptions of their pupils and conversely pupils' evaluation and perception of other pupils and their teachers. The general term for the study of these features is 'micro-ethnography'. This approach recognizes that important messages are being conveyed in the non-verbal and minute interactional aspects of classroom life and tries to decipher what these may be and how they affect learning. These micro-ethnographic approaches have made extensive use of audio and video tape recordings.

In a series of studies R. P. McDermott (1974; 1977; 1978) has developed and refined this approach to the study of classrooms. McDermott makes use of close observational techniques for examining classroom processes and draws on both anthropological and psychological research findings to interpret the data. He has used this approach to examine the achievement of poor reading skills (McDermott 1974), how the way in which teachers and pupils 'make sense' of each other creates specific social contexts for learning (McDermott 1977), and the social processes involved at getting turns at reading in one American elementary school (McDermott 1978). This research represents some of the most detailed work on classroom interaction and has clear implications for classroom organization.

Micro-ethnographic research using audio and video tape recording techniques demands a fairly high level of technical sophistication. It is likely that this research will take time to set up. Cameras are indeed highly obtrusive and can have a marked influence on people's behaviour. The analysis of video recording is itself not an unproblematic affair. Despite these difficulties and reservations teachers can gain much from a close examination of classroom video tape recordings.

In this section we have explored some of the contributions of the ethnography of schooling to understanding the social, cultural, and interactional aspects of schools and classrooms. In doing so we highlighted the kinds of techniques employed by various researchers. The teacher researcher may pick up some possible topics for research and ways of exploring those areas by reading the studies referred to here and in the further reading section at the end of this chapter.

## Ethnomethodology, conversational analysis, and doing teaching

These linked approaches offer those involved in educational research fresh and exciting ways of investigating classroom interactional processes. Ethnomethodology and conversational analysis have opened up questions about learning, understanding, effective communication, and miscommunication. Ethnomethodology originated in the west coast of the USA, particularly California, during the 1960s and 1970s. A group of sociologists who shared a similar qualitative and interpretative approach to investigating the social world began to do small-scale studies on the ways in which people ordinarily interacted with each other in everyday situations. A focus upon the 'methods' by which individuals make sense of, construct, and thereby give meaning to the world emerged as a hallmark of this approach.

Ethnomethodology shares some basic premises with qualitative sociology and ethnographic approaches to social research more generally. Ethnomethodologists stress that the social world is made up of shared meanings and shared viewpoints. So much so that if actors changed places they would quite likely see the world in much the same way and that our knowledge of the world is generated through interpretations. There have been two main trends in ethnomethodological research which the teacher researcher might consider. First, a number of ethnographic studies of institutions and social processes have been carried out which are based upon the assumption that people's actions can be explained only by making reference to the context within which they take place. As such these studies were concerned with how individuals acquired the cultural perspectives of their societies and displayed them in the course of their daily lives. Second, 'conversational analysis' emerged as some of the most elaborated and extended body of research coming out of the ethnomethodological tradition. Conversational analysis (CA) focuses upon the organization of talk in everyday social life and conversational analysts, most notably the late Harvey Sacks and a group of researchers including Gail Jefferson, Jim Schenkein, W. W. Sharrock, and R. G. Anderson, attempt to consider how a sense of orderliness and coherence is displayed in conversational exchanges. The most striking feature of this approach is the technical machinery developed to analyse naturally occurring talk. One of the earliest attempts in this direction was Harvey Sacks's work on telephone conversations to a suicide crisis agency, where he treated the calls themselves as an object for description and analysis. Conversational analysts use raw data, not refined or invented data. They make a series of assumptions and procedural points on the nature and organization of talk.

1  Talk is organized by parties to that talk.
2  This orderliness and organization of talk must be displayed in the raw data.
3  Talk is sequentially organized and speaker change recurs and occurs.
4  Talk displays a turn-taking system and turns are not fixed but vary.
5  Describing conversational events must be context specific.
6  The insistence that data must be recorded as accurately as possible and collected from naturally occurring settings, usually by means of audio or video tape recordings.
7  The emphasis upon the sequential and interactional organization of talk reflects a major departure from much linguistic and conventional sociolinguistic approaches.
8  The unit of analyses for conversational analysis becomes not the sentence, but rather the utterance.
9  In analysing conversational interaction it is argued that the focus must be on participants' orientations to utterances in terms of previous utterances.
10  As a result of the first nine points it is clear to see that members have a methodological resource for making sense of talk; CA attempts an elaboration of this.

Conversational analysis is nothing if not a highly technical and extraordinarily detailed approach. Conversational analysis offers the teacher researcher a novel and valuable way of focusing upon classroom talk. In an important article Sharrock and Anderson (1982) have outlined an argument and a rationale for a focus upon classroom talk. Talk, they argue, is fundamental to all of the activities that sociologists claim to be studying, and in turn if we are to understand these activities, of which teaching and learning are a part, we need to develop an understanding of talk in the classroom. Furthermore, Sharrock and Anderson make some specific points about the way in which this can be done in terms of a focus upon how talk is organized in particular lessons in particular ways. This requires researchers to look at the ordinary, the routine, and the normal aspects of doing teaching. If research does not tell us this, they argue, then it cannot deliver much by way of insight into how lessons are organized and subsequently how learning takes place.

An impressive body of research now exists in the area of classroom studies which makes use of ethnomethodology and conversational analysis. We will briefly consider some of these studies in order to provide the reader with a flavour of the nature of this kind of research and what light it can throw upon classroom organization and learning. For purposes of this discussion it is useful to distinguish between studies of the social organization of classroom lessons, and studies of the turn-taking system and conversational organization of classroom lessons.

### The social organization of classroom lessons: Mehan, Cicourel

A growing number of American researchers influenced by the ethnomethodological perspective began to investigate the traditional areas of the testing of children and the assessment of children's abilities and performance. Mehan (1973: 309–28) focuses upon what he describes as 'children's language-using abilities', highlighting the ways in which speakers and hearers apply their linguistic, social, and interpretive knowledge in routine everyday situations, especially those in classrooms and more particularly testing situations. In a study of some formal testing situations in American kindergarten schools, Mehan found that the tests failed to capture the child's reasoning abilities and obscured understanding of the extent to which the child had understood the questions and hence how well the child had done because they were clearly based upon the teacher's subjective interpretations and narrow definitions of measurement. Mehan illustrates his point with an amusing but none the less telling example from one of the testing situations he examined.

> Another question instructs the child to choose the animal that can fly from among a bird, an elephant and a dog. The correct answer (obviously) is the bird. Many first-grade children though, chose the elephant along with the bird as a response to that question. When I later asked them why they chose that answer they replied 'That's Dumbo'. Dumbo (of course) is Walt Disney's flying elephant, well known to children who watch television and read children's books as an animal that flies.
>
> (Mehan 1973: 315)

Thus a child's response does not always indicate a lack of ability, but rather the use of an alternative scheme of interpretation to that being used by either teacher or tester. Mehan provides the following observation on this sequence:

> These descriptions demonstrate that the child can exist simultaneously in

a number of different 'realities' or worlds ... that is the factual world of everyday life and the world of fantasy. The child who says that animals can fly and talk is (from the adult point of view) mixing and blending the characteristics of fantasy and everyday worlds. The test, however, assumes that the child is attending to stimulus only from the viewpoint of the everyday world in which dogs do not talk and elephants do not fly. The test assumes further that the child keeps the world of play, fantasy and television out of the testing situation. Yet as these anecdotes demonstrate, the child of age 4–6 does not always keep his realities sequentially arranged. Because the child may be operating simultaneously in multiple realities, valid interrogations must examine why he answers questions as he does and determine what children 'see' in educational materials; testers must not use answers exclusively.

(Mehan 1973: 317)

These issues and many more are taken up in an important and influential collection of papers deriving from some American research. *Language Use and School Performance* by Cicourel *et al.* (1974) reports on the social organization of language use in both the testing and classroom situation in first-grade and kindergarten classrooms in two school districts in southern California, as well as some of the home settings of the children. The studies report on a range of situations and the richness of this work can be appreciated only by actually reading them. For our purposes there are two features which deserve attention. First, the major point of many of the studies contained in this volume suggests that a considerable proportion of the teachers and the testers operated with highly limited versions of the child's competence. The authors show through the analysis of verbatim transcripts and video tape recordings how, given the child's stock of knowledge at hand and cultural capacities, the answers to the often ambiguous questions can be demonstrated to be highly ingenious and acceptable. So much so that the 'facts' of the test scores and children's classroom answers are not a direct reflection of the individual child's abilities, but rather a reflection of the social processes and interactions and interpretations of both teachers and pupils. Second, of major interest here is the methodology these researchers employed. They made use of in-depth observations, audio and video tape recordings of testing and classroom settings as well as interviews with the teachers. The authors developed what they describe as a system of 'indefinitive triangulation'. This involved recording the classroom or testing situation and playing these materials back to the teacher later and discussing the data with the teacher after the event, as it were.

The whole thrust of this volume is the fact that children's cognitive abilities must be set against teachers' perceptions and children's interpretive skills within the testing and classroom context. Children's 'performance' then needs to be seen as an outcome of all these features.

*Conversational analysis, turn-taking, and classroom talk: French and French*

As we noted above, conversational analysis has developed a conceptual machinery for unravelling the organization of conversation so that it may be described and analysed. It is easy to see how such a detailed focus upon transcripts of tape-recorded lessons scrutinized in such a way will reveal the properties underlying the order of such lessons. The organization of classroom talk, the nature of turn-taking, and the conversational strategies employed by both teachers and pupils can help to throw light on such diverse issues as participation profiles of individual children or pupils, gender imbalances, miscommunication, starting a lesson, dealing with latecomers, the assessment of pupils' reading abilities, the achievement of success or failure in the classroom, and so on. All of these areas have been considered by those researchers influenced by ethnomethodology and the programme of work developed by conversational analysts. One example will serve to demonstrate the value of such a focus on classroom talk.

Jane and Peter French have been working on the organization of class-room talk and its effects on learning in a number of different settings for a considerable period of time. Their research has been based around the analysis of transcriptions of tape-recorded classroom lessons together with their own observations of the settings concerned. The study by French and French (1984) may be considered since it shows how a focus upon the verbal interactional dimensions of the primary classroom might in fact be the cause of the gender imbalances reported by many researchers in schools. In mixed-sex schools and classrooms, research has shown that boys tend to receive greater attention than girls. Boys tend to have more direct involvement and interaction with the teacher than girls and certainly do better in science subjects than girls. The study undertaken by French and French involved the analysis of the verbatim transcription of a fourth-year junior school lesson. The lesson was a teacher–class discussion of 'What I do on Mondays and what I would like to do on Mondays'.

This study like many others showed the same kind of gender imbalances between boys and girls. However, unlike other researchers these authors do not see the situation simply as a result of sexist bias, or even poor classroom management, but instead in *interactional* terms. This they do by means of a concentration upon the distribution of interactional turns between boys and girls. Taking this view, the responsibility, if this is not too strong a word, lies with both the teacher and the pupils who collaboratively produce the activities of the lesson. In the lesson reported a focus upon the numbers of turns of boys and girls showed that a disproportionately high number of turns were taken by a small sub-set of four boys. Furthermore, the ability to obtain a turn to talk was frequently associated with ability to offer 'newsworthy items' which was a resource that was exploited by some children more than others. It is through such interactional manoeuvres as presenting newsworthy items and taking up unusual positions that boys were able to secure more of the teacher's attention. The major significance of French and French's study lies in its suggestion that gender imbalances within the classroom may not be simply or only due to the sexism or psychological predispositions of the teachers, but in part the ability to manipulate the turn-taking machinery.

## Implications for the teacher researcher

In this final section on major approaches to classroom talk and interaction we consider the contributions of ethnomethodology and conversational analysis. The kinds of research developed by these investigators are particularly suited for adoption by the teacher researcher. Quite simply the teacher need do no more than tape record and transcribe one of her lessons. In other words, both the ways of researching classrooms and the kinds of analyses represented in this section are amenable to ordinary teachers themselves. As Payne and Cuff (1982: 8) have pointed out, the most important elements of the attitude needed by teachers to do this is that they suspend some of their own common-sense assumptions about classrooms and teaching. By making the familiar strange it is possible to get closer to the phenomena themselves and in doing so develop tighter and more detailed descriptions and analyses.

Such approaches will inevitably increase teachers' awareness and under-standing of classroom processes. In this final section of this chapter we try to show how the teacher might go about looking at her own or other teachers' classrooms and suggest some possible topics and areas to focus upon. To conclude we outline some of the issues involved in transcribing.

## A practical guide to observing, recording, and investigating classroom talk and interaction

We have been focusing upon the classroom as a social environment in this chapter and have paid special attention to the importance of analysing classroom talk and interaction. The teacher researcher can profitably make use of any of the approaches we have highlighted. Indeed, a focus upon the nature of classroom talk and interaction can be achieved without the teacher's even having to move from her own classroom. A focus upon the transcriptions of class lessons can reveal the complexity and subtlety of much classroom communication. Furthermore these materials can be used in conjunction with other kinds of data which the teacher might have collected in the past or proposes to collect in the future.

While there is much the teacher can do this is not without its difficulties. The major problem here, as elsewhere in school-based teacher research, is the problem of the familiar. The data which the teacher researcher collects on classroom processes may be all too familiar to her. This familiarity may mean that the teacher neglects or simply passes over as uninteresting important features. It is important to bear in mind therefore that familiarity with the data, while clearly an advantage, is not without its disadvantages.

## Some possible topics for research

Throughout this section of the book we have offered suggestions about the possible areas and topics the teacher researcher might wish to follow up. We have not been prescriptive since the teacher herself must consider the particular and immediate context of her own teaching in defining a project area. The ten questions listed below are areas the teacher researcher might like to consider in the light of the preceding discussion in this chapter. These questions might be regarded as some initial preliminary questions requiring some general observations which can in turn become more focused at a later stage. In approaching interaction and communication patterns in any classroom the teacher researcher might like to consider these ten questions as a checklist of items to make notes on. The following examples of topics is intended only as a guide to possible areas for investigation in greater depth.

1 What types of classroom language are employed?
2 What are the characteristics of teacher talk?
3 What are the characteristics of pupil talk?
4 What form does teacher questioning take?
5 What form does any class discussion take?
6 How large are the main working groups or group?
7 How does the teacher direct learning?
8 What is the balance between formal or informal talk?
9 How are turns to talk or rights to talk distributed?
10 How much teacher talk and how much pupil talk is there?

These questions can act as a guide for some general observations. We will now consider a series of more focused topics which it is possible to explore.

## Control over classroom communication

Teachers are able to exert a considerable amount of control over classroom communication in terms of what is said (topics), over the way what is said is received (relevance), and how much may or may not be said (amount). Teachers adopt a number of strategies to aid them in this regard. It is important to consider the ways in which these strategies may influence learning.

A possible topic of investigation arising from a focus upon control over classroom talk might be a consideration of the differences in teacher styles and classroom organization upon the degree of 'conversational freedom' children are allowed, and the quality of adult–child interaction in the classroom that might ensue.

## The right to speak

In our culture children in a number of situations may clearly be said to have limited rights to speak when co-present with adults in interaction. This superordinate-subordinate adult–child relationship is manifest in one of its clearest forms in the teaching situation. The way in which the turn-taking machinery is exploited by different children, different groups of children, or by boys compared to girls is important in order to discover the nature of learning in any one situation.

## What does the teacher want?

Teachers in the course of their day-to-day activities are involved in what has technically been described as 'recapitulation', 'getting the children to respond', 'feedback', and so on. Mehan (1973) has discussed in some detail the kinds of 'searching practices' the children he observed were engaged in where the teachers or adults involved provided further information for them to respond to original questions. Such activities and strategies can be analysed for the kinds of conversational mechanisms and the cultural knowledge they exhibit. This is of special interest because such activities are characterized by the co-presence of parties with unequal access to the very conversation they are engaged in.

## Sociolinguistic barriers

In one of the best general introductory texts on language schools and classrooms, Stubbs (1983: 76–83) offers some topics for investigation. Notably he suggests that it is possible and important to consider what 'sociolinguistic barriers' may exist between schools and their pupils and specifically teachers' attitudes to children's language. This is especially important in the multicultural context. Teachers' attitudes about 'right' and 'wrong' language can have many consequences and can generate in pupils negative images of their language and consequently their social worth in the classroom. These are certainly whole-school issues as well as areas of concern for individual class teachers. The development of any school language policy could certainly benefit from the investigation of these areas because attitudes to language are indeed crucial in determining both the classroom environment and the organization of classroom communication.

These are simply a few suggestions for the possible focus of a research project. Other areas that may be considered might include language use and special needs, gender imbalances, subject or task-oriented classroom talk, the nature of child–child talk and interaction, adolescent talk, and many more. Whatever the focus and however the teacher researcher explores the materials she collects, the experience will be fruitful and the data exceptionally rich. Policy and practical implications will certainly follow. To conclude this chapter we need to explore the technical aspects of putting classroom conversation into a readable and presentable form, that is the job of transcription.

### Transcribing: transcription symbols and systems

One of the typical features of qualitative ethnographic research is that it produces vast quantities of seemingly unmanageable data. An important aspect of the research process surrounds how the researcher is actually going to present the data. The questions here relate to the overall nature of the research design as well as to the data-collection techniques employed and the kinds of data which result. These questions need to be borne in mind whether the teacher is relying upon field notes, interview materials, or transcriptions of classroom lessons. Questions of degree of detail, accuracy, and comprehensiveness will vary according to the situation and the materials involved. Generally speaking, if the research is to be focused upon 'classroom interaction' and 'lessons' a transcript which is sufficiently detailed to enable the kinds of analyses we have been talking about will have to be produced. It follows that the teacher researcher needs either to make use of an existing system or develop her own system and symbols for transcribing the materials. Sometimes researchers describe the transcription conventions they have used (Payne and Cuff 1982: ix; French and French 1984: 134). We offer below our own system for transcribing lesson tape recordings. This scheme has evolved during our work with teachers over the years; it can of course be adapted and modified. The main point, however, is that a reasonably high degree of consistency is achieved and that the same conventions and symbols are used in the same way throughout the transcript.

### Some transcription symbols and conventions

| | |
|---|---|
| T. | Usually for purposes of anonymity it is best to identify |
| C. | speakers by means of T. for teachers, C. or P. for pupil; |
| P. | individual children's or pupils' names can of course be used provided they are changed yet keep the gender of the speaker clear. |
| ... | A pause; dots signify length roughly in seconds. |
| (1.5) | Alternative symbol for pause timed in seconds and tenths of seconds. |
| [ ] | Indicates overlap of talk at point of overlap. |
| // | An interruption of one speaker. |

| ( ) | Denotes an unidentified speaker or utterance. |
| (( )) | Indicates that the transcriber does not know or cannot effectively make out what the utterance is. |
| L-A-W-N-S | A speaker spelling out a word. |
| YES | A phrase or word spoken loudly with emphasis. |
| —— | An alternative symbol for indicating loudness or emphasis. |
| – | Indicates a hesitation or pause. |

The difficulties involved in transcribing and the time spent should not be underestimated. Indeed, this should be built into the research design itself and taken into account when planning the research so that sufficient time is in fact left for it to be done properly. There are no tried and tested rules for transcribing. Transcribing is for the most part a slog. However, it does have one major advantage. The length of time the researcher has to spend with the data in order to transcribe them accurately means that she is also developing familiarity with the data.

From our experience the mechanics of transcribing can be seen to involve the following series of stages and tasks.

1 Listen to the complete tape at least twice through without attempting to write anything down. This will provide the transcriber with a sense of the materials as a whole, the rhythm, tone, and substantive content of the talk together with an 'ear' for who is talking at what point.
2 The use of headphones gets the researcher or transcriber closer to the data and eliminates any distracting extraneous background noise.
3 Transcribing proper will involve listening to short 'chunks' of talk and noting it down, and playing and replaying the tape backwards and forwards in order to get an accurate transcript.
4 Once a reasonable transcript has been made from the tape the researcher or transcriber should listen to the tape again as a whole while going through her own transcript of it and making any additions or corrections as she goes along, stopping the tape at the appropriate points in order to facilitate this.
5 If possible, it is always useful to get another person to listen to the tape and cross-check the transcript.

Transcribing is time-consuming and is often seen as an unrewarding exercise. All the same, it is a necessary process and demands the same kind of commitment and serious approach that any other aspect of the research itself involves.

## Summary

In this chapter we have provided an overview of the main approaches to classroom talk and interaction and have stressed the importance of seeing the classroom as a social environment. In many ways the points we have been making in this chapter relate to the wider aspects of a teacher's professional responsibilities. Research into such areas can only enhance this. The prospect is an exciting one and we hope only that some teachers will be prepared to take up this challenge.

## Suggested further reading

A vast amount of research has been carried out into classroom interaction. Many different approaches have been used and a variety of topics explored. S. Delamont (1983) *Interaction in the Classroom,* 2nd edn, London: Methuen, is one of the best introductory texts dealing with the classroom as a social environment and covers many of the perspectives outlined here. One of the best accounts of systematic observation as a research technique applied to classrooms can be found in P. Croll (1986) *Systematic Classroom Observation,* London: Falmer Press, while criticisms and evaluation of both the Flanders FIAC system and systematic observation have been made by D. Hamilton and S. Delamont (1974) 'Classroom research: a cautionary tale', *Research in Education* 11, 1–15; D. I. McIntyre (1980) 'Systematic observation of classroom activities', *Educational Analysis,* 2, 2: 3–30, and R. Walker and C. Adelman (1975) 'Interaction analysis in informal classrooms: a critical commentary on the Flanders system', *British Journal of Educational Psychology* 45, 1: 73–6. Debate over the ORACLE project is continued in R. Barrow (1984) 'The logic of systematic classroom research: the case of ORACLE', *Durham and Newcastle Research Review* 10, 53: 182–8; and by J. Scarth and M. Hammersley (1986) 'Questioning ORACLE', *Educational Research* 28, 3: 174–84. The importance and influence of anthropological perspectives in classroom research is examined in two articles: S. Delamont and P. Atkinson (1980) 'The two traditions of educational ethnography: sociology and anthropology compared', *British Journal of Sociology of Education* 1, 2: 139–52; A. Vierra, C. Boehm and S. Neely (1982) 'Anthropology and educational studies', in A. Hartnett (ed.) *The Social Sciences in Educational Studies: A Selective Guide to the Literature,* London: Heinemann. Studies derived from the ethnography of communication tradition can be found in D. Cazden, V. John, and D. Hymes (eds) *Functions of Language in the Classroom,* Columbia and London: Teachers College Press. For those unfamiliar with sociolinguistics, P. Trudgill (1974) *Sociolinguistics: An Introduction,* Harmondsworth: Penguin, remains one of the best introductions, while R. Wardhaugh (1986) *An Introduction to Sociolinguistics,* Oxford: Blackwell, though longer and more detailed, covers a lot of different studies and is worth consulting for reference purposes. The most accessible overview of sociolinguistic approaches to the classroom is the short book by Michael Stubbs (1983) *Language, Schools and Classrooms,* 2nd edn, London: Methuen. A. D. Edwards and D. Westgate (1986)

*Investigating Classroom Language,* London: Falmer Press, could profitably be read after Stubbs's work. Edwards has taken up the issue of ethnicity, multicultural issues, and education in two important and readable works: A. D. Edwards (1979) *The West Indian Language Issue in British Schools,* London: Routledge & Kegan Paul, and A. D. Edwards (1983) *Language in Multi-Cultural Classrooms,* London: Batsford. The classic and highly influential essay by William Labov is reprinted in this country as W. Labov (1969) 'The logic of non-standard English', in N. Keddie (ed.) *Tinker, Tailor ... the Myth of Cultural Deprivation,* Harmondsworth: Penguin. A collection of articles demonstrating the value of ethnomethodology and conversational analysis in the study of classroom activities can be found in G. C. F. Payne and E. C. Cuff (eds) (1982) *Doing Teaching: The Practical Management of Classrooms,* London: Batsford.

# Chapter seven

# Space and interaction in schools and classrooms

## Introduction

In this concluding chapter to Part II of the book we focus upon the spatial dimensions of schools and classrooms and try to show why space and place might be an important focus of research for the practising teacher. We will consider the importance of space in the learning situation and offer a 'hands-on' appreciation of how the classroom teacher might begin to go about looking at space in her own or other schools and classrooms. As such this chapter builds upon what we have already said about looking at classroom interaction and the main traditions of classroom research we outlined in Chapter 6. By way of conclusion we examine Sally Lubeck's (1985) comparative ethnography of two early education settings in America, *Sandbox Society,* first in order to consider the ways in which both time and space dimensions structure activities in the schools, and second because her study raises many of the issues of research design we tried to unravel in Chapter 2. Her book shows some of the ways in which ethnographic and field research methods can be applied to educational settings. While not holding up this study as a definitive model of the research process, it offers many insights and might act as a useful benchmark for the prospective teacher researcher. Furthermore it is an important contribution to understanding the pre-school educational process.

## Space and place as a research focus

By referring to space and place, or to spatial arrangements and spatial organization, we are pointing to the complex relationships between the physical, interactional, and symbolic factors which shape and influence everybody's lives in countless and complex ways. From how close we sit next to strangers on a train, to the ways in which we organize and arrange the furniture in our classrooms, space is a crucial aspect of human social life. How people use, orientate towards, and make sense of such features as spaces, places, and the physical features of these settings, contributes to the orderliness of social interaction. In other words spaces and places have 'social properties' and we all have a stock of common-sense knowledge which tells us how to act in particular settings, what to expect in them, and the likely consequences of interaction in such settings.

Spaces and places contain symbolic messages and social information. Social researchers ask a series of questions. What is it that a particular spatial arrangement is actually saying? How do people construct spaces to give off messages and how does this influence the interaction which takes place in them? The answers to these questions move us towards considering some of the most basic social and cultural features of our societies.

As a topic of research interest, space allows us to ask a series of important, but often neglected, questions. For example, how do people attend to and make sense of the features of spaces and places? How do people physically conduct themselves in particular spaces and places? How do they act, stand, queue, walk, etc? How are territories or boundaries developed, maintained, and crossed? Answering such questions is no easy matter since for the most part the rules governing our behaviour are simply taken for granted and unstated.

How human beings orientate towards and structure the visible and invisible boundaries we refer to as space, environments, territories, or places and how we interact and react within these features has long been a topic of interest to social scientists. E. T. Hall (1969) for example began his studies by asking why it was that Arabs in the USA felt uncomfortable while co-present with Americans during interaction and, conversely, why it was so many Americans felt uncomfortable with 'strangers' abroad. Others, notably Oscar Newman (1973) and those people having an interest in the architectural features of our society and the ways in which these features have affected us, pose questions about the correlation between crime rates, housing styles, and the composition of many urban environments. On the other hand, more recently researchers like Goffman and Scheflen have examined in detail the ways in which people co-ordinate their face-to-face interactions in both public and private places, 'upstage' and 'backstage', manipulating these features to their own advantage. In the world of education, most notably in the *Plowden Report* (1967), the influence of the spatial arrangement and organization of classroom activities was spelt out. Other social scientists, notably anthropologists and sociologists, were focusing upon what was described as 'territoriality'.

In a series of works, E. T. Hall was concerned with unravelling the use of space as a 'specialized elaboration of culture'. As such he was concerned with the dynamic use of space and the ways in which human beings could shape and control communication and interaction through the use of both the fixed features and semi-fixed features of space. Examples of the fixed features of space would be things like buildings, houses, schools, those features that it is not possible to move; semi-fixed features on the other hand are environmental factors that have the capacity either to increase or to decrease the amount of social interaction with others or will affect the nature of that interaction: hence actors can develop certain amounts of control over these features. Hall can be credited with developing the suggestion that space is indeed a sociocultured phenomena. Different settings create different patterns of interaction, different cultures have different codes and rules for the use of spaces and the physical proximity of different kinds of actors.

Hall follows the distinction drawn by Osmond (1959) in his study of the development of mental hospitals between the notions of *sociofungal* and *sociopetal* space as ways of describing two quite distinct kinds of spatial arrangements. Examples of sociofungal spatial arrangements would be railway station waiting-rooms, or the classical/formal Victorian English classroom; the concern and emphasis in these arrangements is to keep people apart by establishing degrees of distance between participants. Sociopetal space, on the other hand, can be found in the typical French pavement café or indeed the progressive, informal English primary school. Here the spatial arrangements have the reverse effect of actually encouraging social interaction, developing informality, closeness, and co-operation. Joiner (1976), for example, from his study on the spatial arrangement of small offices shows how objects such as reception areas, lobbies, and so on can be used to develop impressions of the setting those on the outside of the organization will receive. In a similar fashion, the sociofungal arrangements of many open-plan schools are designed theoretically to provide a more flexible, less constraining, learning environment. It is clear to see how all aspects of our lives are influenced both by the nature of the physical spatial arrangements we find ourselves in and our interpretations of them and orientations towards them. It can be argued that these are crucial variables in the learning process and that as part of a teacher's professional responsibility these aspects of schools and classrooms demand close scrutiny. However, before we consider the ways in which the teacher researcher might embark on investigation of the spatial dimensions of classrooms, let us broadly consider the grounds for wanting to do so in the first place.

## Spatial dimensions of schools and classrooms

Schools and classrooms may be conceived of as 'arenas of interaction'. School buildings, classrooms, areas, and locations in school are interpreted and identified by different people in different ways. Teachers and pupils routinely cope with and manage the physical arrangements in schools. The ways in which they do this has all manner of consequences. Dealing with these aspects of life is fundamentally an interactional affair; it is in this way that space and learning are linked. The ways in which objects and classrooms are organized and arranged is not arbitrary; indeed the organization of a classroom often reflects the kind of spirit in which learning can take place and can furthermore be said to reflect conceptions of knowledge. The organization and layout of a school or classroom tells as much about the character of the school and the orientations of participants. The aim of research on school and classroom spatial organization is pragmatic. Such research should aim to unravel the ways in which space and learning interact so as to reveal some of the educational consequences of the spatial and physical organization of the immediate environment. This knowledge will enable the teacher researcher to reflect back upon professional practice.

The spatial organization of a school or classroom provides possibilities for learning but at the same time constraints. The school buildings and classrooms themselves express and embody conceptions of teaching and learning. In looking at the spatial organization of any school or classroom, the teacher researcher will need to bear in mind the overall assumptions which are likely to influence any one situation. For example conceptions of children, the status of the pupils, interpretations of schooling in formal or informal terms as subject- or child-centred, together with teachers' and pupils' attitudes will all affect the nature of classroom interaction and the influence of the spatial organization and physical context upon this. The pervasiveness of these features and their perceived importance is illustrated by the way in which this issue has received considerable attention in the educational and professional literature. This is reflected most notably in the primary area and the so-called 'progressive' approach to primary education and, of course, in the debate on open-plan schools. Space has also been a focus of attention in unravelling the reasons why girls do not achieve as boys do in science subjects, particularly mathematics.

The implications of the *Plowden Report's* (1967) recommendations were quickly felt. Discovery learning and the rejection of the compartmentalization of knowledge meant that the physical and spatial organization of many primary schools was changing. Increased 'activity work' meant provision within a classroom for often a number of different activities taking place simultaneously. Similarly the introduction of the 'integrated day' or 'team teaching' were attempts to provide greater flexibility within schools and individual classrooms, as well as encouraging greater pupil autonomy. Consider for a moment some of the implications of Dearden's definition of the integrated day

Learning takes place in an open or openly interconnected space where the teachers move from individual to individual, or draw aside groups according to an overall and agreed programme. Something like the traditional class and its teacher still residually exists at the beginning and end of the day. This is the homebase from which children and teachers alike move out to wider contacts.

(Dearden 1971: 51)

or of Rintoul and Thorne, on the features of open-plan organization in the primary school

1 The organisation of classroom spaces so that children can learn as individuals and in small groups for some time,
2 The integration of subjects so that different activities may be going on at the same time.

(Rintoul and Thorne 1975: 13)

However, this is really only one side of the coin, the professional side of the professional themes and practical arrangements issue. This points to the way in which teachers have constantly to translate the educational theory, ideas, and professional themes, into what they can do in practice, within the constraints in which they work and in relation to their own interpretation of these themes. As Hamilton puts it with regard to open plan, though the point has more general applicability,

Open-plan schooling, like any other kind of schooling, is not simply a cluster of theoretical assumptions, still less a set of individual practices. Its realisation is a combination of both practices and theory.

(Hamilton 1977: 107)

From the professional literature then, spatial organization in school is an important matter. Primary teaching is no longer here seen as being about instruction in places of instruction, but rather about developing and creating environments for learning, where teachers provide direction, stimulation, and encouragement. These are professional themes and the extent to which they influence and affect practice is not unproblematic. As we said above, teachers have to translate this, which they do in various ways, in the light of their definitions of the area, the children, their past experiences, and their jobs. It is in this way that the social organization of space in schools and classrooms reflects the practical routine day-to-day considerations of teachers. It is clear to see how the organization of space in any school or classroom situation often reflects the philosophical and pedagogical assumptions underlying practice. It is one of the tasks of the teacher researcher to get beneath the surface of this.

Possibly the earliest and best-known research that has been conducted in the area of space and education is the work of Robert Sommer, a social psychologist. In a series of studies Sommer was concerned with unravelling the influence of seating arrangements and classroom spatial organization on the levels of pupils' participation. In one study of an introductory psychology class, the students sitting directly opposite the instructor were found to participate more than those on the sides (Sommer 1967: 489–503; see also Sommer 1969). In classrooms where desks were arranged in straight rows students in front were found to participate more than those in the rear, and students in the centre of each row participated more than those on the side. It is argued that these and other findings back up what is known as the *expressive contact hypothesis* which relates direct visual contact to increased interaction. Sommer's concern was primarily practical, being involved mainly with the problem of the ecology of classroom participation; his work rests upon the implicit assumption that increased participation makes for better teaching and is therefore geared towards establishing the kinds of physical arrangements that will best facilitate this.

Sommer's approach was one of the first systematic attempts to consider these issues. However, there are problems surrounding this research. There appears to be little recognition of the fact that different groups, and indeed individuals within any one group, will have their own ideas about spatial arrangements. In many ways Sommer's work relates to standard classrooms, but in reality how many classrooms are 'standard'? As we noted in Chapter 6, one of the persistent criticisms of Flanders' interaction analysis system (FIAC) was its inability to cope with non-standard and informal classrooms (Walker and Adelman 1975: 73–6).

Rivlin and Rothenberg (1976), however, conducted their research in a rather different manner. This study is noteworthy not so much for its conclusions, but rather the methodology it adopted. Rivlin and Rothenberg in their study of space in open classrooms in the USA made use of descriptions of the rooms and the users of the rooms and the location of individuals within the room in relation to other individuals. The researchers made observations of two public elementary schools using open-plan classroom approaches located in large urban areas of the USA. The authors described their methodology in the following way:

> The specific techniques that were used included repeated observations of classrooms, repeated *tracking* (following the complete days of individual children), interviews with teachers, children and parents and use of a model of the classroom in conjunction with an interview with students.
>
> (Rivlin and Rothenberg 1976: 481)

The researcher also made use of a behavioural mapping and time-sampling technique which focuses upon the location of any one individual at specified periodic moments. Their use of triangulation by means of interviewing and discussions after the event is also interesting here.

A different line of research is pursued by the well-known American educational researcher Ray Rist (1972) in his study of irregularities in an American ghetto kindergarten classroom; Rist speaks about the 'social distance' that the teacher in his study was able to maintain between herself and her pupils so that a 'some can do it and some can not' attitude developed. Rist's study was based upon lengthy periods of observation in the kindergarten classroom of a group of black children; he also conducted interviews with both the class teacher and the principal. Rist argues that the actual spatial arrangement of the classroom echoed the kinds of social distinctions which were developed between the teacher and the pupils. Rist offers some revealing observations on the ways in which spatial arrangements in the classroom can further contribute to inequalities and underachievement.

> The permanent seating of the children in the classroom on the eighth day of school took on additional significance when it is noted that they appear to have been seated based on a number of social-class criteria independent of any measurement of cognitive capacity and ability to perform academic tasks.
>
> (Rist 1972: 274)

Rist's study points to the way in which aspects of the spatial organization of classrooms, in conjunction with other factors, can have a considerable effect on the pupils' learning.

More recently in an ethnographic study of the social organization of space and place in one urban open-plan primary school in northern England, Hitchcock (1982) found that the teachers were involved in the elaborate creation of boundaries in a school where there was a general absence of walls and 'classrooms'. Teachers in this school faced a problem. On the one hand there was the theory and professional themes of open-plan teaching, and on the other hand they were faced with the realities of teaching in their school in a 'difficult', 'downtown', inter-city neighbourhood. As a consequence, teachers developed a series of practical responses and adaptations to the open-plan context of the school. In other words, this research showed how the professional themes of what should and ought to be going on in open-plan schools such as this were mediated and translated into what could go on and be made to work in these types of location by the teachers themselves. This researcher found three general processes that teachers became involved with in translating the professional themes of the school into the practical arrangements of day-to-day teaching. First, the teachers might be described as being engaged in a process of 'normalization'. The teachers had collaboratively learnt to recognize and interpret certain events in school as being 'normal for here'. This had the effect of rendering a whole range of activities as being non-problematic while elsewhere they could quite easily have been regarded as being highly problematic. Second, the teacher had also learnt to disregard certain kinds of disorderliness and disciplinary problems as a direct response to the visibility of action within the school. Finally, the researcher observed that the widespread practice of the retreat into the home-base seemed to be a response to try and compensate for the absence of walls by using their home-bases, and the five-feet-high partitions of which they were composed, as barriers and partitions within which particularly sought-after behaviour could be encouraged and developed (Hitchcock 1982: 76–84).

The responses and adaptations made by these teachers have important consequences for the amount and kind of learning that takes place in school. Many published studies point to the importance of space and place in schools and classrooms. Furthermore this research displays a great amount of variation in the methodology employed and data collected. Rivlin and Rothenberg (1976) and Lubeck (1986) made use of flow charts. Rist (1972) used non-participant observation and Hitchcock (1982) used participant observation. In the following section we will examine some of the ways in which the teacher might go about investigating space in schools and classrooms.

## How to research space and place in schools and classrooms

While observation is likely to be the major source of data for the teacher researcher interested in considering the importance of space and place in schools, perhaps more than any other topic, the question of classroom and school spatial arrangements lends itself to the triangulation of sources of data and methods of data collection. Moreover, the spatial organization of classrooms and its relation to learning may indeed crop up as part of another research topic or curriculum evaluation exercise. In this sense focusing upon space may constitute a small part of an overall study, or in contrast, the main issue in a single investigation. We will outline some of the main issues involved in researching space. However, to begin with the teacher researcher needs to bear two crucial points in mind.

First, it needs to be recognized that patterns of interaction in classrooms do change and develop over time. Any research into the spatial dimensions of schools and classrooms will have to take this into account. Second, it is important to give due consideration to the typicality or representativeness of the group, class, or subject being observed. It is important therefore for the teacher researcher to consider a range of situations in order to get a fair picture of what is happening.

There are likely to be three main ways in which data can be generated on the spatial arrangements and organization of schools and classrooms. Observation, and in particular participant observation, the use of diaries, and interviewing could all be used here. However, a range of visual materials as we will point out below, are particularly helpful when examining this area.

The teacher's familiarity with the setting can be both an advantage and a disadvantage; the kinds of observations made will therefore have to consider this. The observations may be quite formalized or alternatively they may be more descriptive and extended accounts of a classroom setting or particular area. Observations could also be made of the development of a class lesson or activity focusing upon descriptions of the physical layout and of the classroom and the movements of teacher and pupils. The researcher should aim to produce as detailed descriptions as possible from these observations.

The diary offers the teacher an excellent means of gaining fairly detailed descriptions of the routine features of teacher–pupil interaction and the use of space in classrooms. The teacher simply records the timing and activities she has engaged in during the course of a school day, paying attention to the relationship between timings, locations, and the participants involved. The teacher researcher can do this in her own classroom or alternatively ask another teacher to keep a diary of these features of classroom life. Of course if a number of diaries are kept the teacher researcher can engage in a comparative exercise, when similarities, differences, and patterns could be established across the materials.

The unstructured or semi-structured interview can provide the opportunity to reconsider some of the materials the teacher has collected via observations, a diary, or some other means. Here the teacher researcher can seek to clarify, for example a teacher's perceptions of the spatial dimension of a particular classroom. The interview might also be used to develop further lines of inquiry. Here it will be useful to have developed beforehand a checklist or an *aide-mémoire* of the salient features it is intended to explore in the interview. In many cases this interview material will act as supplementary data. Whatever method or combinations of methods are used to explore this area, the general aim ought to be the production of as rich and detailed descriptions as possible. With this in mind let us examine some of the data available for the teacher researcher to collect, the ways in which it may be collected and the kinds of questions which may be raised. The list below sets out some of these aspects.

1 Photography and video tape recording
2 Layouts, maps, plans, and diagrams
3 Relationships between locations and activities
4 Boundaries
5 Seating arrangements
6 Tracking teachers and pupils and time-sampling
7 Gender dimensions of classroom activities
8 Subject or classroom tasks and spatial arrangements
9 Workshops with staff and parents

*Photography and video tape recording*

As we mentioned in Chapter 3, still photography has for a long time been considered to be one of the basic tools of the ethnographic fieldworker. Visual records of all kinds may help the researcher to develop a closer feel and appreciation of the setting. There is certainly scope for the use of photography when investigating classroom spatial arrangements. Photographs can add depth and richness and are useful as descriptive resources from which the teacher may tease out ideas and lines of analysis. The photograph, however, can never hope to capture the dynamic ebb and flow of classroom life. This might mean that photographs are more useful for some kinds of classrooms than others. Static, frozen images of classroom activities must always be placed within the ongoing and constantly moving patterns of classroom interaction. In this sense, the use of audio-visual techniques have very definite advantages. Many schools nowadays have access to a 'back-pack' video camera outfit and certainly a number of schools have video tape recorders and playback provision. If video tape recording a classroom lesson for whatever purposes, the teacher will have to bear in mind the nature of the lesson, the subject involved, age and orientation of the children, and the teacher's style, together with the possible effects the presence of a camera will have upon the interactions themselves. Moreover, the teacher will also need to pay attention to the angle or angles from which the filming is done. This is especially important if the teacher uses a fixed tripod. Questions surrounding the possible exclusion of certain areas in the classroom or groups of children need to be considered alongside the kind of film that will emerge from placing the camera at the back, front, or sides of the classroom. While many of these problems are minimized when the classrooms in question are conventional ones, they are conversely increased in, for example, informal infant or primary schools. We have worked with video tape recordings of classroom lessons where the backs of children's heads have been virtually all that one saw of the children. Despite these difficulties the video tape recording of classroom lessons can provide the researcher with an important moving record from which to consider the spatial ecology and social organization of space within the classroom.

*Layouts, maps, plans, and diagrams*

Many teachers and other researchers find the construction of classroom layouts, maps, plans, or diagrams of locations within a school or classroom a particularly valuable exercise (see for example Hitchcock 1982). The following examples show the kinds of diagrams and plans it is possible to construct from the school and classroom situation. The degreee of detail will depend upon the nature of the topic under investigation. Although not absolutely essential, these layouts and diagrams should be as near to scale as possible. Obviously the degree of detail in these will depend upon what the researcher is looking at.

Figures 7.1, 7.2, and 7.3 show the kinds of features it is useful to indicate on a sketch map, plan, or diagram of a particular classroom or part of a school. The teacher researcher also needs to remember that the semi-fixed features of space recorded on the plans and diagrams can and do change. This might mean that more than one plan will have to be produced for a single classroom. If the school's original architect's drawings are available these too can help to develop a sense of scale. It will be necessary to include a key to the items contained on these plans. A few of the things the teacher researcher might want to include would be seating arrangements, position of furniture and desks, numbers of children in the classroom or group, and the main lines of travel or apparent 'thoroughfares' within the classroom.

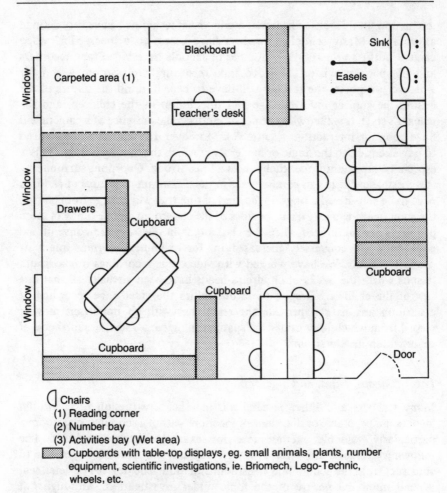

Chairs
(1) Reading corner
(2) Number bay
(3) Activities bay (Wet area)
Cupboards with table-top displays, eg. small animals, plants, number equipment, scientific investigations, ie. Briomech, Lego-Technic, wheels, etc.

**Figure 7.1** An Infant School Classroom

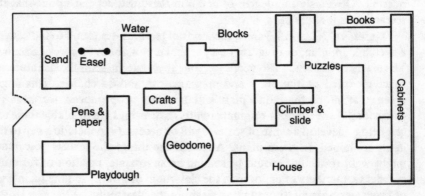

**Figure 7.2** Floor plan of Harmony Preschool          *Source:* Lubeck (1985: 84)

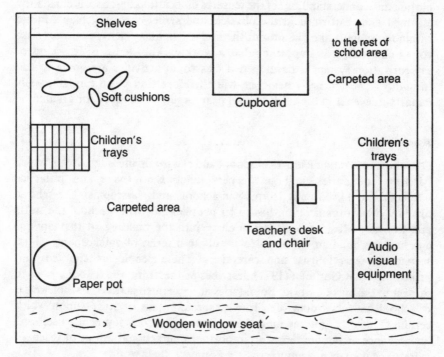

**Figure 7.3** Plan of a home-base in an open-plan primary school.

*Relationships between locations and activities*

Human beings are indomitable categorizers. We routinely devise categories for people, places and activities. The importance of this lies in the observation that certain categories are seen to 'go together'. Teachers, in the course of their routine work, see certain categories as going together, knowing this categorization system enables the smooth running of organized social activities. Schools in this sense are made up of complex interconnections of locations and activities. Teachers and children come to have specific understandings of the way things get done where and how. The teacher researcher concerned to uncover the spatial dimension of schools and classrooms might focus upon the expectations regarding locations, behaviour, and categories of people within the school system. Such a focus will enable us to see any discrepancies between the intended uses of particular locations and the way in which they are used in practice. All the time the teacher is concerned to describe what is actually going on in any school or classroom situation in relation to how the participants themselves orientate towards what they see to be happening. Here it is interesting to see the ways in which artefacts, furniture, signs, posters, and so on play a part in altering people to the actual nature of a particular location. In other words, participants' understandings of the features of locations in school is constantly affirmed and reaffirmed in the physical and symbolic arrangements found within the schools and classrooms themselves. In many cases, especially with young children, it is important that a working knowledge of this kind of categorization system is developed if classroom activities are going to run smoothly. The teacher researcher will therefore find these fundamentally important, even if in the event they appear largely to be taken for granted.

### Boundaries

One of the interesting features of school and classroom life is the way in which barriers, boundaries, and gatekeepers function to shape and influence interaction and eventually learning in schools and classrooms. The school, like any other organization, has to let people know where school life starts and finishes. Most schools secure entry into the building so that anyone entering the building will have to negotiate a series of gatekeepers, school secretaries, receptionists, and caretakers. These people are charged with protecting what Goffman (1971) describes as the 'front' the school wishes to present to the outside world. Boundaries are generated across the whole realm of school and classroom life. They generate arenas or stages upon which certain kinds of interactions take place. The development, use, and maintenance of boundaries is an important interactional aspect of teachers' work since it enables them to create an order to their worlds.

### Seating arrangements

These are obviously important aspects of class management. The issue here surrounds the ways in which seating arrangements, proximity of pupils to the teacher, and the position of the teacher in relation to the class or the group are seen to shape and influence the nature of interaction within the classroom. Sommer's work (1967; 1969) sought to establish a relationship between levels of participation and seating arrangements in the classroom. A number of studies on the gender dimensions of schooling and girls' poor performance in science subjects compared with boys point towards the marginality of girls in many mixed-sex classrooms in terms of being outside the 'action zone' (Turner 1982: 45). Again the teacher will need to prepare seating plans carefully, asking questions about the degree of choice the pupils are able to exercise, and also the kinds of interaction patterns that might seem to be related to where the pupil sits.

### Tracking teachers and pupils and time-sampling

In order to get at the normal use of space in any one classroom and the routine ways in which teachers and pupils make use of this space and interact with each other, a number of teachers in the past have made use of what might be described as tracking. This is an observational technique which involves an observer/researcher monitoring the teacher, pupil, or groups of pupils in the course of a single lesson, or whole school day in order to see the interactions and activities they become engaged in and the consequential use of physical space and places. While this technique will obviously produce fairly detailed data, the researcher has first to develop some way of noting, coding, or identifying the actions and locations in question. Here the researcher would do well to remember the kinds of criticisms that were made of systematic observation schedules like those of Flanders and ORACLE in Chapter 6. Our point would be that any attempts to track or log the teachers' or pupils' interactions and use of space would need to be combined with other more qualitative data. However, this tracking, mapping, and coding can be as flexible or as controlled as the researcher sees fit. Sally Lubeck (1985), for example, shows how this can be done in order to produce 'flow charts' of individual children's movements; use of spaces and activities in the course of the school day. Often a time-sampling technique can be incorporated into this approach whereby at certain prearranged regular intervals the teacher is logged in terms of her position or location in the classroom, or the tasks that the pupils are engaged in. Rivlin and Rothenberg (1976) in the study mentioned earlier made use of what they described as 'behavioural mapping', a 'naturalistic time-sample technique for describing patterns of activities and use of physical space'.

Another opportunity open to the teacher researcher is to focus upon one child's day and to follow the child through an ordinary day noting the interaction patterns, locations, and activities the child becomes engaged in. With care and an eye for detail, a fairly comprehensive 'natural history' of the child's day can be painted from which the teacher researcher can draw inferences about the importance of and orientations towards the spatial organization of school and classroom.

## Gender dimensions of classroom activities

There has been considerable research done into the different kinds of educational experience of girls and boys together with research into the reasons for girls' poor achievement in maths and science subjects compared with boys, see for example the Equal Opportunities Commission Research Bulletin 6 (Spring 1982). Clarricoates (1980), and Stanworth (1981). Most research has focused upon aspects of the hidden curriculum, teacher and pupil attitudes to subjects, and a general sexist bias in education. An important focus for the teacher researcher might be upon the gender dimension of school and classroom spatial organization. It may be that seating arrangements and the spatial/physical arrangement of the classroom will influence interaction patterns differently for boys and girls. If teachers are seen to spend more time with boys than girls how much of this might be to do with the spatial organization of the classroom? There is certainly much more research needed in this complex area, some of which may be done by teachers themselves. The point is, however, to consider the influence of gender variables in conjunction with other factors, including the spatial organization of the classroom, as influencing learning and, moreover, attitudes to learning.

## Subject or classroom tasks and spatial arrangements

Another important aspect concerns the actual subject of the lesson or alternatively the nature of the tasks the pupils are engaged in. The teacher researcher needs to bear in mind the general ethos surrounding the subject or activities in question and the teachers' and pupils' perceptions of what is involved. Clearly different kinds of lessons are likely to display different uses of space and spatial arrangements of classrooms when using these materials.

## Workshops with staff and parents

Finally it is worth making the point that the teacher researcher need never be on her own. Staff meetings with parents are useful points at which to bring up observations and ideas. Alternatively workshops designed to discuss particular issues may be arranged. Many teachers in the primary section have people helping them in the classroom, and as such they offer an important source of information on the setting as well. The workshop is a useful way of reminding ourselves where our research comes from.

These are just some of the ways in which the teacher might begin research into the spatial organization of schools and classrooms. The data obtained in the ways we have outlined above will probably need to be supplemented by other sources of data, using different techniques. The remaining question surrounds the analysis of these kinds of materials. The visual character of the data and descriptions which the teacher is likely to generate when looking at space and place raises some special issues. The teacher may wish to consult, for example, the highly influential work by Goffman (1971) *The Presentation of Self in Everyday Life* or to consider the guidelines, suggestions, and kinds of focus outlined in some of the published studies, for example King (1974: 201–9) or Hitchcock (1982).

By way of conclusion not only to this chapter on the spatial dimension of schools, classrooms, and learning, but also to this part of the book, we consider an American ethnographic study of early childhood education, or what we would describe broadly as nursery education.

## Case Study: Sally Lubeck, *Sandbox Society*

*A focus upon time and space in ethnographic research*

It seems fitting to end our discussion in this part of the book and our examination of space and education in this chapter by focusing upon one study. We have chosen Sally Lubeck's interesting and well-written book for a number of reasons. First, this book is based upon a doctoral thesis and shows how research for degrees may be turned into a published work. Second, the study makes use of the case-study, ethnography format and clearly shows how the researcher in such work can move backwards and forwards between description and explanation/analysis, an important theme of qualitative research we have encouraged teachers to develop throughout this part of the book. Third, by focusing upon two schools Sally Lubeck develops comparisons and hence shows how ethnographic research can throw light upon more general processes. Fourth, the overall research design of this work is clearly presented and while displaying certain weaknesses can provide the teacher researcher with a useful model or benchmark from which to develop her own work together with an insight into the research process itself. From within the context of early education in the USA the book deals in a sensitive way with the complex aspects of time, space, and interaction variables. *Sandbox Society* is an excellent example of the ethnographic approach to educational research.

Sally Lubeck's book is based upon studies of pre-school settings in suburban America. One is a pre-school centre where the children and teachers were white, the other is part of a Head Start programme with black teachers and children. The study was based on a year's fieldwork and her main focus was upon activities, materials, and teacher–pupil interaction together with the use of time and space. She aimed first to try and understand how poor minority black children actually adapted to a 'distinctive social history', how these adaptations were in fact reproduced in the black Head Start classroom, and how these were transmitted to the next generation. Second, she aimed to understand, conversely, the processes by which main-stream white middle-class cultural values were adopted and transmitted in a white pre-school not a mile away from the black Head Start school. Lubeck paints a picture of two very different experiences of pre-school education, of two different orientations to pre-school education, and ultimately pre-school education of differing quality. She comments on her book that

> The study that needs to be told is one that has no obvious beginning and seemingly no end, and so its rendering is but a pinprick in time. It is a story of a single city in the United States, a story of a suburb of that city, a story of two early education programs in that suburb, a story ultimately of the few people in the act of re-creating the social order by transmitting their values, attitudes and life orientations to the next generation. There,

185

near the sandbox, in this littlest of worlds, children take in cues of who they are and of what the world they will inhabit is like.

(Lubeck 1985: vi)

In order to try and unravel this complex issue Lubeck went for an anthropologically informed ethnographic study based upon the controlled comparison of the two classroom settings we described above. Her perspective sought to 'look at the day-to-day processes by which adults teach children to adapt to the reality which they themselves experience' (Lubeck 1985: 1). While the delineation and analysis of time and space relations, as lenses through which the social organization of a group or culture may be observed predominates in anthropological literature, this is largely missing from research in pre- and early school settings.

## *The research of 'Sandbox Society'*

If the teacher is writing for the purposes of some degree or other course, what is known as a review of the literature is normally regarded as a central aspect of the project or dissertation. It is useful in any case for the teacher to locate her research in current trends, ideas, and practices. Lubeck provides such a review of related literature in Chapter 2 of the book. This is important for a number of reasons, but perhaps most important of all is the way in which such a review of relevant related studies can serve as a comparison with the present research findings. This helps to locate a piece of research within the context of a broad research problem. The researcher aims here not at the production of extended, detailed reviews of every single study of the topic that she can find, but rather to set the scene noting the salient themes, topics, and findings of the research.

We have mentioned throughout this book the possible use by teachers of a pilot study in conducting small-scale school-based research. Lubeck conducted a four-month-long pilot study which involved close descriptions, many field notes, and some intensive in-depth formal interviewing of teachers in the context of a traditional integrated pre-school setting in an inner suburb of a large mid-western city. This was an exploratory study, but Lubeck had a major problem. She wished to investigate and develop, prior to conducting the case studies proper, a research methodology which would allow her to stop the action sufficiently 'in an environment where the wash of movement, activity and interaction could be overwhelming to the prospective observer' (Lubeck 1985: 51). How can the researcher, especially the qualitative ethnographic researcher whose work depends on involvement, be protected from being totally swamped and overwhelmed by the density of the data themselves in such settings? Lubeck's pilot study, which involved spending over 100 hours 'in the field' and the development of a series of flow charts of the activities of individual children, enabled Lubeck to come to some appreciation of the flux and to explore the possibilities of developing multiple methods for 'stopping the action'.

Lubeck's book is based upon a comparison of two case studies, one of a traditional white middle-class pre-school, the other a black Head Start centre. Lubeck developed the traditional role of participant observer taking field notes and making observations. She would record child–child and teacher–child interactions, analyse the classroom schedules and layouts of the school and, by means of flow charts, plot the children's activities and use of space. Lubeck also became involved in helping out in the routine day-to-day activities of school life. Noting the issue of validity in ethnographic research, Lubeck attempted to build in some validity checks. One of the important checks Lubeck employed here was to ask the teachers to read her field notes and in fact left space on the notes themselves for teachers to respond and to agree or disagree. As she became more established in the setting she began to discuss what she was seeing more openly with the staff. Lubeck's study is a good example of the way in which the researcher constantly moves backwards and forwards between description and analysis, between what is the case and why it is the case. Furthermore, the study shows how careful comparison of cases can be used to reveal crucial factors in children's pre-school educational experience which can influence their later educational careers and performance. Lubeck's study is important not only for the way in which the research was designed and carried out, but also for the contribution it makes to our understanding of time and space within an educational world.

## The use of time

Lubeck argues that in effect differing uses of time reflect different conceptualizations of time. In many ways much conventional educational research seemed to suggest that schools and classrooms were first educational institutions, and the participants, especially the pupils, were individuals. The ethnographic approach stresses that schools are socially generated organizations made up of complex layers of meanings which are created by the shared interpretative work of groups of people. Furthermore, a person's history and culture provide them with an orientation to the world and a way of handling that world. Lubeck suggests that time was used and understood in the two classrooms she explored in different ways and, as such, there were differing educational consequences (Lubeck 1985: 69). What is important for Lubeck is that each of the two schools she observed devoted differing amounts of time to differing activities, which, in turn, Lubeck is able to link to the individualistic orientations of the white middle-class pre-school and to the emphasis upon kinship and peer group loyalty on the part of teachers in the black Head Start school. Lubeck produces comparisons of the daily routine schedules in the schools and the amounts of time spent on each activity. Time-tabling differences show that in effect the Head Start school seemed to be reinforcing group values whereas the white middle-class pre-school was encouraging individual development. By using this approach Lubeck was able to examine the different weightings given to particular activities.

One of the neatest examples here is the way in which the concept of 'free play' is used and interpreted in very different ways in the two school settings. In the white middle-class pre-school it is clear to see how, in fact, much of the children's day is devoted to free play allowing the children the possibility and freedom to direct the nature of the activities they become involved in themselves. This resulted in minimal direct overt control by the adults in this school setting. By way of contrast 'free play' takes on a rather different character in the black Head Start school. Here free play involved the children playing on their own much of the time, enabling the staff to get on with administrative and other activities. These differences taken together with the amount of time devoted to 'free play' in the two schools point to some quite significant differences. Lubeck comments on this situation thus:

> Whereas the Head Start teachers value and practice reciprocal relations among peers, the pre-school teachers assume that their primary function is to establish relationships with the children and to facilitate their growth. Case histories reveal, however, that this is not merely a matter of educational training or of knowledge of psychological principles, rather it is an orientation that reflects their own socialization; each teacher had been the product of a nuclear family where the mother had not worked and where she had been the principal child rearer in the home.
>
> (Lubeck 1985: 81)

Again, Lubeck moves backwards and forwards between the situations she observes and the developing analysis of them. She demonstrates the ways in which methods of data collection and different types of data can be brought to bear on the same issue. Here we find a good example of triangulation since participant observation, staff case histories, interviews, conversations, and flow chart data are all combined to support and to check out the researchers' ideas, adding depth and density to the study.

*The use of space*

The problem for the ethnographer and educational researcher interested in space is well put by Howard Becker when he comments that we need to 'stop seeing only the things that are conventionally "there" to be seen' (cited in Wax and Wax 1971: 10): in other words to stop taking for granted what most of us take for granted most of the time. Again, in overcoming this problem, Lubeck made use of a multi-technique approach mixing observations with conversations, to build up data, extract ideas, and reflect upon them as the research progressed. This could then be related to earlier work in the area.

Lubeck focuses upon two different yet related apsects. First, descriptions of the physical arrangements of the classroom, that is the planned environment, noting the kinds of changes which take place day to day and week to week. Once more Lubeck makes excellent use of diagrams here to identify the uses of space in the settings. But these descriptions might only be able to give limited accounts of the dynamic uses of space in the actual school day. Alongside these general descriptions went intensive observation of how the spaces were used in practice, a matter of seeing through. For example she is able to comment upon the white middle-class Harmony Preschool that

> The environment is carefully planned and modified slightly from week to week. For example, a balance beam is set up next to the sand table one week; the beam is pushed against the wall to make way for a water table the next. ... The teachers keep material not in use in large cupboards against the back wall. These are unlocked each day, and different activities are set up in the different areas. ... Notably teachers and children share the same space. No separate area or desk is sectioned off for the teachers only. This utilization of space appears to be a physical manifestation of the form of social interaction practiced in the classroom.
>
> (Lubeck 1985: 84)

Second, the fluidity of the picture needed somehow to be captured. Here Lubeck makes extended use of flow charts which are constructed to demonstrate the movements of individual children as they went about the classroom together with timings of their use of given spaces. This was conducted over periods of time in order to establish some kind of consistency. Figure 7.4 shows a flow chart for 'Sue' taken from Lubeck's study.

Conversely it is possible to construct a flow chart of the teacher's movements in the classroom. This will reveal the amounts of time the teacher spends in particular locations and with groups of children or individual children. Flow charts of both children and teachers can then be compared thereby highlighting subtle and often taken-for-granted aspects of classroom organization.

## Summary

This chapter has made a case for the importance of space and place in schools and classrooms as issues worthy of attention by the teacher researcher. We have tried to show some of the ways in which the teacher researcher might profitably go about investigating this area and concluded the chapter by considering one study undertaken in this area. Since *Sandbox Society* (Lubeck 1985) is an important study it demonstrates what can be achieved by adopting the ethnographic qualitative framework for research in schools and classrooms we have been unravelling and advocating. It is possible to question the validity of Lubeck's findings and to criticize her theoretical

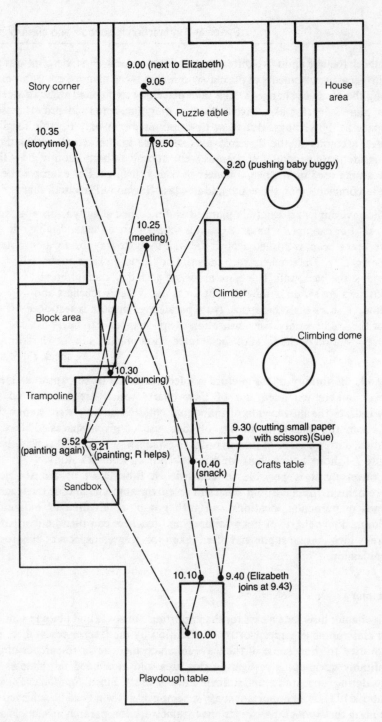

**Figure 7.4** Flow chart for 'Sue', Harmony Preschool

*Source*: Lubeck (1985: 47)

perspective, but the study is fundamentally a good example of ethnographic research design in school and classroom locations. We have tried to show in this short review how research works out in practice by focusing upon both the research design of Lubeck's study and some of her substantive findings. It is to be hoped that the complex yet simultaneously exciting aspects of ethnographic research in education will have been conveyed to the prospective teacher researcher. There is, of course, one important caveat. Sally Lubeck had all of the advantages together with the disadvantages that accrue from the role of outside researcher, and it would, of course, be difficult for the practising teacher to emulate such a piece of research. The teacher researcher will find much of interest in the findings of Lubeck's study, but also much by way of insight into the ethnographic research process itself. On these grounds it provides a fitting conclusion to our introduction to the main aspects of ethnographic qualitative research for the teacher researcher we have been unravelling in this part of the book.

We come now to reconsider the reality of teachers researching their own and others' schools and classrooms. Part III of the book seeks to unravel the links between research and practice in the context of the contemporary situation of the class teacher. This situation is one of conflicts of interest, confusion, rapid change, yet constraints of time, resources, and energy. Bearing these situations in mind, Part III clarifies the question of responsibilities, finding out, writing up and the dissemination of school-based research, and finally the context of school-based research in the 1980s and the future.

## Suggested further reading

There is no one text which deals exclusively with research into the spatial organization of schools and classrooms; however it may be useful to begin by considering some of the professional statements made in the *Plowden Report* (1967) *Children and their Primary Schools,* London: HMSO, and L. Weber (1971) *The English Infant School and Informal Education,* New York: Prentice-Hall, but both deal with the early years of schooling. Of the observational studies available, those by A. C. Berlak *et al.* (1976) 'Teaching and learning in English primary schools', in M. Hammersley and P. Woods (eds) *The Process of Schooling: A Sociological Reader,* London: Routledge & Kegan Paul and Open University; K. Evans (1974) 'The head and his territory', *New Society,* 24 October; and G. Hitchcock (1982) 'The social organisation of space and place in an urban open-plan primary school', in G. C. F. Payne and E. C. Cuff (eds) *Doing Teaching: The Practical Management of Classrooms,* London: Batsford, are of interest. General issues surrounding school architecture and learning are considered in M.Seabourne and R. Lowe (1977) *The English School: Its Architecture and Organisation, 1870–1970,* London: Routledge & Kegan Paul; and D. Bealing (1972) 'The organisation of junior school classrooms', *Educational Research* 14, 3: 231–5.

# Research and Practice

## Introduction

In this final part of the book we come to consider the practical aspects of teachers doing research and the changing nature of the context in which this will take place. Three sets of issues concern us here. While we treat them separately it will be clear to see how they are all linked to each other. First, we consider the question of access to research settings at a variety of levels and the ethnical problems of school-based research and the particular responsibilities of the teacher researcher. Second, we unravel the problems associated with writing up and disseminating school research and offer advice with practical guidelines. Finally, the current background against which teacher research operates is explored and some important questions for the future are posed. Although these may appear to be separate issues, a common theme connects them all: the links which the teacher has to a wider community both inside and outside school. Perhaps the most important issue which we raise, in general terms, is the question of the responsibility which the teacher researcher has to the subjects of the research and the wider profession.

In Chapter 8 we deal with access and ethics. In Chapter 9 we consider how to find out information during the research process, and how to approach writing up the material collected. In Chapter 9 we also deal with the crucial question of the dissemination of teacher research to colleagues and the wider educational community. By way of conclusion we tackle some of the issues raised by the recent changes in educational policy and provision and provision in Britain in the 1980s. This background of educational change in Britain has important implications for any research, of whatever description, the teachers is likely to engage in. We argue that during this period of change it is vital that research and reflection undertaken by the teacher is given its rightful role as one means of improving practice. We consider the role of school management and the local educational authorities in supporting research. Changes in INSET provision are also discussed. The chapter concludes by providing a summary of the main themes of the book.

# Chapter eight

# Access and ethics in school-based research

## Introduction

As the final part of the book is concerned with research and practice, in this chapter we try to unravel some of the complex but crucial aspects of the conduct of school-based research by the teacher. These issues ultimately come under two headings, namely access to the area or field being explored and the responsibilities and conduct of the researcher while doing the research. Access and ethics are therefore crucial aspects of teacher research and are as important as anything else we have been discussing in this book. Having said this the question of access and ethical responsibilities of researchers is no simple matter. While many of the questions we raise here have come up in previous chapters it is important for the teacher researcher to take a clear look at what is involved in gaining access to research situations and the kinds of responsibilities she has to the subjects of the research.

## Access to research situations

In Chapter 3 we emphasized the importance of entry to a field situation in ethnographic research and the need for the researcher to develop a credible role in the field. The problem will surround the ability of the researcher to develop a reasonable argument for doing a particular piece of research and gaining acceptance and co-operation from the parties concerned. Of course in school-based research a distinction would need to be drawn between those teachers who are already in the situations they wish to explore and those who are outside the immediate settings they want to focus upon. The further away from the research area the teacher is, the greater the problem of access.

Until fairly recently most research in schools has been carried out by outside professional researchers. In many ways these researchers were able to control the research process and, unlike many teachers, left the scene of the research once the data had been collected. However, teacher research raises quite different problems of access which can be so basic that the teacher researcher will have to consider them at the research design and initial preparatory stages of the project. To begin with the teacher will need to identify at an early point the relevant persons from whom permission will need to be obtained. A lot of work in the past has been held up or even had to be abandoned because an initial consideration of the question of access was not properly thought through. There may be said to be some fairly simple rules which are worth following in these matters.

First, the researcher must establish points of contact and individuals from whom it is necessary to gain permission. At this point it is important to establish exactly what activities are going to be observed and what documents will be examined. It may be necessary to obtain the support of immediate superiors or supervisors in order to facilitate this.

Second, the researcher must be as clear and as straightforward as possible in articulating the nature and scope of the projected study. This will have the effect of clarifying the demands which are likely to be made on the individuals or groups involved. Large complicated questionnaires can lie uncompleted on teachers' desks for some time, or an expected interview does not take place because it has been arranged at a particularly busy time. If the demands of the research are clearly established in the beginning then some of these problems may be offset.

Third, it is worthwhile trying to anticipate in advance any potentially sensitive areas or issues the research may focus upon and explain in advance how these are likely to be dealt with in the research.

Fourth, the teacher researcher must be sensitive to the hierarchy of the school or organization concerned, even if this is their own. Experience has shown that research projects have met problems when their aims and methods of data collection have conflicted with a superior's perceived area of jurisdiction and responsibility. As Holly (1984: 100–3) has observed, there may in fact be an in-built opposition between democratically conceived research and hierarchically structured schools! This may be a particular issue in research concerned directly with the relationships between practice and policy. The aim must be to resolve any such conflicts before you begin the research or as soon as potential areas of conflict arise during the course of the work.

Finally, the teacher researcher must also be aware that the aims and objectives of 'applied' or 'action' research are often to change practice in a particular direction. Such research may, whatever its good intention, appear to other colleagues to threaten or provide confirmation of their own professional practice. Hutchinson and Whitehouse (1986), arguing that the ultimate aim of such research is subversive, have advocated a more flexibly timetabled school day so that staff can discuss professional issues including that which can arise from teacher-based applied or action research.

However this is only a partial solution to the problem and we might add, given the current climate, difficult to realize. Certainly current changes and developments in schools, most notably the emergence of 'directed time', will put even greater pressures on the researcher influencing access and discussion.

Researchers, whether teachers or not, must take account of the fact that their activities take place within special social, political, and cultural contexts.

Even if therefore the object of the research may be restricted to helping the researcher's own practice, the above considerations need addressing at an early stage; even more so if the research design and conclusions have implications for other colleagues.

Teacher researchers may experience conflict between their own perceived, professional, and personal development and those of the school, local education authorities, or in the future, school governors. These differences may be difficult to reconcile. However, they will all influence access to the situations under study and the responses and feedback the teacher researcher is likely to obtain.

As we stated earlier, these rules are not hard and fast. Individual circumstances must be the final arbiter. As far as possible it is better if the teacher can discuss the research with all the parties involved. On other occasions it may be better for the teacher to develop a pilot study and uncover some of the problems in advance of the research proper. If it appears that the research is going to come into conflict with aspects of school policy, management styles, or individual personalities, it is better to confront the issues head on, consult the relevant parties, and make rearrangements in the research design where possible or necessary. It should by now be clear to everyone that in the future one will have to argue clearly and with conviction about the positive values of school-based research.

## The ethical conduct of school-based research

The teacher researcher, like all other social researchers, is a moral agent with views, opinions, values, and attitudes. It follows that the teacher conducting research in schools will be faced with ethical and moral dilemmas. What lengths can researchers go to in investigating their subjects? What rights do the subjects of a piece of research have? How can trust be established or confidentiality and anonymity be guaranteed? These and other questions will all emerge when considering the ethical conduct of school-based research.

It is generally recognized that specific ethical problems will emerge from the use of one or other research strategy or data-collection technique. The thrust of this book has been to explore the potential of interpretative research methodologies for school-based research. These approaches are described as qualitative or ethnographic. Since the researcher in such approaches is the major instrument or funnel through which data are obtained, it follows that qualitative research will pose special ethical questions for the teacher. Because the researcher is so close to the subjects of the research it follows that one of the main ethical questions posed by qualitative educational or teacher research is the researchers' responsibilities towards the subjects themselves, in our case teachers and pupils.

Participant observation is a good example to begin with. Participant observation can in fact take two forms. While we would encourage teachers to be as open as possible about their research and observation there are occasions and situations, even within an overt observational piece of research, when the teacher researcher will be involved in covert participant observation. This refers to a situation where, as Bulmer describes it,

> the researcher spends an extended period of time in a particular research setting concealing the fact that he is a researcher and pretending to play some other role. In such a situation, the identity of the researcher and knowledge of his work is kept from those who are being studied, who have no knowledge that they are being studied.
>
> (Bulmer 1982: 4)

There are arguably many situations in the course of ordinary school life where pupils are observed by teachers without the pupils' knowledge. Covert or overt participation as a research strategy will place the teacher in very different circumstances and therefore raises different ethical issues. These questions are not unique to educational research or teacher school-based research, and over the years an important debate has emerged surrounding the limits to deception in social research and the ethics of covert participation and this debate is worth considering briefly.

Bulmer (1982) has collected together a number of key articles in this debate. On the one hand there are those researchers like Erikson (1967: 366–73) who have argued that disguised observation actually compromises both the researcher and subject to an unacceptable degree. This in effect can amount to much the same thing as a doctor carrying out surgery on a patient without the patient's permission. For Erikson, disguised observation is simply bad science. In contrast however, Douglas (1976) has defended what he describes as 'investigative social research' as being quite often relatively harmless, and sometimes even necessary, being the only way to research some locations and situations.

Quite often ethical and methodological issues are inextricably interwoven in qualitative research as Jennifer Platt (1981c) and others have pointed out. Doing participant observation or interviewing one's peers raises ethical problems that are directly related to the nature of the research techniques employed. The degree of openness or closure of the nature of the research and its aims is one that directly faces the teacher researcher. For example the teacher researcher might wonder where formal observation ends and informal observation begins? Is it justifiable to be open with some teachers and closed with others as Hitchcock (1983b: 19–35) and Burgess (1984b) ask? How much can the researcher tell the pupils about a particular piece of research? Alternatively is it actually possible to involve the pupils in a study (Pollard 1987: 95–118)? When is a casual conversation part of the 'research data' and when is it not? Is gossip legitimate data and can the researcher ethically use material that has been passed to her 'in confidence'? The list of questions is endless yet they can be related to the nature of both the research techniques involved and the social organization of the setting being investigated.

These problems generated some heated discussion in the social sciences and studies by Festinger *et al.* (1956), Humphreys (1970), and Stanley Milgram's (1974) famous study of obedience, all point to the limits of deception in social research. Even if prospective teacher researchers follow Erikson and reject disguised research as both unethical and not applicable to their own very different relationship with the subjects of their research, problems of responsibilities will not go away. At the end of the day these questions come down to trust, confidentiality, and anonymity.

As we pointed out in Chapter 3, a central ingredient in the successful completion of ethnographic research is the establishment of good and effective field relations. This will involve the development of a sense of rapport between the researcher and subjects which will lead to feelings of trust and confidence. Inevitably the researcher will receive much information on trust from subjects and the researcher will have to develop some way of safeguarding the anonymity of the subject by, for example, the use of pseudonyms. It may even be necessary for the teacher researcher to assure the subjects that pseudonyms will be used in any subsequent written material. Where records or reports of individual children are concerned, it is of course absolutely essential to maintain anonymity thereby safeguarding the pupils involved. It is quite important for the teacher to step back from the research situation and to analyse carefully what the appropriate ethical response to a situation might be. The principals of confidentiality and anonymity can however resolve many of the ethical dilemmas the teacher researcher may find herself in. If the research has built up a good trusting relationship with the subject themselves this will carry with it certain rights, obligations, and responsibilities. Yet on the other hand the researcher might have more power, status, or authority than the subjects or might even hold widely differing values. All this would suggest the need for some kind of code of practice for school-based research. We would suggest that any such code would need to be based upon a recognition of three interrelated sets of responsibilities the teacher researcher has.

1 Responsibilities towards participants in the research.
2 Responsibilities towards professional colleagues and the teaching community.
3 Responsibilities to the sponsors of the research.

Balancing these responsibilities is hardly ever achieved with total satisfaction. It can be a complicated juggling act. One set of responsibilities can be met only to discover that they conflict with others. This has led many of the professional social science associations to attempt to develop acceptable 'codes of conduct' for their members to follow. The British Sociological Association's *Statement of Ethical Principles and their Application to Sociological Practice,* (1970) are possibly the most relevant to the kinds of situations the teacher researcher is likely to encounter and we have formulated a series of ethical rules for school-based research based upon this statement. While these 'rules' cannot cover every situation the teacher might encounter they will go some way towards resolving ethical problems of school-based research.

## Some ethical rules for school-based research

### Professional integrity

1 Ensure that the research you propose is viable, that an adeqate research design has been established, and appropriate data-collection techniques chosen.
2 Explain as clearly as possible the aims, objectives, and methods of the research to all of the parties involved.
3 If using confidential documents ensure that anonymity is maintained by eliminating any kinds of material or information that could lead others to identify the subject or subjects involved.

### Interests of the subjects

1 The researcher must allow subjects the right to refuse to take part in the research.
2 The researcher must demonstrate how confidentiality is to be built into the research.
3 If any or part of the research is to be published the teacher may need to gain the permission of the parties involved.
4 If the teacher is involved in joint or collaborative research then it is important to ensure that *all* researchers adhere to the same set of ethical principles.

### Responsibilities and relationships with sponsors, outside agencies, academic institutions, or management

1 If the research is 'sponsored', the researcher must be clear on the terms of reference and their own and their subjects' rights in relation to the finished research.
2 The teacher must be aware of the possible uses to which the research may be put.

(based on British Sociological Association 1973)

## *The teacher researcher or observer*

Given the issues that the above discussion raises about the ethical problems that arise from participant observation and allied qualitative techniques, what is the correct role for the teacher researcher? A teacher researcher cannot, in investigating her own or her colleagues' practice, achieve the role of 'non-participant observation' that King (1978) adopted in his study of infant classrooms. Unlike a researcher such as King, the teacher researcher is normally always an active participant in a given situation. Nor are they likely to be able to achieve the role of 'participant as observer' that researchers into school practice such as Hargreaves (1967) and Lacey (1970) adopted. The teacher is normally a researcher and an informant at the same time.

In a sense the nearest model or ideal type in qualitative research to that of teacher researcher is that of the complete participant. Here the researcher disguises her aim and opts for a covert operation to secure the necessary data. Now it would be possible though not desirable for teachers to adopt this model. Apart from some of the ethical issues already raised, the adoption of such a role would limit severely the scope of the research. For example it would make interviewing other subjects virtually impossible. Again access to certain kinds of data may be difficult to obtain unless an explanation is given. Of course one can take the question of openness to absurd lengths and being an active participant means that one is bound to observe relevant material for data collection all the time. The key question here is that would being covert compromise the researcher in her professional duties? Another way of looking at this is would the data collected and results have been different if the research had been open, not secret?

The normal relationship between the roles of 'insider' (observation) and 'outsider' (analysing data) with the researcher stepping into one role and then out into another are also difficult for the teacher investigating practice. The sharp distinction between the two roles is considered crucial to avoid the researcher becoming over identified with the group she is studying and assist data collection.

Teachers must however be identified in given situations with fellow subjects by the very nature of their work and culture. Yet it can be argued that the role of participant observer involves a clash of roles that can be resolved only if that of the 'outsider' is emphasized.

Teacher researchers need therefore to be aware of the two roles that participant observation involves and be able to overcome any conflict during the research process by adopting as open an approach as possible.

## Summary

In this chapter we have tried to outline the problems of access and ethics in school-based teacher research. These difficulties are not unique to teacher researchers but ultimately face all social research. The teacher researcher has to make up her own mind that she has resolved these issues satisfactorily. We would, however, not want to end on a negative note since much of positive value can emerge from a close look at the questions of access and ethics in school-based research, as Burgess has indicated:

Ethical and political dilemmas are not confined to one particular stage of the research process. Indeed ethical issues highlight the problems that occur throughout the research process. However, the way in which the teacher researcher resolves these problems may involve him knowing more about himself, the way in which he works, and the processes that occur within the institution in which he is located?

(Burgess 1980: 171)

## Suggested further reading

The whole issue of the ethical conduct of social and educational research is a complex one. Some key methodology texts that make reference to ethics which are worth consulting include M. A. Rynkiewich and J. P. Spradley (eds) (1976) *Ethics and Anthropology: Dilemmas in Fieldwork,* New York: Wiley, and R. Wax (1971) *Doing Anthropology: Warnings and Advice,* Chicago: University of Chicago Press. Works relating to ethical issues arising from general ethnographic, qualitative research techniques include M. Bulmer (ed.) (1982) *Social Research Ethics: An Examination of the Merits of Covert Participant Observation,* London: Macmillan, which contains many of the classic articles in the debate, and R. G. Burgess (1984) 'Ethical problems, ethical principles and field research practice' in R. G. Burgess, *In the Field: An Introduction to Field Research,* London: Allen & Unwin. Particular research strategies raise special ethical issues. J. Powney and M. D. Watts (1984) 'Reporting interviews: a code of good practice', *Research Intelligence,* September, contains some sound practical advice. On the other hand J. Platt (1981) 'On interviewing one's peers', *British Journal of Sociology* 32, 1: 75–91, has some sobering thoughts. Ken Plummer has approached the ethical questions raised by the use of personal documents: 'A research morality', in K. Plummer (1981) *Documents of Life: An Introduction to the Problems and Literature of a Humanistic Method,* London: Allen & Unwin. Increasingly the ethics of school-based research and the subsequent 'ownership' of knowledge has featured in many reports: the accounts by S. J. Ball (1985) 'Participant observation with pupils', in R. G. Burgess (ed.) *Strategies of Educational Research: Qualitative Methods,* Lewes: Falmer Press; R. G. Burgess (1984) 'The whole truth: some ethical problems in the study of a comprehensive school', in R. G. Burgess (ed.) *Field Methods in the Study of Education,* Lewes: Falmer Press; and A. Pollard (1985) 'Opportunities and difficulties of a teacher-ethnographer: a personal account', in R. G. Burgess (ed.) *Field Methods in the Study of Education,* Lewes: Falmer Press, are all excellent.

# Chapter nine

# Finding out, writing up, and dissemination

## Introduction

Once the teacher researcher has worked through the issues of research design, data collection, and data analysis and has in effect finished the research, the question of what comes next looms large. Usually the term 'writing up' is applied to the translation of the raw research and its findings into a readable and professional account. Linked with this process of writing up are a number of activities surrounding the location of further information and literature on the teacher's research area. This might loosely be described as finding out and refers specifically to the location of relevant literature and information. Teacher research, as we have argued, comes from and inevitably goes back to professional practice. It is vital that the research the teacher has done does not remain stuck on a shelf and forgotten. 'Dissemination' is the term used to describe the transmission and communication of research findings. In this chapter we concentrate therefore upon finding out, writing up, and the dissemination of the teacher researcher's findings and ideas. As such this discussion should prove of value not only to teachers doing independent research but those doing research as part of a further qualification in the form of a report, dissertation, or thesis.

It will perhaps be best if the reader considers this chapter alongside the sections on research design in Chapter 2 since many good pieces of research have floundered on bad storage of material, inappropriate use of libraries, or poor presentation. The needs of the modern teacher undertaking research or evaluation means that a flexible yet systematic approach is required. Part of this approach therefore relies upon the skills of information collection, storage, and presentation. One of the underlying points of school-based research is that the teacher researcher will at some point confront professional colleagues with the findings and implications of the research. Certainly the style of this presentation will be important since many of the teacher's colleagues will not be familiar with an 'academic' style of presentation. Alternatively an increasing amount of teacher research is being published in the professional journals and here the principles of article writing and presentation will need to be adhered to. The result of developments in the teacher researcher movement has meant that existing models of writing up have been modified and new ways created. It is therefore important for the reader of this chapter to recognize what aspects will apply to any particular case. This will depend upon the nature of the research the teacher has been conducting, the aims and objectives of that research, and the prospective audience or recipients of the research findings. We begin by examining the more conventional and formal aspects of writing up and presentation and conclude by examining some of the alternative approaches which have developed and the problems associated with the dissemination of school-based teacher research. However, to begin with finding out and writing up involves at a very basic level study skills and this is the point at which we start.

### Study Skills

In the course of any piece of research the teacher is going to come across published reports, articles, official information, and a range of document-ation. In dealing with these materials ways of note-taking, skimming and speed-reading, and reading for effective understanding will be helpful. We have all tended to acquire our own versions of these skills whether it be at school, college or work. Few of us have either done this systematically or understood the underlying principles. These are skills which can always fruitfully be reconsidered. Two useful texts here are *Use Your Head* (Buzan 1982), which provides a good introduction to study skills and note-taking and is very useful during the planning stage of a piece of research, and *Read Better, Read Faster* (DeLeeuw and Deleeuw 1965), which offers an excellent introduction to the techniques of 'skimming' and more effective reading generally.

Once the researcher develops these study skills it will become apparent how much easier many of the tasks of finding out and writing up will become. Many of the initial ideas, theories, and suggestions for school-based research will come from issues prompted by existing research, reports, or other sources of information. The teacher researcher of course always has to relate this back to her own circumstances. At this point it is important to know how to go about organizing a literature search.

### How to organize a literature search

In Chapter 5 we highlighted some of the aspects of using documentary sources and pointed to the problems involved in locating written and oral sources. Here we will concentrate mainly upon published materials including books, articles in journals, and theses. A prerequisite of most research is the presentation of a written report, often in the form of a thesis or dissertation; in-service courses and evaluation projects will also entail some form of oral or written report. It will of course be necessary to find, collate, and evaluate this material; three questions will therefore appear at the start of a piece of school-based research.

1 How and where can one find the relevant publications?
2 How can one avoid getting lost in the material?
3 How can one record information about the material in a clear and systematic way, which can be used days, weeks, months, or even years later with success?

We will try to answer some of these questions. The starting-point is of course with the library.

### Access to libraries

In Britain the teacher will have access to both public and academic libraries including university, polytechnic, and college libraries. These will vary considerably in the range of books and journals stored and services provided. In Britain all public and academic libraries can draw upon the services of the British Lending Library, which can arrange for inter-library loans of books and journals not immediately available from their own shelves. You may need to ask for special permission to use the services of academic libraries, especially if you wish to borrow books, but outside the city central libraries they will provide the best source for bibliographies, abstracts, and collections of key journals. A visit to the libraries concerned and a talk to the library staff about the range of services and facilities provided is a good first step. A useful guide here is *Study and Library Facilities for Teachers: Universities, Institutes and Schools of Education*, Hull Institute of Education (annually).

### Planning a library search

A review of the relevant literature as well as often being a course requirement is an important element of a researcher's work. This will mean initial and subsequent library searches. At the start it is important to bear in mind the following points.

1 Define precisely the topic to be studied as clearly as possible. The initial library search will more than likely open up new avenues making a subsequent visit necessary.
2 Be clear about the parameters of the search and avoid becoming side-tracked. The comments we made on 'locating a field' in Chapter 4 are valuable here for this reason.

   Further questions arise. Is the research going to be limited to British publications? Is it going to be limited to recent publications on a given topic, for example over the past ten years? (It is of course important to be flexible on these issues as the research develops.) Authors, bibliographies, and reviews of literature are often useful introductions to the key works in any field, since they put the researcher in touch with general findings, ideas, and current thinking on particular issues, thereby providing an important background framework.

3 The most usual cataloguing system used in British libraries is the Dewey Decimal System, though libraries often modify the basic layout to suit their own requirements.

4 British libraries use either a card index or microfiche index (or both) as a means of cataloguing their stock. It will be organized under both subject classification and author's name so that one can follow up leads from two angles. Both will indicate where physically in the library the books and materials are shelved by the use of a classification number. When beginning a library search on a new topic with only minimal knowledge, the subject classification provides the best way to locate a book or article. For example, if the teacher was beginning research on the topic of *Appraisal and Target Setting*, the obvious starting-point would be the subject classification index under *Education*, and then the sub-heading *Education Management*. However, one may find that another related sub-heading *Teachers* or *Teacher Performance* may be of use. It is important to be prepared to widen the search within the sub-classification if necessary and even move into a new classification area. In the example given above this could be *Management*.

One of the most daunting and indeed frustrating aspects of research is finding relevant literature. Hours can be spent searching through dusty book shelves in dark basements to turn up only one or two texts of any use and these might turn out to have only one or two relevant sections. Obviously this is an element of the research and writing process but it can become very time-consuming and is often not cost-effective. What is needed is a systematic approach. The research community and libraries have recognized this and produced bibliographies, abstracts, and guides to finding materials. However, these are themselves daunting publications; we have therefore listed below some of the key guides and publications it would be useful for the teacher to consult.

*Bibliographies*

Books

1 Walford, A.J. (ed.) (1982) *Guide to Reference Material* (4th edition).
2 *British National Bibliography* (since 1950). This is a cumulative series of volumes so it is important to consult the index. The Dewey decimal number is also recorded in the BNB and because classification numbers sometimes change it is necessary to check these for each year.

3 *United States Library of Congress, Books* (quarterly) *Periodicals*
4 *British Education Index* (quarterly). Since 1976 the more general format of this has been replaced by one which makes it essential to use the detailed subject index..
5 *British Humanities Index.*
6 *Ulrich's International Periodicals Directory.*

## Abstracts

The main difference between an abstract and an index is that abstracts provide useful summaries of the work listed. The researcher could initially consult Ulrich and Walford cited above and then discuss what abstracts are available for the particular subjects to be investigated. We have listed below some of the main abstracts.

1 *Child Development Abstracts and Bibliography*, University of Chicago Press, since 1972.
2 *Current Index to Journals in Education.*
3 *Language Teaching and Linguistics Abstracts*, Cambridge University Press, since 1975.
4 *Psychological Abstracts*, American Psychological Association, since 1927.
5 *Research into Higher Education Abstracts* since 1982.
6 *Sociology of Education Abstracts* since 1965.

## Theses

A lot of research conducted by teachers themselves appears in theses and dissertations for degrees. The following works are therefore worth consulting in order to see what research has been done in a particular area.

1 *Current Research in Britain*, British Library Board.
2 *Dissertation Abstracts.*
3 *Index of Theses* (submitted) ASLIB annually with supplements since 1950.

## Keeping Records

An essential aspect of any research activity is the systematic organization of the information and materials which have been collected. This is especially important where literature and references are concerned. References and notes written down on bits of paper stand the risk of getting lost or destroyed. A simple card index system is the easiest solution. We discussed the issues surrounding the organization of field notes in Chapter 3 and many of the points we made there apply here. The researcher needs to develop an organized and systematic approach to ordering information collected outside the field so that it can be retrieved easily at a later point. The best size of card for this purpose is eight by five inches. Additional sheets can always be stapled to the cards later. The cards should list all the bibliographical details, provide accurate copies of any quotations, and list contents of books or articles. It is important to provide all the details of the book or article including the author's surname, forename, date of publication, title of the book or article, publisher or title of the journal, place of publication, page numbers, and volume and part numbers. For purposes of securing a book through the inter-library loans system, the ISBN number is useful. Hence reference to a book would look like this

Milman, D. (1986) *Educational Conflict and the Law*, Croom Helm, Beckenham, ISBN–7099–3521–8

and reference to an article in a journal would look like this

Barrow, R. (1986) 'Empirical research into teaching: the conceptual factors', *Educational Research*, 28, 3, November, pp. 270–7.

If the teacher researcher keeps these records properly and consistently as the reading and research goes on, it will make the process of referencing the final report much easier. It is useful to draw a distinction between references and a bibliography.

References have to be made in the text to any source which is cited in the report, while a bibliography is placed at the end of the report and lists in alphabetical order all of the sources which have been referred to and consulted during the course of the research and referenced in the report. However, reports come in a number of forms. They can list all known current material on a given topic, the sources consulted in a piece of research whether used in the text or not, or they can list works of a particular author. In preparing a report of research the kind of bibliography the teacher researcher includes will depend upon the nature of the research.

Referencing often causes difficulties and the main reason for this is that there are a number of different methods of referencing. The teacher researcher will in the course of reading discover a variety of referencing systems. What is important for the teacher researcher is that the method of referencing adopted is consistently adhered to. One of the most straightforward methods, and one which is common in scientific and social scientific writing, is the 'Harvard system'. Using this system the complete references to an article or a book appears at the end of the article or book. The author's surname and date of a piece of work is given in the text and would read for example, as 'Stenhouse (1975) has argued ... '. If that author published more than once in a given year letters are added as in 1975a, 1975b, etc. The main advantage of this system is that it does not hinder the flow of the argument. The full list of references should be given at the end of the chapter, article or book (in alphabetical order) and page numbers can be added in the text in the case of a substantial quotation or a passage that draws heavily upon one author's work.

While this is common for reports and articles and in the scientific works it may be inappropriate for dissertations and theses and it is important to consider the regulations involved prior to beginning the research. A particular institution may wish you to follow the numbered note or British system where each bibliographical reference is numbered (1), (2), (3) etc. according to its appearance in the text. A full complete entry should be given either at the bottom of the page (normal in theses and dissertations) or at the end of the chapter, article, or book. This would include the author's name and title, though specific references can be appropriately abbreviated, using short titles. The question of the appropriate use of quotations, correct forms of footnoting, and the use of bibliographies is clearly discussed in Turabin (1980).

Particular attention needs to be paid to the use of quotations in a text. The problem is most marked with secondary sources which are useful for supportive illustrations and information. It is best to avoid using long quotations since these take up much valuable space that could otherwise be used for the teacher's own ideas. The point to bear in mind is that a string of quotations, however well edited, is no substitution for the teacher's own empirical work and ideas. Even when conducting a literature review, attempts to paraphrase the works being reviewed and to develop a synthesis of the materials and ideas around some key points is much better from both the teacher's and the reader's point of view.

As far as footnotes are concerned the form most appropriate to the particular piece of research needs to be worked out. Once this has been decided it is important to be consistent and not to let the footnotes become a bugbear. Generally reports and articles need no or few footnotes and these are usefully placed at the end of the piece. Longer studies need more extensive footnoting either at the end of a chapter or, as is normal in the case of a thesis, at the bottom of each page. In the latter case the writer will need to find out from the institution involved what the particular 'house style' is. The same applies to articles submitted to journals for publication.

## The writing process

As we have already noted, mastering an understanding of research design and techniques of data collection is only one side of the research equation. The other side involves the teacher researcher communicating her findings, ideas, and suggestions to an audience. This is just as important as the actual research itself. The teacher researcher will therefore have to consider seriously the way in which her findings are to be written up and presented. This is, after all, part of the process of reflection upon professional practice. The first question to consider is the nature of the written report itself and second, the nature of the audience for whom the report is intended. In this sense the teacher researcher will be subject to some of the same rules that apply to the presentation of academic work. Part of the problem lies in the nature of the research and kinds of data collected. Becker and Geer (1982) highlight the differences involved in presenting different types of data.

> When fieldwork ends, the observer will already have done a great deal of analysis. He must now put his material into such a form that a reader will understand the basis on which he has arrived at his conclusions. While statistical data can be summarised in tables and descriptive measures can often be reported in the space required to print a formula, qualitative data and their analytical procedures are often difficult to present. The former methods have been sytematised so that they can be referred to in this shorthand fashion and the data have been collected for a fixed, usually small, number of categories. The presentation need be nothing more than a report of the number of cases to be found in each category.
>
> (Becker and Geer 1982: 24)

The major dilemma facing the teacher researcher making use of qualitative materials is therefore how best to avoid an exclusive reliance upon illustrative and anecdotal examples. Ethnography has at its heart description, but this description is theoretically informed. Description must always therefore be balanced with analysis. This is undoubtedly a skill that is learnt. We stressed that the teacher researcher will often be simultaneously involved in the processes of data analysis while collecting the data. The final text then will not only display these elements of the research but the teacher's abilities to communicate in written form effectively. At the end of the day the model which the teacher researcher adopts for the written presentation of the research will depend upon the data obtained, the problems being studied, and the audience who will read the report. There are a number of ways in which the teacher researcher can present her 'findings' and we will now consider some of these.

## The research report

The writing of a research report is perhaps the least problematic though not necessarily the easiest form of research discourse. It is possible to provide a plan of the research report highlighting the key aspects and ingredients of such reports.

The classic model for a research report

1  An outline of the research project

2  A review of previous work in the field in order to place the new research in context.
3  A precise statement of the range and scope of the research outlined.
4  A description of the methods employed in the research.
5  Clear presentation of the data and a discussion of implications.
6  Summary and conclusions.
7  List of references. (Based on Nisbet and Entwhistle 1984: 253)

Obviously the form that a research report will take depends very much on the nature of the research and the data involved. It may be that an appendix is used to place conveniently material that would clutter the main text so that it can be referred to by the reader. The framework provided by Nisbet and Entwhistle (1984) is a useful one. By their very nature research reports are concise illustrations of the whole of the research and the researcher needs to convey this in as clear and readable a fashion as possible. If the teacher researcher is dealing with a more practical or applied concern then the relationship of the research to school or classroom practice will become a key element of the report. Also uppermost in the mind of the teacher researcher will be the audience being addressed. This may therefore involve the researcher in clearly defining any technical or specialist terms, and providing as far as possible a jargon-free text.

In applied research the question of presentation and organization of research material is therefore a crucial issue as the intention of such research is to improve practice by directly involving those within the educational process to reflect upon, evaluate, and perhaps change their practice. In such research a useful organizing principle is often to be found within the issue or series of issues. This usually leads to a different approach to the dissemination of research findings from what is common in more conventional research. One is looking less for universal generalizations than for discrepancies between what people say and do and between school policy as stated and school policy as practised. Another difference is that the balance advocated earlier between description and analysis, action and structure might be difficult to achieve with more applied research (Walker, 1985). Stake, for example, has argued that in an evaluation study 'what the evaluator has to say cannot be both a sharp analysis of high priority achievement and a broad and accurate reflection of the programme's complex transactions. One message crowds out the other' (Stake as quoted in Walker (1985: 163). In endorsing this Walker adds perceptively that

> the same point is generally true in research studies: the kind of investment of time and other resources necessary to complete a survey or testing programme, or to carry out a detailed enthography, rarely leaves room for a full portrayal of the whole context within which the study was made, a choice has to be made between breadth and depth.

(Walker 1985: 164)

Applied educational researchers have experimented with a number of different ways of communicating research information. Teacher researchers should however be alerted to the problems raised by the heavy selection of materials and the consequent potential for distortion. Criteria for the selection of data must always be spelled out.

## Theses, dissertations, long essays, and school-based projects

In a number of situations the teacher researcher may well be working with a supervisor or another professional. In this situation a working relationship develops between both parties. An action plan for writing up for a degree or professional qualification might take the following form:

1 A preliminary 'brain-storming' session with sheets of paper writing down key ideas and concepts. Out of this should emerge a basic plan of the shape of the written text, including main and supportive theoretical constructs and concepts. However, as we observed in Chapter 3 when discussing the analysis of qualitative materials, a thorough knowledge of and acquaintance with the materials is crucial. This will mean reading them through many times.

2 A more detailed plan can then be attempted which should include a chapter or themes, each broken down into main and subheadings (even if in the actual project the researcher may not wish to use these). It is also possible at this stage to detail paragraph content in note form.

3 A review of the research data and comparison with the plan, looking for omissions and inconsistencies in argument. Care must be taken to ensure a flow between narrative, data presentation, and analysis so that as few loose ends as possible are left, or when they are left, that account is taken of them.

4 A final working plan will now appear which should be carefully looked at again not only for omissions which may still occur and for weakly supported and over- or under-theorized descriptions, but also for examples of over-use of quotations, for ideas that may be a favourite 'hobby horse' but are not relevant to the current research (the prejudice syndrome) and above all for ensuring that what you mean to say is in fact conveyed adequately by the text in front of you.

This of course does not exhaust the problems involved in the writing process but provides a helpful checklist. In the end though writing is a creative act and it is important to retain some of this creativity. One of the ways in which this can be done is by using the case study format for writing up school-based teacher research.

*The case study format*

The case study has been a widely used approach in many disciplines both academic and practitioner. As a consequence the term has come to mean different things to different people. For most people the case study's major characteristic is its concentration upon a particular instance in order to reveal the ways in which events come together to create particular kinds of outcomes. The organizing principle involved is the isolation of a set of events and relationships which are described within a given framework of ideas and procedures which are appropriate to cases of that kind. Put another way a case study evolves around the in-depth study of a single case, event, or a series of linked cases or events over a defined period of time, the aim being to try and locate the 'story' of a certain aspect of social behaviour in a particular location and the factors influencing this situation so that themes, topics, or key variables may be isolated and discussed. What may be described as the 'situation' – the immediate present and past factors, interactions, and ideas surrounding the event or set of events in question – becomes the focus of attention. It follows from this that a case study, as a product of social or educational research, is likely to have the following characteristics:

1  A concern with the rich and vivid description of events within the case.
2  A chronological narrative or description of events within the case being studied and leading up to that case.
3  An internal debate between the description of events and the analysis of events described.
4  A focus upon particular individual actors or groups of actors and their perceptions and accounts.
5  A focus upon particular individuals and particular happenings within the case.
6  The integral involvement of the researcher in the case.
7  A particular mode of presentation that is able to capture the parameters of the case.

While the case study approach involves a certain kind of research orientation to inquiry it also offers quite a productive framework for writing up school-based research. Figure 9.1 therefore offers a guide to the way in which a case study may be both carried out and written up in the context of an in-service BEd degree (CNAA) at Humberside College of Higher Education and Doncaster Metropolitan Institute of Higher Education.

## Dissemination

One of the major issues in the whole area of INSET work, short courses, and teacher school-based research is the problem of the dissemination of the

All correspondence to be addressed to the Chief

...tudy of a school, the parents, the local
...es concerned with welfare. The study
...lustrate and (b) evaluate the way in which a
...ol responds to issues, problems, or situations
...pupils' progress or behaviour at school.

...propriate method to use is the 'case study' approach so that
...signment is related to either
 a particular issue confronting the school, or
 a particular set of circumstances affecting an individual or
 group of pupils.
Your study would normally fall into three sections.
1 A discussion which contexts the issue/problem you have
  chosen which draws upon relevant background material.
2 The narrative of the case study as known by you including the
  actions and viewpoints of different parties involved, e.g.
  parents, teacher(s), headteacher, EWO, social worker, etc.
3 An analysis and critical evaluation of the responses of the
  different parties involved in the particular issue or problem.
  Your conclusion might highlight possible alternative responses in the light of your own experience and relevant
  background reading.

Note
This approach assumes that the study will be concerned with information which is normally
available to the school/teacher and therefore need not entail a special investigation into an
individual child's background or circumstances. You will normally be expected to use your present
school for the study; however some students may wish to base their study upon a school where
they have had previous professional experience.

**Figure 9.1** Case Study on school, community and agency relationships

information and findings so gained. Very often we have heard teachers
complaining about 'one-off' courses and about the ways in which insights and
practical knowledge gained from courses get forgotten or lost in the
individual's school system, and how frequently it is not shared or discussed by
the school as a whole or the relevant staff. This situation is especially
regrettable where visits to other schools are involved. The problem is basically
one of the dissemination or sharing of professional knowledge. The research
the teacher becomes engaged in is just as susceptible to these problems as the
whole range of INSET work by teachers. The problem is exacerbated with

teacher research since the complete report may in fact disappear as part of a degree, or certainly be too long for easy digestion by other staff in school. The whole area is therefore one which needs careful consideration. One way of approaching this is to ask two key questions.

*First, if teachers do learn from each other how can research and reflection be made more widely available to practioners?* Within an individual school it should be possible to do this via staff meetings, committees, memoranda, and course materials. Groups of schools can even form networks which can undertake joint research, exchange ideas, and help to validate any research findings and to develop evaluation. By doing this it will become possible to build up a bank of information on local practice which could provide valuable and even generalizable material for comparative studies in educational practice. Some of these networks do exist locally and often arise and an *ad hoc* basis after an in-service course for example, but a more systematic approach would get around the problem of good work and practice being known only to a few interested people. In Chapter 10 the possible role of LEAs in this area will be discussed. Two main kinds of dissemination systems exist, one based on internationally or nationally stored resources and the other based on a particular school or college. ERIC (Educational Resources Information Centre) and BLEND (British Library Electronic Network Development) are examples of the former. BLEND is a form of electronic publishing originally intended for scientists but some experiments are taking place to include teacher researchers (contact BLEND Project, Loughborough University, Leicester). An example of the second bases of dissemination is the Sunnyside Project which developed the idea of establishing data bases in a school research programme using both action research and case study approaches. Two data bases were developed. One was a collection of resources housing documents, tapes, books, etc. which were built up to support the project within the school; this collection concerned data on both the content and the processes of the project. The second data base was housed in the mainframe of the computer and project team members devised a record format which was relevant to the conducting of action research; these records were regularly updated to form a projected data base (Bell and Colbeck, 1984).

The idea of action research utilization was also explored in a Schools Council Programme 2 Feasibility Study (Bell, 1982). Here three types of data base were cited:

1 *INTERACTIVE* – that is an individual or personal data base housed on a micro-computer.
2 *COLLABORATIVE* – that is groups or networks sharing information between institutions using micro-computer links.
3 *INDEPENDENT* – that is a central agency with a mainframe into which the various findings of individual or collaborative action research and

evaluation can be housed and then utilized by those with access to the mainframe.

*Second, can action research provide the necessary objective standards required for sufficient generalizations to be made?* Partly the answer to this question lies in the kind of research undertaken and partly in the way in which it is disseminated and used. For example, as we have argued, the case study approach is one which does not aim for universal generalizations and is focused on specific problems. However, when a large number of case studies on a particular issue have been done it is very likely that some practical generalizations could be drawn. Furthermore, if individual teachers or groups of teachers had access to other teachers' research on a topic of mutual interest they might find it useful for corroboration or for comparison. The establishment of local, regional, and national data bases for such research results will be very important if school practice is to advance as a result of teacher-based research in the future.

Bell has recently advocated a form of action research called 'action inquiry' which merges elements from both action research and case study approaches to develop a more coherent strategy in assessing professional knowledge (G.H. Bell, 1985). He outlines four criteria of rigour and it is important to note that accessibility to data for comment and use by others is a vital element.

*credibility* – the study must be believable by those who are competent to judge the subject of investigation
*transferability* – the study must be able to promote the exchange of experience from one practitioner to another; lessons must be capable of being learned from the evidence provided.
*dependability* – the study must be trustworthy through having gathered evidence by reliable procedures.
*confirmability* – the study must be capable of being scrutinized for absence of bias by making its evidence and methods of analysis accessible.

(G.H. Bell 1985: 181)

By doing this, Bell argues, another dimension can be added to the concept of the teacher as researcher. 'Action inquiry' is therefore aimed at developing new knowledge, solving practical difficulties, and validating available knowledge.

Another angle to this question is the relationship between outside researchers and teacher researchers in schools and colleges. Here much research is conducted after negotiation between outside researchers and teachers and it is worth mentioning the 'triangulation' approach developed at the University of East Anglia as a way of conducting research which involves outside researchers, teachers, and others. Here the data collected can be fed back to participants themselves for comment and interpretation.

One of the easiest ways in which some of these difficulties might be resolved for school-based research is through developing and utilizing a framework or schedule whereby teachers can provide a synopsis or an outline of the work they have been engaged in. This would facilitate the dissemination of teacher research and its findings within the school, the Local Educational Authority, or even wider still, nationally. In any case this would seem to be part of one of the central aims of any school-based research as we conceive of it: the development of professional knowledge. The pro forma shown in Figure 9.2 may therefore be seen as a guide to providing the sort of information that other teachers and interested parties may comprehend quickly and easily. Obviously there is considerable scope for the use of word processors here.

## Summary

In this chapter we have been exploring the practical sides of school-based teacher research. Finding out, writing up, and dissemination are important

Name of principal researcher
Names of other researchers
Keywords
Name of school
Name of headteacher
Names of relevant/involved advisers
Names of key individuals
Details of the area

Title of research
Outline of research
1 Aims of research
2 Methodology employed
3 Data collected
4 Kinds of analyses developed
Current stage of research
Findings to date

Policy implications
Curriculum implications
Classroom implications

Future plans

**Figure 9.2** Schedule for documentation of school-based research

ingredients in the total concept of school-based teacher research. We have paid special attention to the development of study skills using libraries, keeping records, and referencing. The writing process was explored and the principal modes were outlined and discussed. It was argued that the case study offered teacher researchers not only a useful approach to research, but also an interesting way of writing up certain kinds of school-based research. Finally the important issue of dissemination of research findings was discussed in terms of some of the examples from action research and case study work in schools and classrooms. A pro forma was included which it is hoped might become more widely used in teacher research in the future.

## Suggested further reading

The art of writing effective notes can be much improved by consulting T. Buzan (1982) *Use your Head*, London: BBC, Ariel Books. Improving your reading techniques can be explored through E. DeLeeuw and M. DeLeeuw (1965) *Read Better, Read Faster*, Harmondsworth: Penguin. R. G. Burgess (ed.) (1982) *Field Research: A Sourcebook and Field Manual* contains the classic account of note-taking 'In the field', written by Beatrice Webb. See also Burgess's article 'Keeping a research diary' in *Cambridge Journal of Education* 11, 2: 75–83.

For those who are involved in writing up theses and dissertations then K. L. Turabin (1980) *A Manual for Writers of Research Papers, Theses and Dissertations*, though written early in the century, remains indispendable, coupled with the article on 'Writing the report' by J. Nisbet and N. J. Entwhistle in J. Bell *et al.* (1984). Teacher research and evaluation has produced some inventive new ways of disseminating the results of research. A useful introduction is provided by Chapter 5 in R. Walker (1985) *Doing Research: A Handbook for Teachers*, London: Methuen.

For information technology and research see G. H. Bell (1982) *Information Technology and Teacher Research*, Working Paper 9, THQL, Project Cambridge Institute of Education. Action learning can be approached through R.W. Revan (1982) *The Origins and Growth of Action Learning*, Bath: Chandwell.

# Chapter ten

# Conclusion

## Introduction

We will now try to draw together some of the salient themes and issues raised in the book about both the current and future state of teacher research. In the book so far we have done three things:

1 In Part I we provided an introduction to the context and practice of school-based investigation by focusing upon the idea of research and what this means for teachers.
2 In Part II we discussed the ways in which qualitative research techniques might be used by teachers in school-based investigation.
3 In Part III we explored the ethical and practical issues that arise in the course of school-based research, concluding with an examination of the writing up and dissemination phase of the research process.

What we have not done so far is to take a broader view of the relationship between the teacher as researcher and the changing context within which such work takes place. The first part of this chapter will therefore raise some questions about the importance of such research in developing more responsive and effective schools. This concluding chapter will also look at the relationship between the teacher as researcher and other groups engaged in research within education and consider the ways in which the work of each group might be co-ordinated. Finally a brief summary of the main ideas contained within the book will be provided by way of conclusion.

## The value of school-based research

Many teachers on in-service courses, at all levels of responsibility, and at all age ranges often raise the question of how to justify what it is they want to do to local education officers, governors, head teachers, and other staff. They need to be able to justify the time and resources which are likely to be involved in research, especially that which is likely to involve more than one or two teachers. They will need to be able to demonstrate the value and significance of such work. In response to this it might be argued that school-based research might achieve three things.

1 Enable heads and staff, individually and collectively, to be better able to appreciate the nature of national policies and the theoretical and empirical evidence upon which they are based. We hope that we have generated a respect for evidence and a critical approach to what counts as evidence in the educational world. A critical approach to implementing change from outside schools might therefore be encouraged. For example, how might it be possible to maintain the best features of the integrated day in primary schools and still meet the needs of the proposed national curriculum?

2 Provide head and staff with the opportunity of acquiring a better understanding of all aspects of their own practice, be it in relation to subject, content, curriculum design, or the processes of successful implementation inside the school itself. One example here might be the implementation of a new programme of science and technology in a primary or middle school. Such a project would need to address the issue of how teachers interact differently with boys and girls as well as developing new curriculum materials and evaluating existing ones.

3 Develop ways of finding out about key priority areas for evaluation and development, or major issues which need attention in terms of resources or curriculum organization and delivery.

While there are clearly many other things which school-based teacher research can achieve, these three areas are going to be uppermost in the minds of those people who have the power to encourage or discourage teacher research. This suggests that an important element in the equation will be management style.

## School-based research and management style

Research can and should be undertaken by individual teachers developing an understanding of their own practice. One of the characteristics of school-based research however is that the subject matter often means that the dividing line between research that pertains to the individual teacher and work which has a wider frame of reference is difficult to determine. For example many primary head teachers if doing research projects on in-service courses very often choose issues which have managerial implications. The same often applies to heads of department in secondary schools. The value of research as a means of tackling issues that are facing a school is one which is attractive but which equally raises the wider questions of management styles. What indeed might be the most appropriate management climate for research of the kind discussed in the book to take place? In all cases the answer must be an open and democratic style. This is especially the case if the initiative for the research in fact comes from the senior management of the school as part of a staff development programme. Clearly both 'applied' and 'action' research will have implications not only for the individual teachers' practice but also for pupils and other teachers alike. The keywords for such school-based research which aims at some form of staff development might be said to be justification, participation, and consultation.

Wakeman, who was involved in a programme of researcher-led staff development at Rotherham school, observes that while 'teachers are willing to cooperate in the discussion of practical problems in school and are favourably disposed to the applied or action research approach, the research needs careful planning' (Wakeman, 1986: 231). All the people involved need to be consulted from the start and the project's means and ends justified. Such a period of negotiation needs to take place not only at the start but throughout the period of data collection and dissemination. All research or evaluation carried out as part of a departmental or school policy review ought to be carried on in an open and democratic manner. Helen Simons (1982) provides a useful set of suggestions on how to conduct 'democratic' self-evaluation. This could be done in two main ways:

1 Using existing structures, that is staff meetings, reviews and policy statements, in a positive way and as part of the overall research design for involving the whole school.
2 Using both school- and college-based in-service courses, either short or long in duration, and so maximizing the cover provided by Grant Related In-Service Training (GRIST) as part of a comprehensive research programme.

**The teacher researcher and the wider research community**

The issue of how education should be improved and the most appropriate ways of implementing the changes necessary has been at the centre of much educational policy in Britain and the rest of Europe, the USA, and other countries in the past two decades. A considerable amount of the research generated within education from whatever source has been directed towards developing ways of making schools more effective and responsive to the changing needs of society. One result of this, as we indicated in the introduction, has been that the character of educational research has been profoundly affected. In Britain the need to address the questions of the most appropriate ways of improving school effectiveness has led to more groups of people involved in education entering the research field more directly. As well as traditional centres of research activity in the universities, polytechnics, and colleges of higher education involved in initial and in-service education, other groups have emerged, notably HM Inspectors of Schools, Local Education Authorities, and teachers themselves. Coupled with this has been a desire on the part of many research agencies outside school to involve teachers in the research process. We clearly have a growing and diverse research community in education.

Another recent change which may or may not prove permanent but which is already having an impact on in-service work, its structure and content is the delegation of in-service to schools and colleges themselves. The traditional providers now find themselves in a more 'market-oriented' situation *vis-à-vis* teachers and their needs. This has many advantages but it raises a number of questions which centre around the issues of financial, intellectual, and organizational resources. Do all schools in themselves have these in adequate amounts in order to undertake the research that is necessary to improve the quality of education in schools?

Few schools would agree that they can achieve the degree of staff development, in-service training, and research necessary without involving outside agencies. Schools will need all the help they can get if they are to change effectively. This has important implications for INSET and its relationship with school-based research. The new INSET arrangements can be used to provide new and creative opportunities for forging links between traditional research and teacher school-based research. The new two-year part-time in-service degree (B.Phil) at Doncaster Metropolitan Institute of Higher Education provides such an initiative which allows serving teachers to acquire research skills and then use them to develop in depth a research programme of direct relevance to their own work. This course provides a meeting-point or 'trading-post' where in-service tutors, advisers, teachers, and other interested parties can meet in the mutual pursuit of better practice. It allows for much greater flexibility than the more traditionally taught degrees.

These hopeful initiatives are taking place in a very uncertain climate. In Britain the debate on the future course of education policy which began in the 1970s has resulted in a policy which 'is widely regarded as the most interventionist and by many as the most radical since the second world war' (Bolem 1986: 314). A rational model of implementing change in schools has been adopted which involves at a national (macro) level the establishment of curricular and organizational goals which are then transmitted down to the local (micro) level through circulars and policy statements of increasing specificity. In addition as Bolem points out the government is 'implementing this policy by direct funding through the specific grant mechanism. This interventionist strategy often carries with it stricter accountability controls, especially in TVEI and TRIST (now GRIST)' (Bolem 1986: 315). This interventionist strategy will have important implications for the way in which in-service training and related work is both provided and delivered. We would argue that the new arrangements can be used as a way of developing research in schools undertaken by teachers either individually, collectively, or in collaboration with outside researchers, as a way of managing and implementing the changes that are now facing schools and colleges. Teachers will need to play central roles as 'researchers, innovators, developers and (self) evaluators'. But this will depend on adequate planning and staff development inside schools. The new powers given to school governing bodies by the Education Act, 1988, adds a new variable to this. But the issue will depend also on the ability of the LEA officers, advisers, and outside academic institutions to provide the time, appropriate structures, and expertise necessary to support the research of teachers in schools and colleges.

The new strategic planning role which the Education Act, 1988, will give to LEAs means that they can play a crucial role here. As Brian Wilcox has pointed out, recent government initiatives in the field of education are likely to have two consequences for LEAs:

> First by making LEAs define more precisely the nature of their activities
> they will be more able ... to specify areas where research would be
> helpful. Secondly, some of the enabling strategies referred to in the White
> Paper, (Better Schools) would help to define collaborative research within
> the LEA context.
>
> (Wilcox 1986: 7–8)

Furthermore, Wilcox has identified a number of possible areas of research into this area itself including research into the national model of planning, examinations, and assessment, in-service education, management of the teacher, appraisal, the Technical and Vocational Educational Initiative (TVEI) and other related areas.

Such a programme would involve considerable co-operation, not only between the LEAs and academic researchers, the National Foundation for Education Research (NFER) and HMIs, but also teachers who will be involved not only as participants within the programmes, but also potentially as researchers and evaluators. In addition, up until now the notion of teachers as researchers has been seen in the context of individual classroom practice but now it becomes possible to explore the 'complementary notion' of teachers as researchers for the LEA. The LEA could also do much to overcome the perennial problem of dissemination of such research by providing funds and establishing networks within the authority. This would have the advantage of making the research more immediate and therefore relevant, even if it still might only have a small audience. The LEAs have well-established routes of communication via meetings of professional groups, INSET networks, LEA working parties, and so on. The use of these is likely to be more potent in their effects on practitioners than more traditional routes via books and journals. With these thoughts about the contemporary situation in mind let us now try to summarize the main themes, issues, and techniques we have been exploring in this book.

## Summary of the book

1 We stated in the introduction that the aim of the book was to develop an appreciation of the value of qualitative research techniques in school-based research. We have argued that not only do these provide accessible and rigorous ways of describing and analysing classroom and school practice, but also the qualitative tradition, by its emphasis on understanding everyday meanings and situations, offers the possibility to individual teachers of reflecting constructively on their own professional practice.

2 We have characterized this kind of approach to research as either 'applied' or 'action research' in that the ultimate goals are better under-standing of educational practices, thereby giving teachers at all levels the opportunity to both reconsider and improve these by qualitative techniques and methods of analysis. These techniques, and the interpreta-tive ethnographic model of research which underpins them, concentrate upon revealing the often hidden meanings behind our common-sense taken-for-granted assumptions or 'conventional wisdom'. This provides teachers with an important resource from which to challenge this con-ventional wisdom and discover any mismatch between what is said and what is done, that is, our words and our deeds.

3 The research that we have been discussing in this book will therefore be empirical in the sense that it will draw its data for the most part, but not exclusively, from the actual classroom or work-place of the researcher. We have, however, not argued that this will necessarily exclude theory, or existing knowledge. Indeed, as we pointed out in Chapter 2, theory and existing knowledge can be either applied to an issue, or developed during the course of a piece of school-based research itself. The best way of viewing this theory–practice relationship is to recognize that where appropriate teacher researchers will draw on models, theories, and hypotheses from both other educational researchers, and from the disciplines of the human sciences more generally. As such these disciplines act as heuristic devices to assist the teacher researcher in the analysis and organization of their materials. This is in our view both the correct and most productive way to look at the relationship between theory and practice in teacher school-based research. Classroom and school-based research undertaken by teachers must have as its principal goal in the first instance the furtherance of the professional practice of teachers either individually or collectively.

4 What has been said so far does not preclude the fact that research concerned with a particular issue may be used as a foundation for more general knowledge about teaching and so aid the development of theoretical knowledge of more universal relevance and significance. For this reason in Chapter 2 we argued that educational research into

practice could not and should not divorce itself from the ongoing debates about the nature of research on the social world. By recognizing this we are better able to make sense of both the past and present context of our society of which education is so crucial a part. As we pointed out earlier in this chapter, teachers need to acquire the skills of critical analysis in order to be able to cope with the rapid and seemingly incomprehensible changes which education is currently facing.

5 Chapter 2 also highlighted the crucial importance of research design as a means of achieving the aims and objectives of a piece of research. We argued that the researcher needed to pose three important questions at the start of any research and to keep them in mind throughout the research. The teacher researcher needs to ask:

(a) What are the goals of the research?
(b) How are they going to be achieved?
(c) How are the findings to be evaluated?

6 We have alluded throughout the text to the relationship between quantitative and qualitative research. Before we finish it is necessary to look at this issue again. As we outlined in Chapter 2, it is not quantitative research techniques in themselves that we have been questioning. Indeed a working knowledge of these approaches, especially of descriptive statistics and numerical methods of data collection and analysis, including surveys and questionnaires, is important and can all be employed in a small way in a qualitative study. But we have attempted to counter the belief, which appears to be very common among teachers starting research, that the quantitative approach is the only legitimate, scientific method available for studying educational practice. It should also be clear that we were questioning that view of research which placed a high premium on data which were quantified by an outside observer to the exclusion of data which were more qualitative in character, collected by inside participants. While positivism has come in for serious criticisms over the last few decades our view is that the major criteria for deciding on which techniques of data collection and research design to employ is their appropriateness to the research situation or 'field' itself. The interpretative or ethnographic model of research design was presented as being the most appropriate for school-based teacher research and qualitative techniques as offering the greatest potential for teacher researchers and those most likely to yield results.

7 While teacher research is often singular and related to individual practice and is thus particular and unique, it is equally important to remember that the teacher as researcher belongs to a wider community of people engaged in education. We have therefore stressed the value and importance of communication and the dissemination of research findings. The development of networks and collaborative research

programmes is now well established and is one way of realizing a data base of empirical work which can be used by other teachers or form the basis of new theories and guidelines for professional practice.

8  In theory no area of practice should be immune from the possibility of research though, as we pointed out in Chapter 2, one needs to work at articulating a problem and designing appropriate means of data collection for evaluation and analysis. The range of topics that are amenable to a qualitative research approach can range from the areas of managing change and gender issues, illustrated in this chapter, which shows the relevance to curriculum and staff development on an LEA or single school basis, to areas of practice particular to an individual teacher. In other words there is considerable scope.

Yet it would be wrong to confine qualitative research to areas of immediate concern. Teacher researchers should be encouraged to develop from micro studies a more general appreciation of the wider context and sources of constraint on educational changes and provision. Indeed it does the cause of the teacher researcher no good at all to restrict the research which should be undertaken to areas that immediately relate to classroom issues. Peter Woods has recently listed a large number of such topics that teachers using qualitative techniques could explore, many of which will lead to very interesting meetings between the school and the world outside, so linking a particular situation with the general context of schooling and as such the more general concerns of the social sciences. These include organizational issues and their impact on staff and pupils, for example mixed-ability groupings; the careers of pupils and teachers, for example the transition between primary and secondary schools; the cultures of various groups, for example the staffroom; the strategies which teachers and pupils use and exploit and the meanings behind them, for example class discipline; attitudes, beliefs, and views about education; school methods; how decisions are made; how schools are managed; teacher career patterns; and factors affecting school performance and achievement (Woods 1986: 10–11). The list is very long yet such a list is not exhaustive. Indeed, one of the few things that we can be certain of is that educational research has a never-ending rolling plan of issues waiting investigation!

Whatever the future of educational research, we hope that this book has illustrated our belief in the value of qualitative research techniques as a central part of teacher-led research and conveyed some of the excitement and promise of such a venture. As a consequence, we hope to have provided an introduction to new and interesting ways of thinking about how to conduct and organize research. There is no doubt that in the future the modern teacher will need to develop the ability to reflect and therefore evaluate and consequently innovate. A knowledge and experience of research can bring just that. A sound theoretical and practical experience of research should in the future become an essential part of any teacher's survival equipment.

# References

Adams, C. and Arnot, M. (1986) *Investigating Gender in Secondary Schools*, London: Inner London Education Authority.

Adelman, C. (ed.) (1981) *Uttering, Muttering: Collecting, Using and Reporting Talk for Social and Educational Research*, London: Grant McIntyre.

Agar, M. H. (1986) *Speaking of Ethnography*, Qualitative Research Methods Series vol. 2, Beverley Hills, Calif: Sage.

Anderson, R. J., Hughes, J. A., and Sharrock, W. W. (1986) *Philosophy and the Human Sciences*, Beckenham: Croom Helm.

Andrew, A. (1985) 'In pursuit of the past: some problems in the collection, analysis and use of historical documentary evidence', in R. G. Burgess (ed.) *Strategies of Educational Research: Qualitative Methods*, Lewes: Falmer Press.

Back, K. W. (1955) 'The well-informed informant', *Human Organization* 14, 4: 30–3.

Ball, S. J. (1985) 'Participant observation with pupils', in R. G. Burgess (ed.) *Strategies of Educational Research: Qualitative Methods*, Lewes: Falmer Press.

Ball, S. J. and Goodson, I. F. (eds) (1985) *Teachers' Lives and Careers*, Lewes: Falmer Press.

Barnes, D. (1969) 'Language in the secondary classroom', in D. Barnes, J. Britton and H. Rosen *Language, the Learner and School*, Harmondsworth: Penguin.

Barnes, J. A. (1977) *The Ethics of Inquiry in Social Science: Three Lectures*, Delhi: Oxford University Press.

—— (1979) *Who Should Know What? Social Science, Privacy and Ethics*, Harmondsworth: Penguin.

Barrow, R. (1984a) *Giving Teaching back to Teachers*, Brighton: Wheatsheaf Books.

—— (1984b) 'The logic of systematic classroom research: the case of ORACLE', *Durham and Newcastle Research Review* 10, 53: 182–8.

Bealing, D. (1972) 'The organisation of junior school classrooms', *Educational Research* 14, 3: 231–5.

Becker, H. (1963) *The Outsiders*, New York: New York Free Press.

Becker, H. S. and Geer, B. (1957) 'Participant observation and interviewing: a comparison', *Human Organization* 16, 3: 28–32.

—— (1960) 'Participant observation: the analysis of qualitative field data', in R. N. Adams and J. J. Preiss (eds) *Human Organization Research: Field Relations and Techniques*, Homewood, Ill: Dorsey Press.

—— (1982) 'Participant Observation: The analysis of qualitative field data', in R. G. Burgess (ed.) *Field Research: A Source Book and Field Manual*, London: George Allen and Unwin.

Bell, C. and Roberts, H. (eds) (1984) *Social Researching: Politics Problems and Practice*, London: Routledge & Kegan Paul.

Bell, G. H. (1982) 'Information technology and teacher action research', in J. Elliott and D. Ebbutt (eds) *Facilitating Educational Action Research in Schools*, London: Longmans.
—— (1985) 'Can schools develop knowledge of their practice', *School Organisation* 5, 2: 175–84.
Bell, G. H. and Colbeck, B. (1984) 'Whole school practitioner research: the Sunnyside Action Inquiry Project', *Educational Research* 32, 2: 88–94.
Bell, J. (1987) *Doing your Research Project: A Guide for First-Time Researchers in Education and Social Sciences*, Milton Keynes: Open University Press.
Bell, J., Bush, T., Fox, A., Goodey, J., Goulding, S., (eds) (1984) *Conducting Small-Scale Investigations in Educational Management*, London: Harper and Row.
Bennett, J. (1981) *Oral History and Delinquency: The Rhetoric of Criminology* Chicago, Ill: University of Chicago Press.
Bennett, N. (1976) *Teaching Styles and Pupil Progress*, London: Open Books.
Berlak, A. C., Berlak, H., Bagenstos, N. T., and Mikel, E. R. (1976) 'Teaching and learning in English primary schools', in M. Hammersley and P. Woods (eds) *The Process of Schooling: A Sociological Reader*, London: Routledge & Kegan Paul and Open University.
Bernstein, B. (ed.) (1971, 1972, 1975) *Class, Codes and Control*, vols 1, 2 and 3, London: Routledge & Kegan Paul.
—— (1974) 'Open schools, open society?', *New Society*, 14 September.
Beynon, J. (1984) '"Sussing out" teachers: pupils as data gatherers', in M. Hammersley and P. Woods (eds) *Life in School: The Sociology of Pupil Culture*, Milton Keynes: Open University Press.
Blishen, E. (1969) *The School That I'd Like*, Harmondsworth: Penguin.
Blumer, H. (1969) *Symbolic Interactionism*, New Jersey: Prentice Hall.
Boehm, A. E. and Weinberg, R. A. (1977) *The Classroom Observer: A Guide for Developing Observation Skills*, New York: Teachers College Press.
Bogdan, R. and Biklen, S. K. (1982) *Qualitative Research for Education: An Introduction to Theory and Methods*, Boston, Mass: Allyn & Bacon.
Bolem, R. (1986) 'School improvement: the national scene', *School Organization*, 6, 3: 314–20.
Borg, W. R. (1981) *Applying Educational Research: A Practical Guide for Teachers*, New York: Longman.
Boydell, D. and Jasman, A. 'The Pupil and Teacher Record', in *ORACLE Project: A Manual for Observers*, Leicester: University of Leicester School of Education.
Brice-Heath, S. (1982) 'Questioning at home and at school: a comparative study', in G. D. Spindler (ed.) *Doing the Ethnography of Schooling: Educational Anthropology in Action*, New York: Holt, Rinehart & Winston.
British Sociological Association (1973) *Statement of Ethical Principles and their Application to Sociological Practice*, London: BSA; copies available from British Sociological Association, 10 Portugal Street, London, WC2A 2HU.
Bromley, D. B. (1986) *The Case Study Method in Psychology and Related Disciplines*, London: Wiley.
Bulmer, M. (1980) 'Comment on "The ethics of covert methods"', *British Journal of Sociology* 31, 1: 59–65.
—— (ed.) (1982) *Social Research Ethics: An Examination of the Merits of Covert Participant Observation*, London: Macmillan.
—— (1983) '"The Polish Peasant in Europe and America": a neglected classic', *New Community* 10, 3: 470–6.
Burgess, R. G. (1980) 'Some fieldwork problems in teacher-based research', *British Educational Research Journal* 6, 2: 165–73.

—— (1981) 'Keeping a research diary', *Cambridge Journal of Education* 11, 2: 75–83.

—— (1982) 'The unstructured interview as a conversation', in R. G. Burgess (ed.) *Field Research: A Sourcebook and Field Manual*, London: Allen & Unwin.

—— (1984a) *In the Field: An Introduction to Field Research*, London: Allen & Unwin.

—— (ed.) (1984b) *Field Methods in the Study of Education*, Lewes: Falmer Press.

Burke, V. (1971) *Teachers in Turmoil*, Harmondsworth: Penguin.

Burke, P. (1980) *Sociology and History*, London: Allen & Unwin.

Buzan, T. (1982) *Use your Head*, revised edn, London: BBC Ariel Books.

Cazden, D., John, V., and Hymes, D. (eds) *Functions of Language in the Classroom*, Columbia and London: Teachers College Press.

Cicourel, A. V. (1964) *Method and Measurement in Sociology* New York: Free Press.

—— (1973) *Theory and Method in the Study of Argentine Fertility* New York: Wiley.

Cicourel, A. V., Jennings, K., Jennings, S., Leiter, K., Mackay, R., Mehan, H., and Roth, D. (1974) *Language Use and School Performance*, New York: Academic Press.

Clarricoates, K. (1978) 'Dinosaurs in the classroom: a re-examination of some aspects of the "hidden" curriculum in primary schools', *Women's Studies International Quarterly* 1: 353–64.

—— (1980) 'The importance of being Ernest ... Emma ... Tom ... Jane: the perception and categorization of gender conformity and gender deviation in primary schools', in R. Deem (ed.) *Schooling for Women's Work*, London: Routledge & Kegan Paul.

Cohen, L. and Manion, L. (1986) *Research Methods in Education*, 2nd edn, Beckenham: Croom Helm.

Cope, E. and Gray, J. (1979) 'Teachers as researchers: some experiences of an alternative paradigm', *British Educational Research Journal* 5: 237–51.

Corsaro, W. A. (1981) 'Entering the child's world: research strategies for field entry and data collection in a pre-school setting', in J. L. Green and C. Wallat (eds) *Ethnography and Language in Educational Settings*, Norwood, NJ: Ablex Publishing.

Cottle, T. J. (1972) 'Matilda Rutherford: she's what you would call a whore', *Antioch Review* 31, 4: 519–43.

—— (1973) 'The life study: on mutual recognition and the subjective inquiry', *Urban Life and Culture* 2, 3: 344–60; reprinted in R. G. Burgess (ed.) (1982) *Field Research: A Sourcebook and Field Manual*, London: Allen & Unwin.

—— (1978) *Black Testimony: The Voice of Britain's West Indians*, London: Wildwood House.

Croll, P. (1986) *Systematic Classroom Observation*, London: Falmer Press.

Croll, P. and Galton, M. (1986) 'A comment on "Questioning ORACLE" by John Scarth and Martyn Hammersley', *Educational Research* 28, 3: 185–9.

Davies, B. (1979) 'Children's perceptions of social interaction in school', *Collected Original Resources in Education* 3, 1.

—— (1982) *Life in Classroom and Playground: The Accounts of Primary School Children*, London: Routledge & Kegan Paul.

Dearden, R. (1971) 'What is the integrated day?', in J. Walton (ed.) *The Integrated Day in Theory and Practice*, London: Ward Lock Educational.

Deem, R. (ed.) (1980) *Schooling for Women's Work*, London: Routledge & Kegan Paul.

# References

Delamont, S. (1976) 'Beyond Flanders fields', in M. Stubbs, and S. Delamont (eds) *Explorations in Classroom Observation*, Chichester: John Wiley.

Delamont, S. (1980) *Sex Roles and the School*, London: Methuen.

— — (1983a) *Interaction in the Classroom*, 2nd edn, London: Methuen.

— — (1983b) *Readings in Interaction in the Classroom*, London: Methuen.

Delamont, S. and Atkinson, P. (1980) 'The two traditions of educational ethnography: sociology and anthropology compared', *British Journal of Sociology of Education* 1, 2: 139–52.

DeLeeuw, E. and DeLeeuw, M. (1965) *Read Better, Read Faster*, Harmondsworth: Penguin.

Denzin, N. (1968) 'On the ethics of disguised observation', *Social Problems* 15, 4: 502–4.

—— (1970) *Sociological Methods: A Source Book*, London: Butterworths.

Douglas, J. D. (1976) *Investigative Social Research*, Beverly Hills, Calif: Sage.

Dumont, R. and Wax, M. (1969) 'Cherokee society and the intercultural classroom', *Human Organization* 28, 3: 217–26.

Durkheim, E. (1952) *Suicide*, London: Routledge & Kegan Paul.

Edwards, A. D. (1979) *The West Indian Language Issue in British Schools*, London: Routledge & Kegan Paul.

—— (1983) *Language in Multi-Cultural Classrooms*, London: Batsford.

Edwards, A. D. and Westgate, D. (1986) *Investigating Classroom Language*, London: Falmer Press.

Erickson, K. J. (1967) 'A comment on disguised observation in sociology', *Social Problems* 14, 4: 366–73.

Equal Opportunities Commission (1982) 'Gender and the secondary school curriculum', *Research Bulletin No 6*, Spring.

Evans, K. (1974a) 'The spatial organisation of infant schools', *Journal of Architectural Research* 13, 1: January.

—— (1974b) 'The head and his territory', *New Society*, 24 October.

Faraday, A. and Plummer, K. (1979) 'Doing life histories', *Sociological Review* 27, 4: 73–98.

Festinger, L., Riecken, H. W. and Schochter, S. (1956) *When Prophesy Fails*, Minneapolis, Minn: Minnesota University Press.

Finch, J. (1984) '"It's great to have someone to talk to": the ethics and politics of interviewing women', in C. Bell and H. Roberts (eds) *Social Researching: Politics, Problems and Practices*, London: Routledge & Kegan Paul.

—— (1985) *Research and Policy: The Uses of Qualitative Methods in Social and Educational Research*, London: Falmer Press.

Flanders, N. A. (1960) *Interaction Analysis in the Classroom: A Manual for Observers*, Ann Arbor, Mich: University of Michigan Press.

— — (1970) *Analyzing Teaching Behaviour*, New York: Addison-Wesley.

Frake, C. O. (1962) 'The ethnographic study of cognitive systems', in T. Gladwin and W. C. Sturtevant (eds), *Anthropology and Human Behaviour*, Washington, DC: Anthropological Society of Washington.

Frank, G. (1985) '"Becoming the Other": empathy and biographical interpretation', *Biography* 8, 3: 189–210.

Frank, G. and Vanderburgh, R. M. (1986) 'Cross cultural use of life history methods in gerontology', in C. L. Fry and J. Keith (eds) *New Methods for Old-Age Research: Strategies for Studying Diversity*, Massachusetts: Bergin & Garvey.

French, P. and French, J. (1984) 'Gender imbalances in the primary classroom', *Educational Research* 26, 2: 127–36.

Frielich, M. (ed.) (1970) *Marginal Natives: Anthropologists at Work*, New York:

Harper & Row.

Fuller, M. (1980) 'Black girls in a London comprehensive', in R. Deem (ed.) *Schooling for Women's Work*, London: Routledge & Kegan Paul.

Galton, M. and Simon, B. (eds) (1980) *Progress and Performance in the Primary School*, London: Routledge & Kegan Paul.

Galton, M., Simon, B. and Croll, P. (1980) *Inside the Primary School*, London: Routledge & Kegan Paul.

Garfinkel, H. (1967) *Studies in Ethnomethodology*, Englewood Cliffs, NJ: Prentice-Hall.

Garkinkel, H. and Sacks, H. (1970) 'On formal structures of practical action', in J. McKinney and E. Tiryakian (eds) *Theoretical Sociology*, New York: Appleton-Century-Crofts.

Gittins, D. (1979) 'Oral history, reliability and recollection', in L. Moss and H. Goldstein (eds) *The Recall Method in Social Surveys*, Studies in Education 9, London: University of London Institute of Education.

Glaser, B. G. and Strauss, A. L. (1967) *The Discovery of Grounded Theory: Strategies for Qualitative Research*, Chicago, Ill: Aldine.

Goffman, E. (1959) *The Presentation of Self in Everyday Life*; London: Allen Lane.

Goffman, E. (1971) *The Presentation of Self in Everyday Life*, Harmondsworth: Penguin.

Goodson, I. F. (1982) *School Subjects and Curriculum Change*, London: Croom Helm.

—— (1983) 'The use of life histories in the study of teaching', in M. Hammersley (ed.) *The Ethnography of Schooling: Methodological Issues*, Studies in Education Limited, Driffield: Nafferton Books.

—— (1985) 'History, context and qualitative methods in the study of the curriculum' in R. G. Burgess (ed.) *Strategies of Educational Research: Qualitative Methods*, Lewes: Falmer Press.

Green, J. L. and Wallat, C. (eds) (1981) *Ethnography and Language in Educational Settings*, Norwood, NJ: Ablex Publishing.

Grelé, R. (ed.) (1975) *Envelopes of Sound: Six Practitioners Discuss the Method, Theory and Practice of Oral History and Oral Testimony*, Chicago, Ill: Precendent Publishing.

Hall, E. T. (1969) *The Hidden Dimension*, London: Bodley Head.

Hamilton, D. (1977) *In Search of Structure: Essays from a New Scottish Open-Plan Primary School*, Scottish Council for Research in Education, Publication no 68, London: Hodder and Stoughton.

Hamilton, D. and Delamont, S. (1974) 'Classroom research: a cautionary tale', *Research in Education* 11: 1–15.

Hammerlsey, M. (1980) 'Classroom ethnography', *Educational Analysis* 2, 2: 47–74.

—— (ed.) (1983) *The Ethnography of Schooling: Methodological Issues*, Studies in Education, Driffield, Nafferton Books.

—— (ed.) (1986a) *Controversies in Classroom Research*, Milton Keynes: Open University Press.

Hammersley, M. (1986b) 'Measurement in ethnography: the case of Pollard on teaching style', in M. Hammersley (ed.) *Case Studies in Classroom Research*, Milton Keynes: Open University Press.

—— (1986c) 'Revisiting Hamilton and Delamont: a cautionary note on the relationship between "systematic observation" and ethnography', Milton Keynes: Open University Press.

Hammersley, M. and Atkinson, P. (1983) *Ethnography: Principles and Practices*, London: Tavistock.

Hammersley, M. and Woods, P. (eds) (1976) *The Process of Schooling: A Sociological Reader*, London: Routledge & Kegan Paul and Open University.

Hargreaves, D. (1967) *Social Relations in a Secondary School*, London: Routledge & Kegan Paul.

Hargreaves, D., Hestor, S. K. and Mellor, F. J. (1975) *Deviance in the Classroom*, London: Routledge & Kegan Paul.

Hexter, J. H. (1972) *Doing History*, London: Allen & Unwin.

Hitchcock, G. (1979) 'Preliminary notes on the doing of fieldwork and ethnography', *Urban Review* 11, 4: 203–14.

—— (1980) *Social Interaction in an Organisation Setting: The Analysis of the Social Organisation of a School*, unpublished Ph.D. thesis, University of Manchester, England.

—— (1982) 'The social organisation of space and place in an urban open-plan primary school', in G. C. F. Payne and E. C. Cuff (eds) *Doing Teaching: The Practical Management of Classrooms*, London: Batsford.

—— (1983a) 'What might INSET programmes and educational research expect from the sociologist?', *British Journal of InService Education* 10, 1: 18–31.

—— (1983b) 'Fieldwork as practical activity: reflections on fieldwork and the social organisation of an urban open-plan primary school', in M. Hammersley (ed.) *The Ethnography of Schooling: Methodological Issues,* Studies in Education, Driffield: Nafferton Books.

Holly, P. (1984) 'The institutionalisation of action-research in schools', *Cambridge Journal of Education*, 14, 2.

—— (1986) 'Soaring like turkeys', *School Organization* 6, 1: 321–6.

Humphreys, L. (1970) *Tearoom Trade,* London: Duckworth.

Humphries, S. (1984) *The Handbook of Oral History: Recording Life Stories*, London: Inter-Action Trust Limited.

Husserl, E. (1965) *Phenomenology and the Crisis of Philosophy*, New York: Harper Tourchbooks.

Hustler, D., Cassidy, T. and Cuff, E. C. (eds) (1986) *Action Research in Classrooms*, London: Allen & Unwin.

Hutchinson, B. and Whitehouse, P. (1986) 'Action research, professional competence and school organisation', *British Educational Research Journal* 12, 11: 85–94.

Hycner, R. H. (1985) 'Some guidelines for the phenomenological analysis of interview data', *Human Studies* 8: 279–303.

Hymes, D. (1962) 'The ethnography of speaking', in T. Galdwin and W. C. Sturtevant (eds) *Anthropology and Human Behaviour*, Washington, DC: Anthropological Society of Washington.

Joiner, D. (1976) 'Social ritual and architectural space', in H. M. Proshansky, W. H. Ittleson, and G. Rivlin (eds) *Environmental Psychology: People and their Physical Settings*, 2nd edn, New York: Holt, Rinehart & Winston.

Keddie, N. (1973) *'Tinker, Tailor ... the Myth of Cultural Deprivation*, Harmondsworth: Penguin.

King, E. (1974) 'The presentation of self in the classroom: an application of Erving Goffman's theories to primary education', *Educational Review* 25: 201–9.

King, R. A. (1978) *All Things Bright and Beautiful? A Sociological Study of Infants Classrooms*, Chichester: Wiley.

—— (1987) 'No best method: qualitative *and* quantitative research in the sociology of education', in G. Walford (ed.) *Doing Sociology of Education*, Lewes: Falmer Press.

Labov, W. (1969) 'The logic of non-standard English', in N. Keddie (ed.) *Tinker, Tailor ... the Myth of Cultural Deprivation*, Harmondsworth: Penguin.

Lacey, C. (1970) *Hightown Grammar: The School as a Social System*, Manchester:

Manchester University Press.

Langness, L. L. and Frank, G. (1981) *Lives: An Anthopological Approach to Biography*, California: Chandler & Sharp.

Lewis, L. (1970) *Culture and Social Interaction in the Classroom: An Ethnographic Report*, working paper 38, Berkeley, Calif: Language Behaviour Research Laboratory, University of California.

Lofland, J. (1971) *Analyzing Social Settings*, New York: Wadsworth.

Lubeck, S. (1985) *Sandbox Society: Early Education in Black and White America – A Comparative Ethnography*, London: Falmer Press.

McCall, G. J. and Simmons, J. L. (eds) (1968) *Issues in Participant Observation: A Text and Reader*, New York: Addison-Wesley.

MacCrossan, L. (1984) *A Handbook for Interviewers*, London: HMSO.

McDermott, R. P. (1974) 'Achieving school failure', in G. D. Spindler (ed.) *Education and Cultural Process*, New York: Holt, Rinehart & Winston.

—— (1977) 'Social relations as contexts for learning in school', *Harvard Education Review* 47, 2: 198–213.

—— (1978) 'Relating and learning: an analysis of two classroom reading groups', in R. Shuy (ed.) *Linguistics and Reading*, Rawley, Mass: Newbury House.

Macdonald, B. and Sanger, J. (1982) 'Just for the record? Notes towards a theory of interviewing in evaluation', in E. House (ed.) *Evaluation Review Studies Annual*, Beverly Hills, Calif: Sage.

McIntyre, D. I. (1980) 'Systematic observation of classroom activities', *Educational Analysis* 2, 2: 3–30.

McIntyre, D. I. and MacLeod, G. (1979) 'The characteristics and uses of systematic classroom observation', in R. McAleese and D. Hamilton (eds) *Understanding Classroom Life*, London: NFER.

Malinowski, B. (1922) *Argonauts of the Western Pacific,* London: Routledge & Kegan Paul.

Mandelbaum, D. G. (1973) 'The study of life history: Gandhi', *Current Anthropology* 14, 3: 177–96, reprinted in R. G. Burgess (ed.) (1982) *Field Research: A Sourcebook and Field Manual*, London: Allen & Unwin.

Marwick, A. (1977) *An Introduction to History*, Milton Keynes: Open University.

Matza, D. (1964) *Delinquency and Drift*, Chichester: Wiley.

Mead, G. H. (1934) *Mind, Self and Society*, Chicago: University of Chicago Press.

Measor, L. (1985) 'Interviewing: a strategy in qualitative research', in R. G. Burgess (ed.) (1985) *Strategies of Educational Research: Qualitative Methods*, Lewes: Falmer Press.

Measor, L. and Woods, P. (1983) 'The interpretation of pupil myths', in M. Hammersley (ed.) *The Ethnography of Schooling: Methodological Issues*, Studies in Education, Driffield: Nafferton Books.

Measor, L. and Woods, P. (1984) *Changing Schools*, Milton Keynes: Open University Press.

Mehan, H. (1973) 'Assessing children's language-using abilities: methodological and cross cultural implications', in M. Armer and A. D. Grimshaw (eds) *Comparative Social Research: Methodological Problems and Strategies*, New York: Wiley.

Milgram, S. (1974) *Obedience to Authority*, London: Tavistock.

Newman, D. (1973) *Defensible Space: People and Design in the Violent City*, London: Architectural Press.

Nisbet, J. and Entwhistle, N. J. (1970) *Educational Research Methods*, London: University of London Press.

—— (1984) 'Writing the report', in J. Bell *et al.*, *Conducting Small-scale Investigations in Educational Management*, London: Harper & Row.

Nixon, J. (ed.) (1981) *A Teacher's Guide to Action Research*, London: Grant McIntyre.

Osmond, H. (1959) 'The historical and sociological development of mental hospitals', in C. Gasken (ed.) *Psychiatric Architecture*, Washington, DC: American Psychiatric Association.

Palmer, V. M. (1928) *Field Studies in Sociology: A Student's Manual*, Chicago, Ill: University of Chicago Press.

Payne, G. C. F. and Cuff, E. C. (1982) *Doing Teaching: The Practical Management of Classrooms*, London: Batsford.

Phillips, S. U. (1972) 'Participant structures and communicative competence: Warm Springs children in community and classroom', in C. B. Cazden, D. H. Hymes, and V. P. John (eds) *Functions of Language in the Classroom*, New York: Teachers College Press.

Pitt, D. C. (1972) *Using Historical Sources in Anthropology and Sociology*, New York: Holt, Rinehart & Winston.

Platt, J. (1981a) 'Evidence and proof in documentary research: some specific problems of documentary research', *Sociological Review* 29, 1: 31–52.

—— (1981b) 'Evidence and proof in documentary research: some shared problems of documentary research', *Sociological Review* 29, 1: 53–66.

—— (1981c) 'On interviewing one's peers', *British Journal of Sociology* 32, 1: 75–91.

Plowden Report (1967) *Children and their Primary Schools*, report of the Central Advisory Council for Education, London: HMSO.

Plummer, K. (1983) *Documents of Life: An Introduction to the Problems and Literature of a Humanistic Method*, London: Allen & Unwin.

Pollard, A. (1984) 'Coping strategies and the multiplication of differentiation in infant classrooms', *British Educational Research Journal*, 10, 1: 33–48.

—— (1985a) *The Social World of the Primary School*, London: Holt, Rinehart & Winston.

—— (1985b) 'Opportunities and difficulties of a teacher-ethnographer: a personal account', in R. G. Burgess (ed.) *Field Methods in the Study of Education: Issues and Problems*, Lewes: Falmer Press.

—— (1987) 'Studying children's perspectives', in G. Walford (ed.) *Doing Sociology of Education*, Lewes: Falmer Press.

Popper, K. (1959) *The Logic of Scientific Discovery* , London: Routledge & Kegan Paul.

—— (1962) *The Open Society and its Enemies*, vol. 2, *The High Tide of Prophecy: Hegel, Marx and the Aftermath*, 4th edn, London: Routledge & Kegan Paul.

—— (1969) *Conjectures and Refutations*, 3rd edn, London: Routledge & Kegan Paul.

Powdermaker, H. (1966) *Stranger and Friend: The Way of an Anthropologist*, New York: Norton.

Powney, J. and Watts, M. D. (1984) 'Reporting interviews: a code of good practice', *Research Intelligence,* September.

—— (1987) *Interviewing in Educational Research*, London: Routledge & Kegan Paul.

Radin, P. (1963) *Crashing Thunder: The Autobiography of an American Indian*, (original edn 1920) New York: Appleton & Company.

Reid, W. (1986) 'Curriculum theory and curriculum change: what can we learn from history?', *Journal of Curriculum Studies* 18, 2: 159–66.

Revan, R. W. (1982) *The Origins and Growth of Action Learning*, Bath: Chandwell.

Rintoul, K. and Thorne, K. (1975) *Open-Plan Organisation in the Primary School*, London: Ward Lock Educational.

Rist, R. C. (1970) 'Student social class and teacher expectations: the self-fulfilling prophesy in ghetto education', *Harvard Education Review* 40, 3: 411–51; reprinted in M. Hammersley (ed.) *Case Studies in Classroom Research*, Milton Keynes: Open University Press.

—— (1972) 'Social distance and social inequality in a ghetto kindergarten classroom', *Urban Education* 7, 3: 241–60.

—— (1973) *The Urban School: A Factory for Failure*, Cambridge: MIT Press.

—— (1975) 'Ethnographic techniques and the study of an urban school', *Urban Education* 10, 1: 86–109.

—— (1977) 'On the contributions of labelling theory to an understanding of the processes of schooling', in J. Karabel and H. Halsey (eds) *Power and Ideology in Education*, New York: Oxford University Press.

Rivlin, L. G. and Rothenberg, M. (1976) 'The use of space in open classrooms', in H. Proshansky, G. Rivlin and W. Ittleson (eds) *Environmental Psychology: People in their Physical Settings*, New York: Holt, Rinehart & Winston.

Rosenthal, R. and Jacobson, L. (1968) *Pygmalion in the Classroom*, New York: Holt, Rinehart & Winston.

Runyan, W. M. (1982) *Life Histories and Psychobiography:Explorations in Theory and Method*, New York: Oxford University Press.

Rynkiewich, M. A. and Spradley, J. P. (eds) (1976) *Ethics and Anthropology: Dilemmas in Fieldwork*, New York: Wiley.

Saran, R. (1985) 'The use of archives and interviews in research on educational policy', in R. G. Burgess (ed.) *Issues in Educational Research*, London: Falmer Press.

Scarth, J. and Hammersley, M. (1986) 'Questioning ORACLE: an assessment of ORACLE'S analysis of teachers' questions', *Educational Research* 28, 3: 174–84.

— — (1987) 'More questioning of ORACLE: a reply to Croll and Galton', *Educational Research*.

Scheflen, A. E. (1972) *Communication Structure*, Bloomington, Ind: Indiana University Press.

Schofield, M. (1968) *The Sexual Behaviour of Young People*, Harmondsworth: Penguin.

Schostak, J. F. (1982) 'The revelation of the world of pupils', *Cambridge Journal of Education* 12, 3: 175–85.

Seabourne, M. and Lowe, R. (1977) *The English School: Its Architecture and Organisation, 1870–1970*, London: Routledge & Kegan Paul.

Sharpe, R. and Green, A. (1975) *Education and Social Control*, London: Routledge & Kegan Paul.

Sharrock, W. W. and Anderson, R. G. (1982) 'Teaching and talking: reflective comments on in-classroom activities', in G. C. F. Payne and E. C. Cuff (eds) *Doing Teaching: The Practical Management of Classrooms*, London: Batsford.

Simon, A. and Boyer, E. G. (1967) *Mirrors for Behaviour: An Anthology of Classroom Observation Instruments*, Philadelphia: Research for Better Schools Inc.

Simons, H. (ed.) (1980) *Towards a Science of the Singular*, Centre for Applied Research in Education, (CARE) Occasional Publications 10, Norwich: University of East Anglia.

—— (1981) 'Conversation piece: the practice of interviewing in case study research', in C. Adelman (ed.) *Uttering, Muttering: Collecting, Using and Reporting Talk for Social and Educational Research*, London: Grant McIntyre.

—— (1982) 'Suggestions for a school self-evaluation based on democratic principles', in R. McCormick (ed) *Calling Education to Account*, London: Open University Press and Heinemann Educational Books.

Sinclair, J. McL. and Goultard, C. M. (1975) *Towards an Analysis of Discourse*.

London: Oxford University Press.

Smith, L. and Geoffrey, G. (1968) *Complexities of an Urban Classroom*, New York: Holt, Rinehart & Winston.

Smith, L. and Keith, P. (1971) *Anatomy of an Educational Innovation*, New York: John Wiley.

Sommer, R. (1967) 'Classroom ecology', *Journal of Applied Behavioural Science* 3: 489–503.

—— (1969) *Personal Space*, Englewood Cliffs, NJ: Prentice-Hall.

Spradley, J. P. (ed.) (1969) *Guests Never Leave Hungry: The Autobiography of James Sewid, a Kwakiutl Indian*, New Haven, Conn: Yale University Press.

—— (1979) *The Ethnographic Interview*, New York: Holt, Rinehart & Winston.

—— (1980) *Participant Observation*, New York: Holt, Rinehart & Winston.

Spradley J. P, and McCurdy, D. W. (eds) (1972) *The Cultural Experience: Ethnography in Complex Society*, Chicago, Ill: Science Research Associates.

Stake, R. (1980) 'The case study method in social inquiry', in H. Simons (ed.) *Towards a Science of the Singular*, Norwich: Centre for Applied Research in Education.

Stanworth, M. (1981) *Gender and Schooling: A Study of Sexual Division in the Classroom*, London: Hutchinson.

Stenhouse, L. (1975) *An Introduction to Curriculum Research and Development*, London: Heinemann.

—— (1981) 'What counts as research?', *British Journal of Educational Studies* 29: 103–14.

Stubbs, M. (1983) *Language, Schools and Classrooms*, 2nd edn, London: Methuen.

Stubbs, M. and Delamont, S. (eds) (1976) *Explorations in Classroom Observation*, Chichester: Wiley.

Swann Report, The, 'Education for all: Report of the Committee of Inquiry into the Education of Children from Ethnic Minority Groups', HMSO Cmnd 9453, March (1985).

Thomas, W. I. and Znaniecki, F. (1958) *The Polish Peasant in Europe and America*, (original edn 1918–20), New York: Dover.

Thompson, P. (1978) *The Voice of the Past: Oral History*, Oxford: Oxford University Press, Opus Books.

Trudgill, P. (1974) *Sociolinguistics: An Introduction*, Harmondsworth: Penguin.

Turabin, K. L. (1980) *A Manual for Writers of Research Papers, Theses and Dissertations*, London: Heinemann.

Turner, G. (1982) 'The distribution of classroom interactions', *Research in Education*, 27 May, pp. 41–8.

Vierra, A., Boehm, C., and Meely, S. (1982) 'Anthropology and educational studies', in A. Hartnett (ed.) *The Social Sciences in Educational Studies: A Selective Guide to the Literature*, London: Heinemann.

Wakeman, B. (1986) 'Action research for staff development', in C. Day and R. Moore (eds) *Staff Development in the Secondary School*, London: Croom Helm.

Walford, G. (ed.) (1987) *Doing Sociology of Education*, Lewes: Falmer Press.

Walker, R. (1980) 'The conduct of educational case studies: ethics, theory and procedures', in B. Dockrell and B. Hamilton (eds) *Re-thinking Educational Research*, London: Hodder & Stoughton; reprinted in M. Hammersley (ed.) (1986) *Controversies in Classroom Research*, Milton Keynes: Open University Press.

—— (1985) *Doing Research: A Handbook for Teachers*, London: Meuthen.

Walker, R. and Adelman, C. (1975) 'Interaction analysis in informal classrooms: a critical comment on the Flanders system', *British Journal of Educational*

*Psychology* 45, 1: 73–6; reprinted in M. Hammersley (ed.) (1986) *Controversies in Classroom Research*, Milton Keynes: Open University Press.

Wardhaugh, R. (1986) *An Introduction to Sociolinguistics*, Oxford: Blackwell.

Warnock Report, The, (1978) 'Special Education Needs,: Report of the Committee of Enquiry into the Education of Handicapped Children and Young People', HMSO Cmnd.

Wax, M. L. and Wax R. H. (1971) 'Cultural deprivation as an educational ideology', in E. B. Leacock (ed.) *The Culture of Poverty: A Critique*, New York: Simon & Schuster.

Wax, R. H. (1971) *Doing Anthropology: Warnings and Advice*, Chicago, Ill: University of Chicago Press.

Webb, B. (1926) 'The art of note-taking', in B. Webb, *My Apprenticeship*, London: Longmans' Green.

Weber, L. (1971) *The English Infant School and Informal Education*, New York: Prentice-Hall.

Whyte, W. F. (1955) *Street Corner Society*, Chicago: University of Chicago Press, 2nd edition.

—— (1982) 'Interviewing in field research', in R. G. Burgess (ed.) *Field Research: A Sourcebook and Field Manual*, London: Falmer Press.

Wilcox, B. (1986) 'Research communities, the White Paper chase and a new research ecumenism', *British Educational Research Journal*, 12, 1: 3–12.

Willis, P. (1977) *Learning to Labour: How Working-Class Kids Get Working-Class Jobs*, Farnborough: Saxon House.

Wolcott, H. (1967a) 'Anthropology and education', *Review of Educational Research*, 37: 82–95.

Wolcott, H. (1976b) *Kwakiutl village and school*, New York: Holt, Rinehart and Winston.

—— (1973) *The Man in the Principal's Office: An Ethnography*, New York: Holt, Rinehart & Winston.

Woods, P. (ed.) (1980a) *Teacher Strategies*, London: Croom Helm.

—— (ed.) (1980b) *Pupil Strategies: Explorations in the Sociology of the School*, London: Croom Helm.

—— (1985) 'Conversations with teachers: some aspects of life history method', *British Educational Research Journal* 11, 1: 13–26.

—— (1986) *Inside Schools: Ethnography in Educational Research*, London: Routledge & Kegan Paul.

Wragg, T. (1983) 'Lawrence Stenhouse: a memorable man', *British Educational Research Journal* 19, 1: 3–5.

Wragg, T. (1984) 'Conducting and analysing interviews', in J. Bell *et al.* (eds) *Conducting Small-Scale Investigations in Educational Management*, London: Harper & Row.

Young, M. F. D. (ed.) (1971) *Knowledge and Control: New Directions in the Sociology of Education*, London: Collier-Macmillan.

Zimmerman, D. H. and Wieder, D. C. (1977) 'The diary–diary-interview method', *Urban Life* 5, 4: 479–98.

# Author Index

# Subject Index